MARITAIN–GREEN
CORRESPONDENCE

The Story of Two Souls

THE CORRESPONDENCE OF
JACQUES MARITAIN
AND
JULIEN GREEN

Edited by
HENRY BARS & ERIC JOURDAN

*Translated with an Introduction
and revised notes by*
BERNARD DOERING

FORDHAM UNIVERSITY PRESS
New York
1988

A translation of Julien Green et Jacques Maritain, *Une Grande Amitié: Correspondance, 1926–1972* (Paris: Gallimard, 1982).
© Julien Green et Héritiers de Jacques Maritain, 1982
© Éditions Gallimard, 1982

Printed in the United States of America

CONTENTS

TRANSLATOR'S INTRODUCTION

BERNARD DOERING

THE FIRST EDITION of *Une Grande Amitié: Correspondance [de Julien Green et Jacques Maritain], 1926–1972* was published by Plon in 1979 under the editorship of Jean-Pierre Piriou, who provided the introduction and notes. Reviewed extensively and enthusiastically in the French press, it soon sold out, and a second edition was prepared, this time by Gallimard.

Having made extensive use of the first edition in my book on *Jacques Maritain and the French Catholic Intellectuals* in 1983,[1] I sent a copy to Julien Green, who in turn sent me a copy of the new edition with the following note: "I have taken the liberty of sending you the complete edition of Jacques' correspondence with me, for a good number of letters have been discovered. I gave permission for my letters to be published for the sole purpose of paying homage to the marvelous man whom I have had the good fortune and the happiness to love." In all, thirty-four additional letters had been discovered, almost exclusively those of Maritain, which filled in the evident lacunae of the first edition. Both authors saved all their letters, but Maritain's system of filing was far less orderly than Green's and often consisted of placing the newly received letter as a marker in the book he was reading or consulting at the time.

The second, complete edition was placed under the editorship of Henry Bars, a close friend of both Maritain's and Green's, who used as an introduction his extensive study of "The Friendship of Jacques Maritain and Julien Green" which had appeared two years earlier in the first issue of the *Cahiers Jacques Maritain*. He expanded the notes considerably and at the end of the correspondence added three entries from Julien Green's *Journal* which contain reflections on the news of Maritain's death. I reread the correspondence in this new complete edition and was so moved by the spiritual luminosity, by the delicate intimacy, by the clarity and beauty of style of these letters that I resolved to make them accessible to an English-speaking public in translation. I have also revised and expanded the notes for such an audience.[2]

There are many famous French literary correspondences. Names like Flaubert, Proust, Gide, Claudel, Rolland, Rivière come to mind. If such letters had never been written or made public, it is not literary history alone that would be impoverished, but literature itself, as well as our understanding of the mind and heart of man. Perhaps some day, as Proust suggested, *téléphonages* will have completely replaced such exchanges of letters, and we will never again be part of the conversations of such minds.

If the letters of Maritain and Green had never been written or made known to us, we would be missing something very special. These letters, of course, are of immense historical interest and value. They are a vivid evocation of a period which antedates most of us or which many of us find receding into oblivion with astonishing and disquieting rapidity, a past so lovingly recalled by Raïssa Maritain in her memoirs *Les Grandes Amitiés* (see 101.3) when writers, artists, musicians, philosophers, theologians, politicians, social activists, and many others gathered each Sunday at the Maritain home on the rue du Parc at Meudon in an extraordinary atmosphere of religious, intellectual, and artistic effervescence. But this is not their principal interest and value.

The correspondence between Jacques Maritain and Emmanuel Mounier was published in the same year[3] as the Maritain–Green correspondence. There is a certain fatherly care on the part of Maritain for his promising young disciple and on the part of Mounier a certain respect and deference, sometimes a bit restive, but there is very little intimacy between them. The subject matter of the letters is almost exclusively the political turmoil of the '30s, the founding and funding of *Esprit* and its editorial policy. In the Maritain–Green correspondence the events of this world hardly enter into consideration. In the 250 letters there is a passing reference to the affair of Action Française; one humorous remark comparing the war between Israel and Egypt to the fight between David and Goliath; hardly a reference to the Second World War, even though both had to find refuge in the United States until the liberation of France; and two references to the assassination of John F. Kennedy in which both express their stupor at the horror of the tragedy and Maritain uses the occasion to remark that Americans no longer believe in the Devil. The Second Vatican Council enters into a number of letters, but mainly concerning the use made of the freedom it accorded and its effect on the souls of Christians. For what is unique about these letters is that they are a conversation which lasted over a period of forty-five years between two souls about the Soul, about its activities, its struggles, and its problems: the pursuit of sanctity, the presence and the dimension of

Evil in the world and the soul's struggle against it, the mystery of suffering, death, and the afterlife. In a series of letters in which one would expect to find the chronicle of an epoch particularly fertile in catastrophes, one finds a conversation about a vision of God and His relation to the human soul. In these letters the reader breathes the rarified atmosphere of spiritual mountain peaks.

The same was true of their face-to-face conversations. One senses the mysterious presence of God, a third, invisible Agent in a triangle of friendship. Julien Green "insists" that "One of the greatest favors God has bestowed on me was to put Jacques [Maritain] on my path in 1925" (see 114.2). His description of their first meeting leads the reader to the same conclusion. "I found myself before one of those men who give the impression of having come from another world. This came from the fact that he never hesitated to speak right off of God, of His relation with our souls, and of the respect He has for them and for their mysterious liberty" (see below, p. 36). Much later, in 1968, Green wrote: "How I would like to see you and hear you speak of all these things, which are the most important things in the world" (Letter 221). The main subject of this letter was the problem of human suffering and the possibility of finding a solution to this problem in the admission that God too could suffer.

It is distressing to reflect that this extraordinary friendship might never have existed. Though certain superficial similarities seemed to indicate that they were made for each other (in their early years they had both wanted to become painters; both were converts to Catholicism after a Protestant childhood; both wrote in a French known for the classical purity of its style; both loved with equal devotion France and the United States, their homeland and the country of their adoption; both were admirers of Charles Péguy; both felt a common distaste for and a common incapacity to adapt to the demands of social life), nevertheless many basic dissimilarities seemed to indicate the improbability of their paths ever crossing, of their ever seeking each other out, or of their ever finding a common ground for friendship.

Green was a convert at fifteen from a strict and depressing Protestantism that haunted all his childhood and left a permanent mark on his personality to a Catholicism that never ceased to trouble him in his soul and in his flesh: "in me nature revolted against the demands of the Church" (see below, p. 36). He was tormented by the rigidity of the Church and by the general laxity and indifference of French bourgeois

Catholicism, so much so that at the time of their meeting, he had just written a *Pamphlet contre les catholiques de France* to take his distance from, and for a long period he gave up the practice of, his faith. Julien Green's faith was that of a mystic (as Maritain insisted, much to Green's surprise), but also a disquieted and tormented faith, prey to painful interior struggles and intermittent crises of discouragement and distress.

Maritain too was a convert from Protestantism, but from a rationalist and indifferent Protestantism that had little to do with his life. He lived intensely the Catholicism he adopted. His faith was serene, without hesitation or reserve. He was at ease with the liturgy and dogma of the Church, and he consecrated a substantial portion of his day to contemplation and spiritual exercises. His faith too was more uncompromising (even intransigent during a certain period) and soon led him to a kind of spiritual realism in which he looked to his faith for solutions to the agonizing social and ideological problems of his time.

Indeed Maritain had always been strongly inclined toward a very literal kind of evangelism and from his student days had manifested a passionate love for the poor and the humble who thirst after justice. Maritain would have preferred by far to give himself over completely to a life of contemplation and to the writing of speculative philosophy. But more and more he felt himself obliged in conscience to turn his pen and his activity to the many grave problems posed by the world and the Church, in an uncompromising application of the principles of the Gospels to the problems of political and social justice. Green, on the other hand, seems to have had little interest in such problems. His preoccupations were with the interior life, with the problems of man's struggle with the evil in his soul, and with his novels, all of which centered in this particular spiritual combat. The passing references in his *Journal* to the events of this world are made because they have some relation to the interior life or are reflections on the vanity of such events. At the end of the many manifestos that Maritain wrote personally or in collaboration with others during the decade from 1926 to 1936, one looks in vain for the signature of Julien Green.

Until the very end of his life Green showed very little concern for the speculative problems of philosophy or theology, and even in the last years of Maritain's life, when Green began to read some of Maritain's speculative writings, particularly those concerned with the problem of the coexistence of Evil and a providential God, he declared himself incapable of following very far the lofty Thomist speculations of his friend and often invited him to come for a visit since he found it much easier to understand such things when Maritain spoke of them to him and answered his questions face to face. The young novelist would never have gone near the eminent Thomist, who was eighteen years his senior, or even thought of doing so, had Maritain not extended an invitation after the appearance of his *Pamphlet contre les catholiques de France.*

Many other things, some of an intimately personal nature, could easily have kept the two men apart, such as the sexual preoccupations of the young novelist and his friendship with André Gide, whose influence on the younger generation Maritain greatly feared and whom Maritain visited, at the urging of Henri Massis, in an effort to discourage Gide from publishing *Corydon,* a defense of homosexuality, which appeared a year before Green and Maritain met.

However, it did not take long for both Maritain and Green to recognize that these differences were in fact quite complementary. The novelist opened to the philosopher new perspectives on the relations between artistic creation and the spiritual life and on the treatment of evil in literature. The philosopher calmed the metaphysical terrors of the novelist, communicated to him a sense of serenity and peace, and provided him with answers that the priests he consulted either refused, or were unable, to give. Julien Green, in fact, chose Jacques Maritain as his spiritual director.

Green came face to face with serenity at a moment when he was living, perhaps more intensely than at any other period of his life, that *sourde inquiétude* from whose spiritual and carnal discomfort he suffered almost all his life. It was Maritain who led him back to the Church, brought him interior peace, and helped him to correct his errors and calm the doubts and moral distress that troubled him incessantly. "The world, which is so frightening, is always there. But you are there too, and the peace that you bring without knowing it" (Letter 108).

Maritain, for his part, recognizing how much the young novelist depended on him, tried to respond as best he could to the call for help that is present in almost all the letters. And he did so with perfect tact, without the slightest pressure or ostentation, finding just the right word at just the right time for the problems of conscience that troubled Green and the problems of grace that obsessed him. And Green does well to insist on Maritain's delicate and sensitive discretion in this regard. For a legend grew up about Maritain, particularly among those who disagreed with him on political, theological, and philosophical matters, occasioned perhaps by some early indiscretions of zeal with regard to Charles Péguy in the first days of Maritain's conversion. This legend was fostered by writers like Bernanos, who, at one point in their uneasy relationship, characterized Maritain as a *convertisseur* who took pride in bagging converts as a hunter might collect heads or antlers to hang on the walls of his den or game room, a legend that pictured Maritain as an insensitively pushy proselytizer. Green's letters certainly give the lie to this legend.

In an interview with Louis-Henri Parias which took place in 1973,[4] six years before the first edition of the correspondence, and in which Green speaks of the many Maritain letters he has kept, he insists time and again on Maritain's delicacy and discretion. He speaks of "the gentleness of his speech, and at the same time . . . it is so difficult to express these things . . . a great courtesy, an extreme discretion. We would speak of religion only when I wanted to." At another point he speaks of Maritain's "humility. . . . How many times did he say to me: 'Don't you think so?' In him there was not the slightest trace of arrogance; he was not intimidating. His charm was the charm of intelligence and courtesy." Or again: "He was very reserved, and I was too. I believe that on occasion we wasted time together. Perhaps he should have spoken to me more directly. He didn't want to. He didn't want to force my hand." On one occasion, when Maritain asked a question concerning Green's personal life, which was not an untoward intrusion, but justified by the nature of their conversation, Green replied with a lie. Maritain knew it was a lie but said nothing. The next day Green wrote to apologize for the lie, adding "I was undoubtedly afraid that I would be led on too far and tell you things I don't want to tell you now" (Letter 28). Maritain wrote back delicately, "You didn't really lie to me, for I understood what you did not tell me" (Letter 29). And in reply to Green's next letter in which he expresses his distress at what Maritain might think of him, Maritain wrote:

> I know too little about your life to permit myself the slightest appraisal of your conscience. But then, I will never judge you. I do not think you are living in sin. I know nothing about that. What I do know is the depth of your heart, and that you are inclined, as a matter of fact, to push scrupulosity too far. . . . I have a feeling that there exist for you in this fearful earthly life, perhaps because you have been called more than any other to catch a glimpse of the other side of the tapestry, certain very dark and dangerous problems. I would give anything to help you solve them [Letter 31].

Maritain never intruded, never forced himself, upon Green. There are a number of long lapses in the correspondence: from August 1935 to March 1939 (when Green was passing through a particularly anguished period and was flirting with Buddhism), from March 1947 to July 1950, from November 1951 to May 1954, and from September 1956 to August 1958. In every case Maritain patiently waited for Green to re-establish contact. These long lapses in correspondence did not seem to disturb Maritain; at least he never mentions being disturbed. What bothered Maritain were the short lapses which made him fear that something had happened to Green, that he might have fallen sick, for example, and Green was always careful to explain them and apologize. The reasons for the long lapses seem to have been understood; explanations or apologies were never given, unless this was done in meetings before the correspondence was re-established.

Such delicacy, such mutual understanding, spare this particular correspondence those violent tempests of discord that are found, for example, in the letters of Claudel or Bernanos. With Green, Maritain never once took the tone of paternal authority he felt obliged to take on occasion with Emmanuel Mounier. If anything, this friendship may seem almost abnormally free from any form of disagreement—the surface seems almost too calm—and the reader can easily be led to wonder if the correspondents themselves did not recognize the banality and the repetitiveness of those overly fulsome expressions of praise and congratulation. Nevertheless, between the lines, one can read, on the part of Green, a desire to maintain a certain necessary independence (which could possibly have had something to do with the lapses in correspondence). For example, though Maritain frequently urged Green to visit the famous Benedictine monastery of Solesmes, twenty-one years passed before Green ever went there. And Green showed no hesitation in rejecting as spiritual counselors most of the priests whose names Maritain suggested.

If this correspondence between souls about the Soul tells us little about the interior life of Jacques Maritain (with the exception of his last years after the death of Raïssa), it illuminates for us the interior, spiritual journey of Julien Green. He bares his soul to Maritain, seeking from him light, comfort, and reassurance about the value of his literary work, about his doubts and fears, about his interior struggles. Maritain replies with a lofty but humble serenity and an assurance which reveals little about his personal interior life. After the death of Raïssa, the roles seem to be reversed. It was Maritain who sought comfort and reassurance from Green. During Raïssa's illness and after her death, since they lived very close to one another, Maritain asked Green to visit him every day. After Raïssa died, when Green tried to comfort his friend by writing to him that from her place in Heaven Raïssa wanted him to be happy, Maritain replied with a letter that opens for us the enclosed garden of his heart. "I firmly believe, as you do, that Raïssa is happy, and that she wants me to be brave. But happy, Julien, how could I be happy? I have lost the physical presence of her whom I loved more than myself. I have witnessed the slow and implacable destruction of her poor body" (Letter 124). Elsewhere he describes for Green the state of "bewildered aberration" (Letter 179) in which he lived without his beloved Raïssa. For all the lofty self-assurance of his speculations on *God and the Permission of Evil* (see 137.1), he writes, on learning of the suffering of Green's sister Anne: "The suffering of the innocent is unbearable for the heart" (Letter 219). He repeatedly seeks from Green the reassurance that he is not falling into a state of senility and that what he writes still makes some sense. After one such reassurance, of which he said he had a terrible need, he confided to Green: "At my age you feel bizarre sensations. You are a stranger everywhere. You are not in eternity, and everything seems to chase you out of time, to deny you your poor little place, your poor little instant in which you existed in the past, and all the while the present instant means nothing at all" (Letter 187).

The last letter in the correspondence is dated October 24, 1972, from Julien Green. Jacques Maritain died on April 28, 1973; Julien Green, a member of the Académie Française, is the only living author whose works have been published in the Pléiade. Both will live on in these letters which take their rightful place among the great literary correspondences of all time.

July 31, 1985

NOTES

1. (Notre Dame & London: University of Notre Dame Press, 1973).

2. The material which I have added to the Gallimard edition appears as entirely new notes, expansion of existing notes, and, in rare instances, insertions in the text of the letters themselves. In all cases, this supplementary material is given inside angle brackets (⟨ ⟩).

Cross references are brief, indicated either by Letter number ("see Letter 19") or by Letter number and footnote ("see 101.2").

3. *Maritain/Mounier, 1929–1939* (Paris: Plon, 1979).

4. In *France Catholique-Ecclesia*, October 26.

JACQUES MARITAIN AT TOULOUSE
see Letters 177 and 180
(photograph copyright YAN, Jean Dieuzaide)

JULIEN GREEN
(photograph Eric Jourdan)

THE FRIENDSHIP OF JACQUES MARITAIN AND JULIEN GREEN

HENRY BARS

A YOUNG AMERICAN, born in Paris at the turn of the century to Protestant parents, a convert to Catholicism at the age of fifteen contrary to all expectation, let himself be persuaded by a strange companion to write a pamphlet against the Catholics of France. This tiny work, published under a pseudonym and dedicated, without the writer's permission, to the six Cardinals of France, made no more noise than a wet firecracker. But a professor at the Institut Catholique, endowed with the kind of antennas that could not be found on the foreheads of his colleagues, picked up the exceptional quality of the author, who at the moment was straying down a very unwholesome path. This was the beginning of a spiritual adventure of a kind that the world will never understand and that would last for almost a half century—not to mention its prolongation *somewhere, out of this world.*[1]

The friendship between Jacques Maritain and Julien Green seems to have held in both their lives a place that was very special and indeed quite exceptional. Maritain had many other friends in the world of arts and letters, and the warmth of his affection, the welcome, and the devotion he showed them are very well known. But there is no doubt whatever that he felt for Green a very special kind of love, which was the result both of his great admiration for the novelist and of far more subtle affinities, even though these two causes were mysteriously related. The name of the philosopher appeared in the earliest publication of the first volumes of Green's *Journal* (1938–1939), even when he was designated by no more than his initials. The volumes that followed and other texts (prefaces, articles) shed more light on their relationship. Maritain, for his part, in his works on art and poetry, let it be known in what high esteem he held this visionary of the human condition. The publication

This essay was originally published, under the title "L'Amitié de Jacques Maritain et de Julien Green," in the *Cahiers Jacques Maritain*, 1 (September 1980), 13–36.

9

of their correspondence has opened their friendship to the full light of day. If indeed that light can never fully escape certain incursions of darkness, it at least reveals the origin, the meaning, and the evolution of that friendship. Even for someone who has read extensively in the works of both authors, the newness of this spiritual landscape, of this story of two souls, is very striking.

The first thing to emphasize is that there was nothing, at the beginning, to turn Green in the direction of Maritain. The fact that they had both come from Protestantism into the Catholic Church was not a point of common interest, for they did not come from the same Protestantism. The one came from Biblical tradition; the other, from religious Liberalism. And at the time of their meeting, the young Green was beginning to break loose from the first fervor of his conversion. This resulted in a tendency toward retraction, which became more accentuated for a number of years, but never really destroyed his affection for the Church. In addition he never felt the slightest attraction for philosophy, and least of all for any Scholastic type of philosophy. "With a clumsiness that was natural to me, I declared to the author of *Antimoderne* that I understood nothing in his books, to which he replied with a smile that this would not keep him from sending me copies of them as they came out and that I was dispensed in advance from reading them" (see below, p. 36). We do not know if Maritain sent all his books, but Green took this dispensation very seriously and for a very long time, if not up to the very end. He tried at times to justify this, suspecting on the part of other friends of Jacques' a disapproval that would have been quite indiscreet (April 10, 1967). Nevertheless he enjoyed the rarest of privileges, for he was attracted to the mystics and had discovered Léon Bloy at the age of eighteen: "I was too young at the time to appreciate the value of this book [*Mon journal*] whose violence was for me no more than a pretext for laughter and mockery, even though I was deeply troubled by the seriousness of this witness" (November 8, 1941).

*

Maritain did not know Green at the time he decided he would like to make the acquaintance of this still almost unknown young writer; for it was he who took the initiative and it seems to me that the initiative remained with him for a long time in the relationship that followed. Before continuing any further I think it preferable to settle once for all a question that could cast a shadow on the rest of my study if I did not seize it by the horns at the very beginning. One reads in his *Journal* a few years later this remark Green made to Gide:

How painful it is to feel so uncomfortable in the presence of people whom we respect, and whom we love too, and from whom we know we will perhaps have to defend ourselves someday, in spite of ourselves. . . . For some of our Catholic friends are like this. . . . With the best intentions in the world, they never see us without the ulterior motive of proselytizing. They worry about our salvation. They think about it, visibly, even when we are speaking to them about entirely other matters [April 10, 1929].

The temptation to think of Maritain is all the stronger in that they had been talking of him at the beginning of their conversation; and it is probable that this was Gide's understanding as well (cf. May 25, 1932); and it cannot be excluded that at the time this was how Green himself felt. But he would write much later when recalling those days: "Maritain had nothing about him of the proselytizer" (229.1). It would be useful, I believe, to quote a few lines from the philosopher where this question is treated from a very general point of view:

The best way to win souls is not by actions that have as their purpose to win those souls, but by actions that have no other purpose than to bear witness to the truth, and bear witness to this truth with the full and over-flowing measure of love. Perhaps it is possible to find here the exact distinction between *proselytism*, which could be defined as an activity of spiritual conquest on a patient (*actio transiens*), and the true *apostolate*, which could be defined as the service of souls, and the awakening of souls to the truth, by the superabundance of activity that comes from union with the truth (*actio immanens*). In the latter case the animating form is love; in the former case it is a sublimated instinct of imperialism [QC 168].

I think that this represents the line of Maritain's conduct from the very first years of his life as a Christian; this does not mean that there was no progress in the way he followed it. One can read in a note to the *Journal de Raïssa*[2] which goes back precisely to those years when he was about to make Green's acquaintance (March 7, 1924): "at that time we insisted a bit too much, I now believe, on the idea of the apostolate. In works of the intelligence it is truth alone that must be kept in view; the rest is granted in addition." And let us add these lines too, written about the same time, "we have always welcomed those who wanted to see us, but we have never sought to make the acquaintance of anyone. This spontaneous rule was a guarantee against any risk of worldliness" (CN 209*n*/151*n*). The landscape that Green paints of his situation in the

Parisian social world around 1925 (Pléiade III, 1457) confirms quite well the texts we have brought together.

In spite of all this, life was still made up of movement and complexity. Maritain wanted to get to know Green, and how could he not be concerned about the salvation of his soul? He was not trying to conquer him, he loved him, he prayed for him surely, from very early on. "He did not hesitate," observes Green, "to speak to me right off of God, of His relation with our souls, and of the respect He has for them and for their mysterious liberty" (see below, p. 36). This language did not have the character of an exhortation, but of a confession of faith in the presence of a being capable of understanding it, even though at the moment Green was moving away from this God about Whom no one had ever spoken to him in this way; and he spoke with authority and at the same time in a way that seemed to bring peace (ibid.). It was the same later on when the moment of intimacy arrived—which was actually quite soon. But now we must go back to the details of the journey and of their relationship.

*

The point of departure then was the *Pamphlet.* "My admiration for the hardness of these beautiful Pascalian contours which contained a kind of trembling distress and the feeling of being suddenly face to face with an exceptionally profound soul made me want to meet the author. He would have liked to slip away; but I ended up finding him."[3]

The pamphlet had appeared in October 1924. At times Green places his first meeting with Maritain in that same year, more often in 1925, and says sometimes that it took place at Meudon (see below, p. 35), sometimes at rue Cortambert where he himself lived (Pléiade I, 1231). The first of Green's letters is dated April 6, 1926, and seems to indicate that they had not yet met face to face (Letter 1). An entry in his *Journal* for the following week mentions a visit he had paid to him the day before and registers the impression he received: "Good, but not enough ferocity" (April 13, 1926). With time he would discover the violence hidden under that gentleness which fooled so many. This was the time when the exchange of letters between Cocteau and Maritain was published. Green was shocked by the manner in which Cocteau spoke of religion (April 27, 1926), but Maritain's answer did not displease him (Letter 2). They saw each other rather frequently, corresponded very often (17 letters in 1926 and it seems that some have been lost). But the principal subject of their letters was the young novelist's work at that time. *Le Voyageur sur la terre* and *Mont-Cinère* were appearing; *La Traversée inutile*, then *Adrienne Mesurat*, would be published in Roseau d'Or. It was during this time, when "they still addressed each other as Sir," that Green offered Maritain the beautiful Greek Bible to which he was so attached and which was to have so astounding a destiny (June 8 and 11, 1965; March 4, 1966).[4]

They still addressed each other as "Dear Sir," but their intimacy developed rapidly; by autumn they had changed to "Dear friend." On June 19, 1927, Maritain called Green by his first name, and Green followed his example a few months later. After a short time more, Jacques joins the affectionate regards of Raïssa to his own. It took more time (December 29, 1934) for Julien to refer to Raïssa other than as "your wife." For "Miss Vera," who remained absent from the correspondence for a long time, it took still longer (September 12, 1939); and it did not seem to be until their common exile in America during those dark years that he would feel a brotherly closeness to this quiet woman (cf. June 18, 1955). At the same time, his sister Anne, who was in exile with him and would come back to the Catholic fold after the war, also became closer to the Maritains; along with her brother, she would remain very close to Jacques after the deaths of Vera and Raïssa. Green had written in his *Journal* a few years earlier: "Yesterday I went to see the Maritains with Anne. We found them just as we had always known and loved them, and when I say the Maritains, that includes Vera, Raïssa's sister, as well. What their affection has been for me no one will ever fully know. One of the greatest favors God has bestowed on me was to put Jacques on my path in 1925. On this I insist" (June 18, 1955). After reading these lines in *Le Bel Aujourd'hui*, Jacques answered with an expression of gratitude (Letter 114). This growth in tenderness and fidelity, amid the contrarieties and heartbreaks of life, seems to me to be in itself a very beautiful story; it takes on incomparable value when interpreted in light of the unique destiny of Julien Green.

*

When he became a friend of Maritain's, Green's faith was already in danger, at least in the sense that the demands of Christianity were becoming for him more and more unbearable. The respect he had for Jacques was so intimately rooted in his heart that after a conversation with him he felt obliged to write to accuse himself of a lie: "You asked me if I intended to live alone and I said yes when I should have said no"

(Letter 28). It was almost no lie at all, Maritain answered him, for he had guessed the situation. What followed this reply, too long to be cited, is too beautiful to be summed up in a few sentences. Let us say simply that Jacques offered his life for his friend. Green was moved; he did not seem overwhelmed. He even excused himself, and in a sense put himself more and more at a distance. Maritain was not discouraged. Not only did his affection increase, but nothing altered the admiration he had for Green's so tragically haunted work. In Roseau d'Or he published the despairing novel *Léviathan*. On *Les Clefs de la mort*, which was published elsewhere, he expressed himself with a perception that very few other critics approached (Letter 33; FP 111/AP 59) and returned to it at the very end of his life (Letter 234).

During those particular years Green was closely associated with Gide and his literary milieu. The Maritain–Gide diptych, sketched out in an article in *Le Monde* in June 1970,[5] is a bit summary, as Green himself admits; it was not completely arbitrary. Gide disappointed him by maintaining that love never made him suffer, "that he does not know what it is" (September 24, 1929), and upset him by insisting on their common Protestant heritage, the pretended source of their love of truth (January 19, 1932). It was not long before Gide in his turn began to put distance between himself and Green, lured away by new comrades sympathetic to Communism (September 25, 1936). Nevertheless Green had for this same Gide a feeling of camaraderie which was almost juvenile (November 25, 1931), quite different from the friendship that had always united him to Maritain. This was Malraux's "Oncle Gide," with whom one attended films and talked shop, that literary glutton, the man who never gave in to resistance but who always returned insidiously on the first favorable occasion—he who much later, after Green's second conversion, would suggest to him "a little detour in the direction of the Devil," and when Green made a vague gesture of partial retreat: "you could at least pretend to" (July 21, 1947). A rare man, certainly, but one who is of little consequence before the honesty of Julien Green.

But from 1928 on, Green had almost given up prayer; he tried to come back to it in 1933, then with more success in 1937 (September 28, 1941). These are the hollow years in the correspondence with Maritain. His editor [Jean-Pierre Piriou] suggests that visits replaced the letters, and that of the letters that were written, some were perhaps lost,[6] all of which is quite possible. At any rate the *Journal* itself says nothing about their relations during the five years that preceded the war. Let us collect a few crumbs from the previous years, sometimes very precious ones.

Readers of the first volume of the *Journal*, in 1938, could without grave risk identify the philosopher with the dinner guest of whom Green wrote on May 1, 1929:

> This is a rare and exquisite person, a truly Christian soul in Catholic armor, and this armor hinders his movements. . . . He stayed with me until eleven o'clock, speaking of everything, with sudden changes from sadness to gaiety and from gaiety to a tone that was almost sorrowful. "Have I made a mistake? Was I wrong to spend my time on all these literary figures?" And on leaving me he seemed sad and bewildered, in spite of his smile.

Such questions, addressed as they were to a young writer who was quite liberated from dogma, do not indicate that this "Catholic armor"— others might say "Thomist"—completely paralyzed this truly Christian soul. This free simplicity in the midst of alternating feelings, the total absence of any intention to entrap, no doubt left their mark on the author of *Léviathan* who would soon write *L'Autre Sommeil* with a depth that Gide would never attain. "Several times in thinking of you I have been kept from committing evil actions" (Letter 32). It is not for us to judge the human heart, but it is difficult not to have feelings about how others act. How much Jean Cocteau, who also drifted away from Maritain, seems of lighter weight and less noble lineage.

I think we must attribute to Maritain the depression that Green felt at times in listening to his pessimistic forecasts, which the course of history would partially confirm (October 1, 1931; June 16, 1933). They counteracted the taste for pleasure and even the happiness which he later claimed (September 25, 1935) to believe he experienced at that time. But they corresponded to a movement in the opposite direction which began to take place in the depths of his soul (February 1, 1944). A kind of dialogue with a head of Buddha (February 7, 1931) would not make full sense until five or six years later. "India is a field of tares where good grain grows now and then" (February 28, 1941). Moreover he began to wonder about the Gospels, especially Christ's words concerning poverty (July 21, 1940). The example of someone like Mercedes de Gournay, whom he had met at Meudon and of whom Maritain had spoken to him, awakened in him distant echoes (March 17, 1934). He listened to Raïssa say that we are still far from understanding all the Gospel and admitted that she was right, even though he had doubts about "the churches which were supposed to be eternal" (December 4, 1934).

Shortly after this there appears to be total silence between Green and the Maritains. But the grain had fallen into the furrow, and as almost always happens in such cases, what is really essential escapes our grasp. The dated journal itself stops for six months on the eve of his final conversion; but it is precisely at this time that the correspondence takes up again, becomes regular, and in its abundance surpasses even the best years: eleven letters of the greatest value between March 15 and November 23, 1939. The discreet and decisive role that Jacques and Raïssa played in this interior denouement, which corresponds to the beginning of the world tragedy, is very noticeable here. They were no more than helpers, all the more efficacious as they were self-effacing: God alone transforms hearts; His friends can only sweep His path.

*

I should now like to return to an aspect of this friendship that it was necessary to pass over a bit at first. Julien Green is a writer; his profession is the art of the novel, in which he gave proof of an astonishingly precocious mastery. Like all artists (even when they hide it, which was not so in his case) he had a concern for his writings that was a bit touchy, like that of a mother for her children. Not that he sought compliments at any price. On the contrary. This creator was, as he often is today, a doubter both of himself and of what he has produced, worried by the thought that he might prove unequal to the creative force that welled up within him; nevertheless he was impatient that, once his works were fully born, they make their way immediately in the world (Letters 15, 23). He had so little ambition to rise suddenly to the top of the literary lists, and his creative and artistic demands were such that he dreaded the impossible probability of doing the same book again and again, or the chance of the facile success that greatly talented authors do not always avoid. Then there were the long intervals between successive novels: eight years between *Varouna* and *Si j'étais vous,* eleven years between *Chaque homme dans sa nuit* and *L'Autre.* It is true that during the years immediately before the war, he lost hope that his books would ever be published (October 11, 1932) and gave free rein to his fantasy. But even this is a form of fidelity to his inner voice, the rule of inspiration to which he made no exception: "My book is completely off the tracks. The locomotive has gone wild. But then too, this derailment is the reward for some very long trips and I had a right to this reward" (March 22, 1933). There was in Green then a kind of involuntary Surrealist, not a systematic one, outside every school, and all the more attractive for that very reason.

Is it for that particular reason that *Le Visionnaire* frightened Maritain? He took the Surrealist experience very seriously (IC 175–76/ 189–90), a thing which Claudel never forgave him; but he knew as well the risks of dangerous delusions that were incurred (May 6, 1943; FP 33–34, 173–74/FP 133–34, AP 74–75). "He is afraid," noted Green, "that all my work should fall prey to the world of dreams. He tells me that in spite of everything I live on a mystical level, and that my view of the world is not a purely human one; he congratulates me for this, but he is worried because of the dream. Formerly such words would have troubled me deeply" (June 9, 1943). Another motive could be supposed for this disquietude, which would nevertheless be very compatible with the one expressed: *Le Visionnaire* is Green's only novel in which a kind of hostility to the Church can be noticed. More curious, and contrasting, was the philosopher's cursive judgment the following year of inviscerated knowledge of man in the art of the novel: "with Mauriac as with Malraux, even with Green himself, there is question of *moral* knowledge more than of *poetic* knowledge" (FP 176/AP 76). Coming after lines full of admiration for Jouhandeau, "who has neither companions nor followers," this judgment has a certain ring of disappointment to it, more noticeable to those who know the superior rank in which Maritain places poetic knowledge and the meaning he gives it (IC 108/124 and passim). "Even with Green himself": this would have been more fitting for the author of *Épaves* than for the inventor of Negreterre, harnessed to what would become *Minuit* (but Jacques did not yet know that story). When much later he wrote, "The great novelists are poets. And they are few" (IC 381/389), he would naturally count Julien Green in that small band of elect (IC 383/399). And, in fact, outside of this *obiter dictum*, this is what he always thought.

As soon as Maritain read *Les Clefs de la mort*, he wrote: "I have to make an effort to remind myself that this is a work of art (and one which I find admirable): it belongs to a higher region. You have been told that there is a certain clumsiness in these pages. In reality one has the impression that your hand trembled a bit—with respect—when writing about such a subject, and there is nothing more beautiful" (Letter 33). A few months later, in the Chroniques du Roseau d'Or, he would use much the same words to characterize this novella (FP 111/AP 59) but without the opening phrase which I want to emphasize now: "I have to make an effort to remind myself that this is a work of art. . . ." This cry in no way implies an underestimation of Green's art. Indeed, the opposite is true: Green is never more an artist than when he makes the reader forget that he is so; a great artist like Gide never succeeded in doing this. With his incomparable powers of intuition, Maritain very early grasped the fact that Green in his total being—with his day-to-day humanity and his romantic creativity indissolubly intertwined—belonged to the invisible world, and that he was at home in the invisible only as it was grasped through the visible itself. This is probably what he wanted to make clear when he said "you live, after all, on the level of the mystics"—an expression which, for my part, I scarcely relish, and about which the philosopher came to say, "this expression is meaningless" (QC 150). This affirmation was all the more audacious in that for many years Green lived a life rather distant from the only spiritual rule that Maritain recognized as true. And Maritain was certainly aware of this fact; but if he was unshakable in matters of doctrine, when there was question of a living person, especially one torn by interior suffering, his "Catholic armor" had nothing about it but the softness and suppleness of love. Nevertheless the expression "after all" raised a problem which Jacques, the speculative philosopher, examined with great care and, doubtless, in silence.

*

Let me now try to analyze the role he played with regard to the novelist considered as such (and also, but later, as the author of the *Journal*). He admired him from the very beginning and without reserve: "I have no doubt that you are in the line of the masters" (Letter 6). A young twenty-five-year-old who hears such things said to him might very well ask himself if he were not dreaming; he might just as well wonder if his speaker were not being a little too polite. But forty-four years later, when the main corpus of his work had been completed, he could read from the pen of the same reader: "For Julien Green I have an admiration without compare. I find it marvelous that an American should be the greatest French writer of our time" (Letter 230). During those years, in the private letters which we have the joy of discovering today, Maritain spoke of most of Green's books, sometimes at length and with the most delicate of nuances. And it can be said that throughout the whole of this very personal relationship, in which so many serious questions were touched upon, Maritain constantly sustained him in his work, sometimes against himself. Here again I must forestall a very realistic supposition, by facing up to it with complete frankness: Was not Maritain's critical judgment biased by his charitable motivations?

Why not recognize the fact? Maritain was the most beautiful example I know of intellectual charity in our century—where, it must be admitted, such charity is not found in abundance. Let us avoid calling up the names of other "Catholic authors," especially those who did not bear this dangerous hallmark. He was capable of the most mordant satire; we have seen enough of that. But I have always seen him, in his writings as in his conversation or in what I know of his correspondence, as trying to avoid hurting anyone. In this respect he in no way resembles his godfather, Léon Bloy. This is due, I believe, to his natural nobility, to the place that contemplation held in his life—that contemplation which "alone reveals the true value of charity. Without it one can know it only by hearsay. With it one knows it through experience" (PS 171/ 114)—and perhaps due also, as he suggests (CN 11/4), to the intimate common life he led with his "two little Jewesses," Raïssa and Vera. His delicacy was extreme; it could not have been other than especially so in the case of someone he loved as much as Julien Green. But this tenderness was also his strength; and his force was never greater than when there was question of *speaking the truth*. The greatest praise he could give to Green, in his final tribute (Letter 230), was that he found in him an "absolute *fidelity to the truth*." We shall see that these words, whose use can so easily turn to banality, have in this particular case implications of singular profundity. What I want to say here is simpler, closer to the language of current use: Maritain would have knowingly done an injustice to Green if he made use of those amiable expressions of courtesy all too frequent among men of letters—which are perfectly compatible with the most intimate cruelty. I think that he was completely incapable of this and that the readers of this correspondence will recognize the absurdity of such a supposition—unless they have no ear at all.

It is another thing to think that every formula Maritain ever used in speaking of these works must be taken at its face value—an idea he would have found absurd. For my part, I do not always agree with him, only most of the time. And what strikes me is the precision of his remarks, sometimes their astonishing unexpectedness, and the absence of any stereotype whatsoever. But this is nothing exceptional in his case; he read as a writer worthy of the name would want to be read, even if he were invited to do it all over again.

This is why I take very seriously Green's request of Maritain that he tell him the "*cold, hard* truth" about *Les Clefs de la mort* (Letter 32). Or those anxious phrases when he was going to send Maritain the manuscript of *Adrienne Mesurat*: "Will the book suit you? I dare not tell you what I think. I know only one thing, that I could not possibly have written it otherwise" (Letter 11). What he thought of his book and dared not say can be guessed; Green was almost afraid of this "rude little book" that Lautey would admire because he felt it was already "born." And Maritain was sure, even before having read it (Letter 12), as he would be astonished a little later on (Letter 40), that Green should be afraid of finding *Léviathan* rejected. To know himself "loved and understood" (Letter 34) was an immense comfort for the young novelist as it would continue to be for the aging man when he ran a great risk in writing a difficult autobiography (Letter 191). He would certainly find other supporters of the finest quality; I would wager that he found few as constant.

For purposes of clarity I should like to speak now of what might be called the literary relationship, that of author to reader and critic, between Green and Maritain. And this is all the more necessary for the first phase of their friendship since the reader and critic is also the director of the collection Roseau d'Or, in which the two novels that established Green's reputation were published. But Jacques Maritain was quite incapable of compartmentalizing what he distinguished more clearly than anyone: what might be called the ontological force and value of a work of art, and its fully human source and scope. He expressed himself at length on this subject in his writings on the philosophy of poetics, especially in his little book *La Responsabilité de l'artiste*, the last chapter of which is not unrelated to his affectionate admiration for Julien Green. Certain views which he proposes there with the most rigorous precision are also sketched out in his letter of September 1, 1951 (Letter 102); and it is not the least interesting aspect of this collection of letters that they point out to us how his personal involvement in the concrete, and sometimes painful, experience of a writer of fiction nourished, clarified, and sometimes inspired a doctrine that a too rapid reader might think sprang completely armed from the Minerva of Scholasticism.

In proposing to open his collection to *Le Voyageur sur la terre*, which at the time was appearing in serial form and which he did not yet know completely, Maritain wrote to Green: "I believe, without attributing to you any systematic objective, that, by the very effect of your own interior life, we are indebted to you for that kind of purification in depth on which the renaissance of the art of the novel depends" (Letter 8). There is a question here of poetic, not moral, purity; Maritain insists absolutely on this kind of purity. No one has more forcefully denounced the falsification that art suffers with the intrusions of a desire to moralize (RDA 35–36, 100–101/39–41, 99–100). *Fidelity to truth*, which he declared was Green's secret, "appears from the very beginning in his fictional work, centered entirely in what can be called the truth of the imagination, and . . . forces him to write only if he *sees* his characters . . ." (Letter 230).

But this interior necessity, which the novelist obeys in virtue of his own poetic ethic, is inseparable from a power that few men possess; and what is its source? "God has set you apart with great gifts. What moves me most profoundly is to see them bearing fruit in His light, close to Him. And indeed, with such gifts of soul, how much you need to cling to Him in prayer!" (Letter 22). "I have a feeling that there exist for you in this fearful earthly life, perhaps because you have been called more than any other to catch a glimpse of the other side of the tapestry, certain very dark and dangerous problems" (Letter 31). These dangers may be connected with the guilty passions which devour the characters, with the author's connivance with them, but perhaps even more so with those invisible powers whose wings may very possibly brush the brow of creative divination itself. It is to the degree that Green's critical consciousness lets itself be obsessed by the drama of passion that he has a "moral knowledge" of it; it is to the degree that Maritain descends to a deeper level, in Green's work itself, that he discerns a preconscious "poetic knowledge." It is never the "Prudent Man, firmly established in his moral virtue" (RDA 35/40), who, in the person of Maritain, addresses the novelist Green, but the Spiritual Man, aware of far less palpable realities. This can be recognized in the judgment he passes on *Léviathan*, where he recognizes that the author has won "an astonishingly difficult match."

> From the point of view *of the novel*, one might reproach your universe for ignoring the debate, the choice, that comes from the glimmerings of man's reason as well as the baitings of grace, and all the agitation of in-

telligence and of conscience that characterizes our human condition. Passions rise like the sun, alone filling the whole sky. But one might answer that the novelist is free to paint only one aspect of what is [Letter 40].

The Prudent Man would knit his brows; the Contemplative would bow with sadness before this "universe of darkness," which is "none other than Leviathan," and reflect that the author has depicted sin as it should be depicted (Letter 40), which may not be the point of view of Green himself.

This was the last of Green's works that Maritain would publish, with a request to insert an introduction with two sections, one expressing the point of view of the author, the other of the collection. The relationship became rather distant, for reasons we have seen. The offer made to publish a novella of his in an issue of *Chroniques* (Letter 56; the date needs correction: 1931 or 1932) had no follow-up; nor did the invitation to collaborate on the *Courrier des Iles* (Letter 54). We are thus deprived of the commentaries Maritain might have made—perhaps he did make them orally—on *L'Autre Sommeil, Épaves*, and especially *Minuit*. Later too we missed what he thought of *Si j'étais vous*, of *Sud*, of *Chaque homme dans sa nuit*. But, as if in compensation, we are overwhelmed by the correspondence about *Varouna, Moïra, Le Malfaiteur*, several volumes of the *Journal*, and the autobiography. I shall not analyze in detail what was written about each of these works. We have already mentioned how relations between the two men grew closer; other reasons (age, the historical moment) imperceptibly but intimately modified their dialogue. What I should like to consider now are the problems they grappled with, which they took up once again, in complete confidence, problems of vast scope, especially one: Is the consecration of a novelist to his work compatible with that search for perfection without which one cannot be called a disciple of Christ?

*

This question tortured Julien Green, even though it remained half-conscious for a certain time. From the day he gave up the idea of becoming a monk, "the weight of the Cross" was lifted from his shoulders (March 30, 1941). At least he thought so, but he noticed quite often that it was not all that simple. Was not the *Pamphlet* a warning addressed to himself in the person of the "Catholics of France"? Even when he was tottering on the brink of unbelief and deprived of the life of the sacraments, and even more so when he returned to the full practice of the Christian life, the call to perfection made itself heard, sometimes faintly, sometimes clearly. Clear or faint, it was the sign of a dead-end street; because in choosing to remain "in the world," he was answering another call, no less imperious, that of a writer—and a writer of novels. It possessed him like another vocation, and it truly was one, but one incompatible with sanctity. In the course of a meeting with Maritain, during the war, he made this remark: "One can imagine a saint painting a picture (Fra Angelico) or composing music. Can one imagine a saint writing a novel?—Why not? I was asked.—Mention one, I replied. Until there is a new order of things, a novel written by a saint remains a kind of ideal. I even wonder if the fact of writing a novel wouldn't be an obstacle to a serious pursuit of the spiritual life" (June 8, 1943). He was not the first to put the question in this way. Mauriac asked it before him; perhaps he even influenced Green in this respect: " 'One would have to be a saint. . . . But then one wouldn't write novels.' . . . But yes!" Maritain replied. "One would write novels if one were born a novelist" (FP 120–21/AP 64).

It would be a mistake to think that Maritain saw things only from the outside. He certainly was not a novelist. But he was a writer of real pedigree, like his godfather, Léon Bloy, and of even better lineage. Most important of all, he had undertaken as a layman to challenge the Prince of this World on his own terrain—by working to resow the seed of the Gospel, without the slightest concession, in that profane culture where the perfume of Bethany had become almost imperceptible in the worldly winds of many centuries: by elaborating a philosophy of nature, a philosophy of history, a philosophy of art and a political philosophy, diversely and supplely joined to a metaphysics guided by light from above. It was a mad undertaking: to bring Christian wisdom down into the street (RJC 50/115). He was not without periods of discouragement, however: " 'Have I been mistaken? Was I wrong to spend all my time on these literary figures?' " (May 1, 1929). The conversions were not always lasting; betrayals were numerous. He began again; he always started over because he had a "heart free enough to suffer what had to be suffered" (RJC 54/119). This is what is meant, in all its fullness, by the expression "integral humanism," which is too often reduced to its political aspect alone: trying to create, in the very heart of the profane, now considered autonomous and taken as such, heroically faced but accepted in the name of divine *philanthropia* (Titus 3:4), something other than the sacral Christianity of the Middle Ages, and if possible better than the Middle Ages, but in fraternal communion with all ages of the Gospel and all the nations of the earth—not only the lands in which these peoples have rooted their genius, but the multiform disciplines by which this genius is expressed in the little space of time accorded here below. Art is one of these forms, and the creation of novels is one form of art. Jacques Maritain, who gave himself without reserve to all that demanded his attention, considered the art of the novel with a respect that theologians never took into account. Julien Green had considerable influence here, Dostoevski too, and a small number of others. Mauriac played no more than the role of a detonater.

It was nevertheless he who ended up proposing the formula that Maritain recalled again and again: "'From now on, the whole question for me comes back to this: *purify the source*'" (FP 122*n*1/AP 65*n*1). But Green protested that purifying the source would be equivalent to castrating the novel (the expression is not his, but, crude as it is, it seems to me to express his thought). Certain novels he was led to read, and we do not know which ones they were, confirmed him in his opinion: this "is nothing but white on white," but he added immediately: "I firmly believe that this kind of book is the fruit of sin and that where there is no sin there can be no novel" (Letter 120). This can be understood in the sense that the datum of experience offered to the novelist is the human species itself in its concrete reality, which is effectively and tragically the universe of sin. But one might ask if he read attentively the little book he acknowledged having received, *La Responsabilité de l'artiste*, in which Jacques analyzed with such care and such delicate nuance the multiple aspects of the problem: he was certainly not the one to mistake its "mysterious character." But, after all, I understand very well that Green did not feel much at ease in the distinction between "formal causality" and "material causality" (RDA 93–94/91–92) where I myself circulate only very slowly and with great precaution. It is even more regrettable that we do not have an answer to the admirable letter of September 1, 1951, which speaks of *Moïra* and *Journal* V: "I see no reason for the scruples you show at certain moments [in the *Journal*]. The book [*Moïra*] is terrifying—just like the human soul; it is constantly dominated by a rational vision that knows no connivance" (Letter 102). Did Green pay any attention to what distinguishes in the novelist the state of "reason" from that of affectivity? Near the end of the letter there is a striking *rapprochement* between the temptation of Luther and that of "every great poet when he is on the brink of despair" (Letter 102). Returning some years later to Mauriac's first assertion ("One would have to be a saint. But then one wouldn't write novels"), Maritain asked: "Couldn't each one of us say the same thing about his particular work in the world? *One would have to be a saint. But then one would not be a politician, or a judge, or a doctor, or a banker, or a business man, or a journalist, or anything else here below,* except perhaps a monk, and the job is still not secure" (RDA 108/104).

Luther considered the monastic calling so unworthy of recommendation that he condemned without remission any religious state whatever. I am not an expert on the Reformation; but is not the profession of philosopher, according to the spirit of the Reformation (I dare not speak of their logic), as radically opposed to the Gospels as the novelist's? Jacques Maritain's undertaking seems to me characterized by the reasoned desire to restore, in the name of the Gospels and in line with Genesis—*et vidit quod esset bonum*—the dignity of every natural activity, but purging it of the poison of the Reformation. He is perhaps not the only one, but I do not know many others who have carried on this work with such certainty, without the slightest naturalist concession. I certainly realize with what energy Green himself rejected Protestantism, from which a mysterious grace snatched, one by one, so many members of his family. But it is the culture to which we belong which has left in so many of us traces of these ancient conflicts. And I hope he will pardon me for saying that a certain tendency toward Port-Royal, in his case as in Mauriac's, is somehow connected with the anguishing problem of the novelist-who-wants-to-be-fully-Christian.

Maritain never put his dialogue with Green in these terms. But he gives me the impression of having given up discussion on this point: "I think we are indeed of one mind" (Letter 121). They could not be in agreement on the theory of the novel or, rather, of the novelist. They were in agreement on Green's works as they actually existed, which was the really important thing. I am convinced that, in writing *Chaque homme dans sa nuit,* Green was giving in to Maritain.

*

In Maritain's eyes, if there is an abyss between genius and sanctity, the experience of poets does not "symbolize" it any less than that of the saints: "Through the effect of a certain fundamental choice accomplished in the heart of man, the poetic experience can either *mimic* the mystical experience or be a *call* to it" (RDA 104–105/101–102), and I think he saw in Green a probable example of the latter case. There is

in Green the artist, in Green the poet, a radical incapacity to cheat—
and nothing separates him more from Gide. In a novel like *La Porte
étroite* is there not a mimicking of sanctity (which in the end makes
sanctity almost intolerable)? With *Les Faux-monnayeurs* and its double
diary (that of Edouard and that of the author), it is something else
again: the novelist, so to speak, multiplies himself and sets himself
completely beyond the grasp of the reader, except for the penetrating
gaze of a spiritual man like ⟨the critic Charles⟩ DuBos whom Gide and
certain of his friends never forgave for that penetrating look of his
which pierced to the very heart of Gide's most mature work. Gide's
reason is a reason that continually slips from one's grasp. Green's reason
is a reason that rebels but never surrenders. It was not by pure chance
that the jangling bell of the celebrated quarrel over the compatibility of
the art of the novelist with a fully Christian life was hung by the
author simultaneously about the neck of *Corydon* and *Numquid et tu.*
Gide wanted to play in all keys at once and make life as difficult as
possible for those of his friends whom Christ had taken in His net:
Claudel, Copeau, DuBos. Mauriac was not exactly a friend; theirs was
a sort of artistico-worldly relationship, which a recent and still fragile
conversion with its air of easy vulnerability made a choice target for
Gide. But in the end I feel a certain gratitude to Gide for having in-
voluntarily and from a great distance provoked Maritain's clarifications.
These clarifications do not make the vocation of the novelist easy; they
make it livable, at the cost of an heroic love of truth in all its aspects:
the truth of the work in its structure, that of the human object in its
creative genesis, that of the writer in his hand-to-hand combat with the
Invisible at the edge of the ford. The creation of a novel is certainly not
the whole of literary creation, but the place of the novel in contem-
porary culture draws, or used to draw, to it the most concentrated attention. But the reflections of the philosopher are far from limited to the
novel alone.

Among the problems he struggled with is one of which Green was
certainly not unaware: Do the purifying incursions of grace into the
soul of the author run the risk of weakening his creative power and
even, "like a parasite, [of] sucking the very life from his art" (RDA
101/92–93)? This is a question that does not admit of a hasty answer.
Varouna is a novel that lets us examine the question in the concrete
since this book was written during the years which saw the preparation
and consummation of that decisive transformation which determined

the style of the second part of Green's life and work. From the very beginning I had the impression of a story that was fascinating in its original intuition, but unfulfilled in its execution. Maritain is less severe than I am, all the while admitting that the first part (*Hoël*) seems to him "less 'inspired' and more 'willed,' with less latitude as far as the interior substance is concerned, and at the same time more sustained in style; it seems to me, if I may be so bold as to say so, too well written. The other two parts are haunting" (Letter 78). If I can trust my memory, since I have been unable to reread the novel, I had the same sensation about the adventure of Pierre and Hélène Lombard, but not about Jeanne's diary, which seemed to me precisely to express conceptions too close to the surface of consciousness. As the philosopher saw very well, the theme of metempsychosis (cf. February 28, 1941) was no more than a kind of fuse; the solidarity of human beings, who are unable to come together in empirical space, is the essential subject, but from my point of view it did not have the time to disappear from the diurnal film of consciousness and be *lost* in the underground passages of the creative instinct, in order to animate the entire work without itself being seen distinctly (RDA 101/93). The form of "journal," which Green had never used in any other novel, is indeed all the more out of place—but what else could he find?—in that the novelist himself practiced this form of expression parallel to his works of fiction. Jeanne's diary makes me think of an involuntary parody, if not an unconscious one, of Julien's journal. His saving spiritual crisis forced the novelist into an impasse—such, at least, is the impression which I retain after many years, and which is enlightened by a return to *La Responsabilité de l'artiste*. It is a work in which the connivance of the author with the *passions* of his characters is at a minimum (even though it was certainly not done with "white on white"); and it is a work in which the creative power seems to me inferior to that of his more troubling stories—like *Minuit* and *Moïra*.

On the other hand, *Le Malfaiteur*, written in good part while his spiritual crisis was still in its incipent stages but already gaining in strength, and suddenly interrupted in May 1938 to make room for *Varouna* (Pléiade III, 1595ff.), lay fallow for more than sixteen years— all his new life-apprenticeship and, in the midst of that long period, the war and exile—to be brought to its completion only after the double indirect confession of *Moïra* and *Sud*. Maritain, who did not know "Jean's confession," understood immediately that this character was the center of the book "in the astounding chiaroscuro in which you have kept him" (Letter 112). And he seems to have applauded, in the novelist's "boundless compassion" for his characters, in the "questioning so painful that it scarcely rises to the lips" (Letter 112), the invisceration of supernatural charity in the very exercise of the poetic gift.

Similarily, in the three volumes of the autobiography: "In reading you I seem to get a glimpse of the light in which the angels see the miseries of the flesh in our poor humanity. It is in no way a question of vocabulary and language (a perfectly pure language can be used to wound and soil the soul). It is a question of interior light—of grace and charity" (Letter 163). "One might say that all those things from which you have suffered so cruelly are a light veil that He [God] has placed before your eyes, with a kind of slightly ironic tenderness, in order to carry out His work, without your realizing it, in the depths of your soul . . ." (Letter 193). And again, apropos of a volume of the *Journal*, alluding to the pretended monastic vocation which a clumsy spiritual director had loaded on his young shoulders and to which for so long a time he was afraid he had been culpably unfaithful: "Father Crété, who is in Heaven, I hope, in spite of his imprudence, must be quite surprised to see by what paths and what extraordinary detours, and at what cost, God has traced out your destiny, and leads you to accomplish, in fidelity to an interior light, a mission which in substance is the very one to which that impatient director felt you were called" (Letter 114). A little earlier he had already written to him: "this desire to leave the world which haunts you is fulfilled in a very profound way by the simple fact of the Faith as you profess it. For what the world cannot tolerate in the Christian, what *separates* us from the world, is the Faith" (Letter 107)—a testimonial which gave great joy to Julien Green (May 29, 1955).

*

As a very young man he had told the philosopher that he could understand nothing in his books (*Antimoderne* and *Théonas* after all were really not all that hermetic . . .). Much later he assured visitors that the work of Maritain was closed to him because of his own lack of initiation into philosophy. His *Journal* and correspondence lead us to believe that this is rather a simplification of the facts. He read books that were very difficult of access. It is evident too that, during Jacques' last years especially, he did his best to understand his friend's publications. And above all in their conversations and letters, they debated rather difficult theological problems. A few months after Raïssa's death, Maritain put to Green this unexpected question about Christ: "When do you think He realized He was divine?" Green gives the impression of being quite taken aback: "I suppose He always realized it—Don't you think so?" (March 6, 1961). Several years went by before Maritain decided to treat in a technical manner this question which had caused such an upheaval at the time of Modernism, and to offer his response to the public (*De la grâce et de l'humanité de Jesus*, 1967). But it is probable that he had been carrying this question in his heart for a long time. Green was perhaps the first person he permitted even to suspect its presence there, which seems to me a moving tribute to Green's understanding of spiritual realities. Similarly, he discussed with him the problem of the "suffering of God" (October 10 and 30, 1968), a topic which he would treat in the *Revue thomiste* but which had haunted him since the time when Father Clérissac was his spiritual director (CN 86/60). Green was at times troubled by such perspectives, *apparently* so out of line with traditional doctrine (but what does it mean "to offend" God, if not to wound Him and hence in a certain sense to do Him harm?). At any rate he wrote on the day after Jacques' death: "with that angelic simplicity of his, and that courtesy of a *grand seigneur*, he succeeded in making me understand difficult truths as if he had just discovered them himself on the instant" (April 29, 1973). And at a much earlier date he had recognized that this way of undertaking to discuss the deepest subjects before audiences that had no special technical formation was far preferable to a condescending attitude and a language systematically watered down to the understanding of everyone (January 9, 1945).

An admirable page by Jacques indeed expresses quite well the contrast between the respective gifts, reflected in their dialogue:

> There is a kind of grace in the natural order presiding over the birth of a metaphysician as there is over that of a poet. The one throws his heart into things like a dart or a rocket, and by divination sees—within the sensible thing itself, indeed, inseparable from it—the flash of a spiritual light where a glimpse of God shines out to him. The other, turning away from sensible things, through knowledge sees, within the intelligible and detached from perishable things, this very spiritual light itself, captured in some conception. The metaphysician breathes an air of abstraction which is death for the artist. Imagination, the discontinuous, the unverifiable, in which the metaphysician perishes, is life for the artist. Though they both absorb the rays that come down from creative Night, the one finds his nourishment in a bound intelligibility that is as multiple

> as the reflections of God in the world; the other finds his nourishment in
> a naked intelligibility that is as determined as the proper being of things.
> They play at seesaw, each in turn rising up to Heaven. Spectators make
> fun of their game; for they are seated on the ground [DS 5/2].

But they also knew how to meet one another; the preceding pages
have tried to show this. "Being a *savant*, and a Thomist, and looking
like the *Beau Dieu* of Amiens had no effect; he never intimidated me"
(October 26, 1966). "I remember that between Jacques and me there
existed no familiarity whatsoever, only tenderness. We never felt the
need to exchange useless banalities. He would ask me about my work,
wanted to see everything I was writing. I sent him the texts. Three or
four days later a wonderful letter would arrive, thought out and composed with care after a most attentive reading" (April 30, 1973).[7] Green
questioned him about Mélanie de la Salette (April 26, 1942), about
Péguy and Bloy (August 28, 1942), about a thousand other subjects,
especially religious ones. Sometimes Maritain answered: "I don't know"
(March 6, 1961). He himself called up old memories, like the visit to
Gide in 1923 (June 29, 1949). Words Maritain had spoken welled up
from Green's heart: about Brémond (November 4, 1954), "God is very
vulnerable" (December 17, 1955). He is reminded of Maritain's features by others, like the poet easily identifiable with Patrice de la Tour
du Pin: a "*baptized* soul" (November 20, 1945: a passage deleted from
certain editions), the "evangelical faces" noticed in the churches of
Soviet Russia (October 18, 1955). When Jacques read such things in
the volumes of the *Journal*, he protested, incapable of seeing himself
in this light (Letters 114, 157). He said he no longer knew "who he
was." "How can we make an examination of conscience? We see
nothing; we cannot see ourselves. Behind the actions we perform there
is always a stranger" (October 20, 1967). But that incapacity to see
himself—indeed, that impatience about putting up with himself—was
precisely an integral part of Jacques' image; all his friends know it.

One of the most precious gifts Julien Green has left to the friends of
Jacques is the portrait he painted of him with such repeated brush
strokes in his *Journal*, from the first pencil stroke, naïve and charming:
"Good, but not enough ferocity" (April 13, 1926), passing through
"the very wise old angel" who explained the trial of Joan of Arc one
evening in New York during the war (June 24, 1943), to "the face full
of light," which turned and looked at Green for an instant after Com-

munion, the day of Raïssa's funeral (November 8, 1960). But the images of the final years are perhaps even more beautiful.

From then on Jacques was alone. He divided his time between the Fraternité at Toulouse, where he ended up "entering religion" completely, and Kolbsheim, where he was welcomed by the affection of his godchildren Antoinette and Lexi Grunelius, with brief stopovers in Paris. He took advantage of these stopovers to visit a few very close friends, especially Anne and Julien Green, not hesitating to climb the four storeys without an elevator, leaning on a supporting arm and stopping at almost every step. Green pictures him for us, "so frail, so bent, but his eyes so full of life, those beautiful blue eyes that sometimes flashed with impatience, that tongue which never stumbled, that un–self-conscious air of a *grand seigneur* who passes with royal ease above everything about him" (November 24, 1962). Or we see him as Heaven's vagabond, stretched out on his hotel bed, his feet "on a piece of paper so as not to soil the gold-buttoned comforter," who smiles as he speaks, corrects a preface, "looks several times in silence at his visitors, as if to speak to us other than with words" (July 2, 1962). Sometimes he says that "he went too far in his work (as others might confess to going too far at table)," affectionately holding Anne's and Julien's hands and speaking to them with tenderness (June 13, 1964). More and more "he is tired, suffers because of his stomach, asks with a look of ineffable purity if he has not become 'stupid' . . ." (March 9, 1968). From then on, "he moves about with a cane, a blanket over his arm" (October 10, 1968). "He wears a little cap, a long gray overcoat, shoes that seem a cross between boots and slippers" (October 5, 1970).

Julien finally learned that Jacques had fallen asleep in the Lord and he wrote: "His hand will never again cover mine affectionately; he will never again throw kisses to Anne and me, when leaving us in the street. This wonderful tramp, the Prince of the Kingdom of God, with his angelic smile and his words, so tender and precise, and with all his soul in the depths of his pale blue eyes" (April 28, 1973).

Jacques Maritain had written, to the great honor perhaps of his colleagues,

> The philosopher is inconsolable at the irreparable loss of the least fleeting reality, a face, a gesture of the hand, an act of freedom or a musical harmony, in which there flashes the slightest glimmer of love or beauty. He has his own solution, I must admit. He believes that not one of these

things passes away because they are all preserved in the memory of the angels; and since, chosen and uttered as they are by pure spirits, they are better off there than in themselves, he believes that the angels will never cease to speak of them to one another and thus bring back to life in a thousand different forms the story of our poor world [SS 208–209/124].

Let us hope that the angels, with whom he seemed to have such an affinity, will give him the task of telling all of us about those moments and the beating of all those wings, so divinely conserved. As long as this perishable life lasts for us, we give thanks to the friend and poet who has let us page through such a beautiful picture book.
October 8–19, 1979

NOTES

1. References to the works of Jacques Maritain and Julien Green are given in parentheses in the text.

The two principal sources for this study are the correspondence between the two writers and the *Journal* of Julien Green. Since this *Journal* has been published many times with differing numbers for the volumes, sometimes with passages added, at other times with passages deleted, it has seemed best to refer to each citation exclusively by its date.

On the other hand, references to the Letters exchanged between Jacques Maritain and Julien Green are (indicated by the number of the Letter in the present volume ("Letter 25") or of Letter and footnote number ("56.3")).

Each of the Maritain works cited has been assigned a siglum corresponding to the French version Henry Bars used. References will be given first to the French text; then, after a slash, to the English translation.

CN   *Carnets de notes* (Paris: Desclée De Brouwer, 1965) / *Notebooks,* trans. Joseph W. Evans (Albany, N.Y.: Magi Books, 1984)

DS   *Distinguer pour unir, ou Les Degrés du savoir* (Paris: Desclée De Brouwer, 1932) / *Distinguish to Unite, or The Degrees of Knowledge,* trans. Gerald B. Phelan (New York: Scribner's, 1959)

FP   *Frontières de la poésie et autres essais* (Paris: Rouart, 1935) / "The Frontiers of Poetry" is found in *Art and Scholasticism and The Frontiers of Poetry,* trans. Joseph W. Evans (New York: Scribner's, 1962), pp. 119–50; "Three painters," "Dialogues," and "The Freedom of Song," the "other essays" of the French volume, in *Art and Poetry,* trans. E. de P. Matthews (New York: Philosophical Library, 1943). References to "The Frontiers of Poetry" will be given immediately after the slash; those to the other essays after the siglum AP.

IC   *L'Intuition créatrice dans l'art et dans la poésie* (Paris: Desclée De Brouwer, 1966) / *Creative Intuition in Art and Poetry,* Bollingen Series 35 (Princeton: Princeton University Press, 1953)

PS   *Primauté du spirituel* (Paris: Plon, 1927) / *The Things That Are Not Caesar's,* trans. J. F. Scanlan (New York: Scribner's, 1931)

QC *Questions de conscience* (Paris: Desclée De Brouwer, 1938)

RDA *La Responsabilité de l'artiste*, trans. Georges and Christiane Brazzola (Paris: Fayard, 1961) / *The Responsibility of the Artist* (New York: Scribner's, 1960)

RJC *Réponse à Jean Cocteau* (Paris: Stock, 1926) / *Art and Faith: Letters Between Jacques Maritain and Jean Cocteau*, trans. John Coleman (New York: Philosophical Library, 1949), pp. 73–120

SS *Science et sagesse* (Paris: Labergerie, 1935) / *Science and Wisdom*, trans. Bernard Wall (New York: Scribner's, 1940).

Though these English versions exist, the translation of the Maritain quotation in this essay are my own. The citations to the printed translations are offered for the sake of convenience, should the reader wish to pursue Maritain's argument in its "original" context.

Pléiade I, II, III, IV, and V refer to volumes of the *Oeuvres complètes*, presented and annotated by Jacques Petit, in the Bibliothèque de la Pléiade (Paris: Gallimard, 1972–1977).)

2. This note, written by Jacques, is found on page 146 of the *Journal de Raïssa, publié par Jacques Maritain* (Paris: Desclée De Brouwer, 1963), and on page 159 of the English translation, *Raïssa's Journal, Presented by Jacques Maritain* (Albany, N.Y.: Magi Books, 1974).

3. This statement is found in Maritain's Foreword to the reissue of Julien Green's *Pamphlet contre les catholiques de France* (Paris: Plon, 1963), p. 9.

4. In these first days of their acquaintance, Green gave Maritain a beautifully bound Bible in Greek. During the Second World War, while the Maritains and Green were in the United States, Jacques and Raïssa had left a number of valuable books locked in a cupboard in their home at Meudon. During the occupation all these books disappeared. Whether or not the Gestapo took them when they searched the Maritain residence is not clear. At any rate, the Bible was not seen or heard of again until June 8, 1965. That evening, while listening to music in his library, Green glanced at his collection of Bibles and, expecting a visit from Maritain the following day, reflected on the beautiful Greek edition he had given Maritain as a gift years before.

The next day, Green, who had gone down to the street to meet the aging Maritain and help him up the stairs, was waiting to cross the street to the place where Maritain was paying the taxicab driver when a young woman approached and asked him if he was Julien Green. She had recognized him from photographs and asked if she might stop by the next day to offer him as a gift a Bible which she had bought in a used book store and which contained his signature below an inscription on the flyleaf of the volume. It was the Bible he had given Maritain almost forty years before.

5. "Tout dire sur soi-même" ["Telling Everything About Oneself"], *Le Monde*, June 6, 1970, p. 1, cols. 1–2; p. 2, col. 4.

6. Professor Piriou makes this suggestion in the first French edition of this correspondence: *Julien Green et Jacques Maritain—Une Grande Amitié: Correspondance (1926–1972)* (Paris: Plon, 1979), p. 67.

7. Henry Bars misdated this reference as May 24, 1973.

THE LIVING JACQUES MARITAIN

Julien Green

It was through my friendship with Stanislas Fumet that I came to know Jacques Maritain in 1925. I no longer know where the meeting took place. Perhaps at Meudon, in that little house which was to play so great a role in so many of our lives. In my baggage as a writer I had at that time nothing but an inflammatory pamphlet against the Catholics of France, and I hardly found a visit to a philosopher a very seductive idea, and when I was informed that this philosopher was a Thomist to boot, I was tempted to sneak off, because I had only the faintest notion of what Thomism was and I put myself instinctively on guard against it. I seemed to glimpse a vast system of definitions defining the indefinable, and besides, what did I have to say to a specialist in the study of the *Summa?*

The man who welcomed me dissipated on the spot all my apprehensions. Instead of a grim pedant, it was a man of exceptional charm who came toward me with outstretched hand. Just by writing these words, it seems to me that time is abolished and that once again I see his thin face tilted slightly to one side, his fine regular features and especially the smiling gaze of his pale blue eyes. However overused it may be, the word "angelic" came irresistibly to mind, and I had the immediate impression of finding myself in the presence of a purely Christian soul. In a second I realized what true interior serenity was, whereas within me there was nothing but deep disquietude.

I was all the more sensitive to such things in that, since the time of my conversion in 1916, I had never spoken to a Catholic about religious problems. In my circles, such things were not to be mentioned. Perhaps they were considered too personal not to be embarrassing. At the University of Virginia I saw only Protestants. After returning to France in 1922, I was taken for a fanatic if I risked the slightest attempt to lead the conversation into these forbidden realms. I finally broke the silence with my pamphlet and suddenly there was this Thomist philosopher who took my strange little brochure seriously and asked me all the questions I was burning to answer. Our confidence in one another was spontaneous.

With a clumsiness that was natural to me, I declared to the author of *Antimoderne* that I understood nothing in his books, to which he replied with a smile that this would not keep him from sending me copies of them as they came out and that I was dispensed in advance from reading them.

If I had only written down everything he said to me in the course of those first hours! I left him with a light heart, and that was the beginning of a correspondence, a long exchange which only the definitive silence of 1973 brought to an end. Alternating with the letters were long visits which helped me round the cape in many a difficult situation. I was young and in me nature revolted against the demands of the Church. In this matter it was grace alone that could be efficacious, and Jacques always showed the most exemplary discretion, trying simply to direct my attention to the writings of the mystics, because he had guessed that for me it was here that the most attractive aspect of Catholicism shone with a special brilliance.

However that may be, this mild-mannered Catholic showed a complete intransigence as soon as there was question of the integrity of the Faith. I saw him in those days as a warrior clad in armor, and not without some interior resistance, in spite of myself, I admired this knight of the absolute, beyond the reach, it seemed to me, of human passions. This impression was very strong. I, who felt myself so vulnerable, had no other way of explaining the luminosity of his gaze, and the ineffable radiance of his presence. When he entered my house, the world was transfigured. The poverty of language becomes very evident when I try to give some idea of these things.

I found myself before one of those men who give the impression of having come from another world. This came from the fact that he never hesitated to speak right off of God, of His relation with our souls, and of the respect He has for them and for their mysterious liberty. No one had ever spoken to me before in the language of an authority so filled with meekness, and, why not say it, so full of love. This was the gift which in my eyes made him unique. He needed but a few sentences to dissipate what I can only call my metaphysical terrors. And I had them, serious ones, but Maritain's presence always brought me peace. Very simply, when he was there, I was saved. Through the years of a youth prey to habitual torments, he maintained the hope that was indispensable for me. These words give some idea of the immensity of my indebtedness to him, the only words I can find, but they reveal only a shadow of what he was.

That being said, would I not betray the image I am trying to leave of him by insisting on his gentleness? To use once again the psychological categories of yesteryear, his place was among the irascible. In the azured pupils of his eyes, I saw his mounting anger flash at the slightest mention of certain injustices, and one felt him ready and eager to close in battle. His adversaries had no trouble finding him: he was there. His words could be devastating, like those of an angel turned furious. This gentleman was one of the violent who bear away the Kingdom of Heaven.

With the coming of age, he changed, but very little; his interior youth seemed to preserve him from the ravages of time. Standing slim and straight till he was sixty, he cast upon the world that gaze of a transparency that set him apart. I do not doubt he knew what effect he had on me that day when he declared in my presence, in one of his characteristic fits of impatience: "God is no imbecile and I am no saint!" But to no avail, and the second part of the sentence remained doubtful in the minds of many. In every situation he gave the impression of someone spiritually overwhelmed, and so the last sufferings of Raïssa provoked in him a kind of quickly mastered indignation. For years Providence seemed to have watched over him in a way that was far out of the ordinary. Then, suddenly, God struck him. Jacques took the blow with a painful astonishment that was transformed into an elevation of his entire being.

I stayed as close to him as possible, but what could I do? However, I believe that from that time on our friendship underwent a deepening that lasted till the end.

How can I forget that day of distress when he asked me to write for him a few lines about her whom he had lost? He read the note, folded it, slipped it into the pocket of his vest and said to me with an indescribably sad and affectionate smile: "A talisman against despair."

These memories make him so present to me that I cannot conceive how I could add to this testimony. If I have surrendered these letters to the public, it is so that they may preserve a reflection of that light in which I have never ceased to see him. May they shine in the eyes of some unknown reader as they still shine today in the mirror of my memory.

MARITAIN–GREEN
CORRESPONDENCE

One of the greatest favors God has bestowed on me was to put Jacques [Maritain] on my path in 1925. On this I insist.

JULIEN GREEN

For Julien Green I have an admiration without compare. I find it marvelous that an American should be the greatest French writer of our time.

JACQUES MARITAIN

I

Paris, 16 rue Cortambert, XVIe

April 6, 1926

Dear Sir,

For a long time now I have wanted to thank you for having considered me for the next issue of *Chroniques.* I recently sent a novella
to M. Stanislas Fumet,[1] and I would be happy if it should prove the
occasion for my speaking with you, not only of the novella itself,
but of many other things as well. I am always free in the afternoons
(preferably between two and five) and I should be glad to come to
see you at Meudon.[2] I hope to have the pleasure of meeting you.
Please, accept, sir, the expression of my respectful affection.

JULIEN GREEN

1. Stanislas Fumet, together with
Jacques Maritain, directed the collection
Roseau d'Or for the Parisian publisher
Plon. (Most of the works in the series
were full-length novels, such as Julien
Green's *Léviathan* or Georges Bernanos'
Sous le soleil de Satan, published under
the title of the novel. These volumes
made up a collection of short stories,
novellas, essays, etc., and were called
Chroniques du Rouseau d'Or and given
a number. The novella referred to here is

"La Traversée inutile," published in 1926;
it is no. 10 in the Roseau d'Or collection.)
⟨2. Meudon was a small town on the
outskirts of Paris where Jacques and
Raïssa had their home. There, every Sunday afternoon, they held open house for
the members of the Cercles Thomistes
and their friends. There, too, they held
periodic religious retreats, having been
granted special permission to keep the
Blessed Sacrament in the chapel of their
home.⟩

2

16 rue Cortambert

Tuesday, May 11, 1926

Dear Sir,

I was still reading *La Vie d'oraison*[1] when your *Réponse à Jean
Cocteau* fell into my hands. I am a slow reader anyway, but then
your book is not the kind to be swallowed at one gulp. At times
indeed it seemed to me rather difficult to understand. I feel some-

thing like an ant before a huge pile of grain. However hungry it may be, it knows full well that it cannot carry off much, so it takes what it can; it drags one grain off to its anthill. As for me, I have picked up this one thing which I will not easily put aside. *"Estote perfecti.* This is the call of love, to which love alone can respond." If you had not written that sentence, your book would still have moved me without any doubt; but that sentence you wrote for me, and I shall keep it and repeat it to myself because it was written according to the Gospels. I would be a bit embarrassed to pay you compliments on the rest of the book. I mean by this that my remarks would have a complimentary tone that I would find disagreeable. You have not helped me to love prayer more, but you have made me much more conscious of what a great grace it is to love prayer. And for this I thank you.

I have finally read your correspondence with Jean Cocteau about his conversion.[2] May I speak with you in all simplicity? The very idea of an open correspondence on such a subject at first disconcerted me, and I have not yet gotten over my surprise. It is difficult enough for me to tell someone about what goes on in my heart and about how it pleases God to act in my regard, but to make the general public a witness to so holy and mysterious an event as a conversion—I don't think I could do that. Perhaps you will say that St. Paul converted on the open road and in full daylight, and that these circumstances cannot be without some meaning and are in some way a kind of lesson for us. This may be true, and my scruples are perhaps the scruples of the bushel with respect to the light, but all this makes no sense. Nevertheless I read your book and liked it very much. Several times I found what I can describe only as a kind of genuflection of thought in the presence of God. It is books like this one that have led me to realize that reason itself can have warmth, movement, and generosity, just like the heart, and that reasoning can touch us and move us if it has its beginning in charity. But I hope that one day I will have the opportunity to speak with you at length about this *Réponse* and in a less general fashion.

I want to thank you again, dear sir, for the kind welcome I found

at your home and for the advice you gave me; I have not forgotten
that we agreed to pray for one another.

Please believe in my most respectful affection.

JULIEN GREEN

1. *De la vie d'oraison*, originally a "small spiritual manual, destined for the members of the Cercles Thomistes" (Jacques Maritain, *Carnet de notes* [Paris: Desclée De Brouwer, 1965], pp. 200–201 (*Notebooks*, trans. Joseph W. Evans [Albany, N.Y.: Magi Books, 1984, pp. 145–146])), was a joint work of Jacques' and Raïssa's, the first edition (1922) of which was not for sale. The work was later published by Art Catholique (1924), but again without the names of the authors. Their names appeared for the first time in the next edition. (The slender volume, translated by Algar Thorold, was published in the United States as *Prayer and Intelligence* (New York: Sheed & Ward, 1943).)

2. Jean Cocteau's *Lettre à Jacques Maritain* and Maritain's *Réponse à Jean Cocteau*, two brochures of 70 and 71 pages respectively, were published together by Stock in 1926; see Green's remark in his *Journal* on April 27, 1926 (*Les Années faciles*, rev. ed. [Paris: Plon, 1970], Pléiade IV) (quoted in 3.2. This exchange is available in English as *Art and Faith: Letters Between Jacques Maritain and Jean Cocteau* (trans. John Coleman [New York: The Philosophical Library, 1948]).)

3

Pax

Solesmes, May 25, 1926

Dear Sir,

I have been thinking of all the questions we spoke about at Meudon, and I say to myself: here is where you will find the answer. I wish with all my heart that you would come to spend a few days in this abbey where the soul breathes in the freedom of the Gospels. I wish you would come to see Father Abbot Dom Delatte,[1] a great soul filled with the spirit of God, and already committed to eternity. Since Dom Delatte is quite old and sickly, it would be best not to put off the trip too long. If you do come, let me know, and I will alert them and ask them to take you to him. If it is ever given to me to be of some service to you, I believe it will be in giving you this advice. And I give it to you in all simplicity because I feel that our conversation has authorized me to do so.

I understand very well the feeling you spoke about, your surprise at the way in which Cocteau made the general public witness to what took place within him.[2] But we must remember that he is in a special situation, having lived up to now always in the public eye, and that he considered it urgent that he bear this witness for certain souls he felt to be in peril.

I am happy that my "response" did not displease you and that you have found something useful in the little book *De la vie d'oraison*.

I cherish deep in my heart the memory of our interview. I think of you often and I feel that God loves you.

I hope we will see each other again. Pray for me. And I have not forgotten our agreement.

Believe in my devoted affection in Xto Jesu.

JACQUES MARITAIN

1. Dom ⟨Olis-Henri-Paul⟩ Delatte (1848–1937), Father Abbot of Solesmes and superior general of the Benedictines in France, went into voluntary exile on the Isle of Wight at the time of the laws passed against religious orders in 1901 by "le petit père Combes." The author of numerous works on philosophy and Scriptural exegesis, Dom Delatte also wrote a *Commentary on the Rule of Saint Benedict*.

⟨Émile Combes was Président du Conseil in the French government from 1902 to 1905. As a senator in 1901, he was champion of the anticlerical policies of the government and proposed the law of the Separation of Church and State, one provision of which was to expel certain religious orders from France and to disband and laicize those who remained, particularly those involved in Catholic education. Apparently the only exceptions to this law were the Daughters of Charity of St. Vincent de Paul.⟩

2. Jean Cocteau had published his *Lettre à Jacques Maritain* after a conversion which he later tried to renounce in part. Green wrote in his *Journal*: "Cocteau's letter to Maritain seemed strange to me. Does one speak of religion this way? The tone is bizarre. What does Maritain think of it?" (April 27, 1926, *Les Années faciles*, Pléiade IV). Maritain, at first discouraged, later answered the question by saying to Green: " 'Have I made a mistake? Was I wrong to spend my time on all these literary figures?' " (May 1, 1929, ibid.). These literary figures were Cocteau, Maurice Sachs, Henri Ghéon, etc.

4

June 7, 1926
16 rue Cortambert XVIᵉ

Dear Sir,

Your letter touched me very deeply, more so than I can tell you, and I beg you to forgive me for not having answered sooner. I have been thinking about Solesmes for years, but I will not go there yet this time.[1] Nevertheless I am very grateful to you for thinking of me and I thank you with all my heart.

May I see you again soon? I know you are very busy, but if you could give me an hour of your time I would be extremely pleased. I am free every day except Mondays, Saturdays, and Sundays.

Dear sir, believe in my affectionate regard.

JULIEN GREEN

1. In fact, Julien Green did not go until 1947.

5

Pax
Meudon, 10 rue du Parc   June 14, 1926

Dear Sir,

I too would be happy to see you again. God needs only a little time to establish real friendships.

Here is the arrangement I propose: I would like to invite you to a little talk that Father ⟨Vincent⟩ Lebbe, a Lazarist, will give to a few friends at our house next Friday at three o'clock; this admirable missionary, an apostle for a native clergy, has brought about miracles of conversion in China (and likewise, they say, miracles pure and simple). He is one of a kind, and I would like you to meet him.

So could you come about two o'clock? This would give us time to chat alone before Father Lebbe and our other friends arrive.

If this arrangement is not satisfactory, write to me at once, and we will make another.

Affectionately devoted in Xto Jesu.

JACQUES MARITAIN

6

Pax

Saint-Jorioz, Haute-Savoie   July 7, 1926

Dear Sir and friend,

A book of yours is the first one I read this vacation. I have just finished *Mont-Cinère* and I must tell you how much I enjoyed it. I find in it not only depth and authority, but grandeur too, and that invisible presence, that uninterrupted contact with the soul, which is the particular quality of real novels. If my testimonial were able to encourage you, I would be most happy; in any case I give it to you wholeheartedly; I have no doubt that you are in the line of the masters.

Might I add that in my opinion the book would lose nothing in being a third longer. On the contrary, this seemed evident to me in the second half.

I stopped at your house before leaving Paris but you were in Alsace. I missed the conversation we might have had.

Write me; you know I will be happy to hear from you.

Pray for me, my dear friend, and believe in my devoted affection in Xto Jesu.

JACQUES MARITAIN

7

July 27, 1926

Dear Sir,

I should have thanked you long ago for your letter and I hope you will be kind enough to excuse my silence. I was very sorry not to be able to come to Meudon before my departure to tell you how much I was moved by Father Lebbe's beautiful stories. I have thought a lot about him and about the miracle of the wheat. Wasn't that precisely in the spirit of the Gospels? But Father Lebbe himself made an even deeper impression on me[1] than his beautiful stories, and I thought, while listening to him, that it was difficult after hearing him not to feel oneself either better or worse. To remain at the same point after having approached such a man would seem too much like a step backward. Don't conclude, please, that I consider myself better, but let me thank you for having introduced me to this missionary.

What you say about my book is a great encouragement to me. A testimonial like yours helps me more than you can imagine. At present I am working in the midst of a disquietude that sometimes borders on despair, but letters like the one you were good enough to write give me back my confidence and make my task easier. Believe me, I am extremely grateful.

I hope to have the pleasure of seeing you again on my return, and I ask you to pay my respects to your wife. Dear sir and friend, accept my respectful and devoted affection.

JULIEN GREEN

1. See *Les Années faciles*, passim, but especially June 24, 1926, for his thoughts on Father Lebbe.

8

Pax
Saint-Jorioz, Haute-Savoie   August 21, 1926

Dear Sir and friend,
This little note I am writing you is dictated by a bit of self-interest. I do not receive the *Nouvelle Revue Française* here, but I notice in a summary of the last issue (which I read in a newspaper)

that you have begun publishing a novel there.[1] If you could reserve its publication in book form for Roseau d'Or, I would be very grateful. Massis[2] must have told you that for a long time now we have been counting on publishing one of your books. I deeply regret that *Mont-Cinère* did not come out in Roseau. I will never be able to tell you how much I value what you are doing and all that I hope for from your work. I believe, without attributing to you any systematic objective, that, by the very effect of your own interior life, we are indebted to you for that kind of purification in depth on which the renaissance of the art of the novel depends. I would encourage you with all my strength. Did you receive the last issue of *Chroniques*? I would be happy to know what you think of it.

It appears that there are now six Chinese bishops. Father Lebbe must be pleased!

Pray for us. My wife sends you her regards. Believe in my affection in Xto Jesu.

JACQUES MARITAIN

P.S. We are returning to Meudon about September 15th for a retreat which Father Garrigou-Lagrange is preaching to a group of friends and which begins on the 26th.[3]

1. *Le Voyageur sur la terre* appeared in *La Nouvelle Revue Française* in two parts and so fascinated Gide that he asked for the page proofs of the second part so as not to have to await its publication.

⟨2. See 25.1.⟩

3. (Reginald) Garrigou-Lagrange, a famous Dominican theologian and author of many theological works, including *Les Trois Âges de la vie spirituelle* (1928), had considerable influence in the Thomistic renewal of theological studies. Pope John Paul II was one of his students.

As the first spiritual director of the Cercles Thomistes, he regularly attended the meetings at Meudon and preached the annual retreats there. ⟨He had great difficulty accepting Maritain's positions on Action Française, the Spanish Civil War, and the Vichy regime. He even tried during the Spanish Civil War to forbid Maritain, as his spiritual director, to speak or write on political or social issues. Though he did defend Maritain's orthodoxy in Rome when conservatives there were agitating for the doctrinal censure of Maritain, he was surreptitiously involved in the attacks on him by such people as Rev. Julio Mienvielle of Argentina. See Bernard Doering, *Jacques Maritain and the French Catholic Intellectuals* (Notre Dame & London: University of Notre Dame Press, 1983), passim, esp. pp. 15, 87, 113ff., 209, 222.⟩

9

August 23, 1926

Dear Sir,

You are very kind to think of me for Roseau d'Or but *Le Voya-geur sur la terre*, which the *Nouvelle Revue Française* is publishing, is not a novel, but only a novella that is a bit long. And I was about to write you to ask this: Gallimard wants to publish this novella in "Une oeuvre, un portrait."[1] I answered a month ago, with the approval of Maurice Bourdel and on the advice of Le Grix, that I was ready to draw up an agreement with him. Recently I saw Aron about this matter, and we discussed the terms of a contract that I will sign on Gallimard's return.[2] All this to get to the point: Do you think Cocteau would be good enough to furnish my portrait? I have asked him, and undoubtedly did so clumsily, but I am somewhat frightened of him and I don't know how to approach him. He nevertheless sent me an extremely kind letter regarding *Mont-Cinère*, and I was deeply touched. To get back to my novella, I am not sorry that it is to be published by Gallimard because it seems to me after all a bit short for a volume in Roseau d'Or, but also because I wrote it long ago (in 1923) and it is quite far from me now. But since you have been kind enough to take an interest in what I write—and I can never tell you how much I appreciate your kindness—let me put this question to you: Why don't I give you my next book? And if that one doesn't suit you, why not the next, or the one after that, if by chance the first two are not suitable? I would be most happy to appear in Roseau d'Or, and as you see, I offer whatever I have. I know that you will be frank with me and that you will not hesitate to tell me if you think my book is no good. But let me thank you once again for your kind attention. For *Le Voyageur* I have no regrets, because I know that, having read it, you yourself will have no regrets in this respect (and yet you cannot imagine how much this *voyageur* resembles me). Excuse me for speaking to you like this about myself.

I think of you with great affection. The other day I was totaling up mentally all the things God granted me this year and I said to myself: "He let me meet Maritain, He let me hear Father Lebbe, He let me read *La Vie de Marie des Vallées*."[3]

Good-bye, dear sir. I am leaving the day after tomorrow for the Pyrenees, but I hope to see you this fall. Please give my respects to your wife.

I hope you are not forgetting me when you speak with God and that you realize the depths of my affection.

JULIEN GREEN

The richness of the Christian—this thought frightens me. To think that the name of Jesus, pronounced in the most distracted or the most blasphematory way, can bring Heaven to attention, increase the fervor of Purgatory, break the heart of Hell (in spite of the joy it might feel in hearing the name of Our Savior profaned)— in a word, stir in its entirety the whole invisible realm of creation. And there are Christians who yawn instead of throwing themselves on their knees and working miracles, and there are lips which close in death *having said nothing* when they could have set free so very many souls! Don't you find this terrifying? Don't be astonished if I always ask you to pray for me and if I plunge my hands into your treasures.

1. *Le Voyageur sur la terre*, appearing first in the review, was later published by Gallimard, with a portrait by Jean Cocteau. Plon then published it in a single volume which also contained "Les Clefs de la mort," "Christine," and "Léviathan." See 32.1.

2. (The four men mentioned are all involved in publishing: Gaston Gallimard was the owner and publisher of Éditions Gallimard; Bourdel was editor-in-chief at Plon, and Aron was evidently one of his managing editors;) François

Le Grix, the director of *La Revue hebdomadaire*, was a very influential reader for Plon.

3. *La Vie et les révélations admirables de Marie des Vallées*, by Emile Dermenghen (Roseau d'Or). This French mystic, who lived in Caen in the seventeenth century, like Father Surin, believed herself in Hell. She was a visionary whose exceptional intelligence made her greatly esteemed by the most notable spiritual personages of the day, including Father de Renty and St. John Eudes.

10

Pax
Saint-Jorioz, Haute-Savoie   September 2, 1926

Dear Sir and friend,

I have not been able to answer you sooner and I am still obliged
to write these lines in haste; excuse me, my work leaves me no
respite.

Yes, by all means, send your next book to Roseau d'Or; as I told
you, we will publish it with joy.

Yes again, I believe that Cocteau will be happy to do your portrait. I am writing to him about it. He is already supposed to do one
of Beucler for the same collection, but I don't think this will cause
any problem at all.

Thank you for all you have written. I was deeply touched.

It is indeed overwhelming to think of the endless consequences
of our most insignificant acts—overwhelming for us who bear the
sign of Jesus—and, what is even more terrible, the consequences of
all our omissions and our negligence. Alas, the universal misery we
see reminds us of them. One would fall into despair if one did not
give over everything, one's soul first of all, to the love of Jesus.
Jacta cogitatum tuum in Domino et ipse te enutriet.[1] As for me, I
am so conscious of my own misery that my only consolation is in
knowing how much the work I have been assigned is beyond my
capabilities. So it is God Who has to take things in hand.

Pray for me, my dear friend. Ask Him to help me in my power-
lessness. I pray for you with all my heart. All my affection is yours.

JACQUES MARITAIN

⟨1. Maritain's Latin is a paraphrase of Psalm 54:23: "Jacta super Dominum curam
tuam, et ipse te enutriet."⟩

II

October 15, 1926
16 rue Cortambert
Dear Sir and friend,

May I ask you a question? Here it is. Some time long ago Le Grix offered to publish my novel in his *Revue*.[1] I held back a bit in my answer, knowing that the novel would be quite long and that Le Grix was known for cutting with liberality, but now Bourdel has informed me that a novel cannot appear at the same time in Roseau d'Or and in a review, since Roseau d'Or is considered a review. He also explained to me that when a book is published by Roseau d'Or, it is as if it appeared simultaneously in a review and in Plon's yellow-covered series (at least, I think, as far as the number of copies is concerned). Yet other people at Plon insist that a book can appear in a review and in Roseau d'Or. You alone can solve this problem, and this is what I am asking you to do. As far as my personal feeling about the matter is concerned, you know what it is: I am writing my book for Roseau d'Or whether it appears in a review or not. You are therefore perfectly free to dispose of my manuscript as you see fit. Especially, don't think you will hurt my feelings by telling me that it cannot appear in a review.

In rereading what I have written I notice that I speak as if the publication of my book in Roseau d'Or were taken for granted. Will the book suit you? I dare not tell you what I think. I know only one thing, that I could not possibly have written it otherwise. If it is bad, it will not be for lack of work, but if it is bad, I am counting on you to tell me so.

At the moment I am sick. I think of you very much. In order to be with you a little I am rereading all there was about you in *L'Invendable* and *Le Pèlerin de l'absolu*.[2] Certain things had so deeply moved me that I wrote you, then I tore up my letter. (The story about the convert of Montpellier, I mean your part in this story.)

Good-bye, dear sir. I will write again when I am feeling better.

Please remember me to your wife and believe in my devoted affection.

JULIEN GREEN

1. *Adrienne Mesurat*, which was published by Plon in 1927, in the Roseau d'Or series, appeared serially first in *La* *Revue hebdomadaire.* 2. The titles of two volumes of Léon Bloy's *Journal.*

12

Pax
Meudon, October 19, 1926

Dear Sir and friend,

Since you want to put me completely at ease in telling me that you do not particularly insist on your novel's appearing in the *Revue hebdomadaire*, I will answer by asking you to keep it for Roseau d'Or, which is—because of the limited number of its copies, its system of subscriptions, etc.—at the same time a review as well as a collection. Once the copies in Roseau d'Or are all sold out, your book will go into the regular stock of Plon publications (yellow cover).

As I already wrote you, it is a joy for me to publish this novel in Roseau d'Or. Even before reading it, I know it has that quality of spiritual nobility which gives a work its greatest value.

I feel bad that you are sick. I myself am not very well these days. But if you have to stay in bed for a while, I will be glad to come to see you. We always seem to have so much to say to one another, and in spite of what is actually said, so much also in silence and in prayer.

But why did you tear up that letter which I would have liked so much to read? Pray for me and believe in my devoted affection.

JACQUES MARITAIN

I could come to see you some afternoon next week!

13

16 rue Cortambert
[October 1926]

Dear Sir and friend,

Thank you very much for your letter. It touched me deeply. I will never let you inflict on yourself such a long trip in order to come to see me, and besides I am quite well now. I had the flu. Wouldn't you like me to come to see you some afternoon next week? I know you are very busy and I won't stay long—in any case don't be at all scrupulous with me. This will be a way of showing me that you accept my friendship.

JULIEN GREEN

P.S. I will be free Tuesday, Wednesday, and Friday of this coming week and every day of the following week except Monday and Saturday. Naturally I will arrive after lunch, since I am busy in the mornings, as I told you.

14

Pax
Meudon, October 26, 1926

Dear Sir and friend,

I am busy every day this week, but could you come next TUESDAY, November 2nd, in the afternoon, say at three o'clock? I will be pleased to see you.

Affectionately yours,
JACQUES MARITAIN

15

November 9, 1926
16 rue Cortambert

Dear Sir and friend,

I'm sorry I have to write you in haste but I just remembered something I forgot to ask you. Again it's about my novel. You told me, didn't you, that it was supposed to come out toward the end of March? I would be very happy for that is an excellent time of the year, and if you could arrange that this date remain unchanged, I would be most grateful. I don't know if you have received any word about its publication in a review, but in any case I would not want at all that, to permit such a publication, the date of its distribution in bookstores be put off or that it be given another number in the Roseau d'Or series. I may seem to attach an inordinate importance to this question of a date, but *Mont-Cinère*, which was supposed to appear near the end of April, did not appear till the middle of June, which even Le Grix admitted was annoying.

I wanted to write an entirely different letter. I had intended to speak to you of your book which interested me so much, but I will have to put that off till another day. I have likewise reflected quite a bit on our conversation.

Believe in my devoted affection.

JULIEN GREEN

P.S. Let me remind you once more that I would be brokenhearted that though my book pleased you, it should appear elsewhere than in Roseau d'Or. I will gladly sacrifice its appearance in serial form so that it might appear in your collection.

16

Pax
Meudon, November 10, 1926

My dear friend,
    (I hope I do not offend you by addressing you in this simple way.) May I ask you to come to Meudon twice next week after dinner (around 8:30)? First on Tuesday, the 16th, then on Thursday, the 18th.

    The first time would be to meet de Massot and Nicholas Nab-akoff;[1] the second, to see Robert Honnert and a few friends, and to speak about a review that Honnert would like to bring out as soon as possible (not a "prestigious review," but a few pages on current events, a sort of continuation of *L'Oeuf dur*[2]), the principal object of which would be to furnish for a certain time a point of encounter for so many young people such as those whom you and I know, believers or those drawn to God, and those who run the risk of becoming discouraged and of wandering away.

Excuse me for bothering you in this matter. I do so only because such a project seems to me so very useful. Believe in my profound affection.

JACQUES MARITAIN

P.S. I just received your letter. I was not worried at all since I had heard nothing, either from Plon or from Le Grix about the eventual publication in the *Revue hebdomadaire*. I am writing immediately to M. Maurice Bourdel to tell him that I insist absolutely on your novel's appearance in Roseau d'Or in March, and that I am opposed to any previous publication in the *Revue hebdomadaire*.

1. Nikolas Nabakov, a Russian musician, was a member of Diaghilev's Ballets Russes and lived in Berlin and the United States. He wrote ballets, an opera, and a *Symphonie biblique*, as well as a cantata for voice, chorus, and percussion, *Le Collectionneur d'échos*, which, according to Julien Green, "he used to howl at the piano for his friends."

2. *L'Oeuf dur*, a review published by young philosophers, lasted for sixteen issues.

17

16 rue Cortambert
[between November 10 and 16, 1926]

Dear Friend,

I would be most pleased to come on the two dates you have mentioned. I beg of you to forgive me for all the trouble I have given you about my next book. You are so kind, and I am afraid I have somewhat taken advantage of you. I am anxious to see you again and to speak with you about your book.

Very affectionately yours,

JULIEN GREEN

18

Pax
Meudon, 10 rue du Parc   December 1, 1926

My dear friend,
  A serious case of the flu keeps me from writing more than a few
lines to tell you that my friend Pierre Van der Meer[1] would like to
do an article on you. He has *Mont-Cinère* and has already spoken of
it in a chronicle. But he would also like to have the pamphlet. In
fact, he would like all you have published and anything about you
that might interest the Dutch public. *And also a portrait to have
reproduced.*
  Address: Pierre Van der Meer de Walcheren,[1] Danielwillinks-
plein 42, Amsterdam.
  Very affectionately yours

                                              J. M.

1. Pierre Van der Meer de Walcheren ⟨was a close friend of Maritain's, who, like Maritain, converted through his association with Léon Bloy and, again⟩ like Maritain, was Bloy's godson. ⟨He was a frequent visitor to Meudon and an active participant in the Cercles Thomistes. For some time he worked in publishing, as a⟩ director of Roseau d'Or at Plon and as a literary editor at Desclée De Brouwer.

19

                                    December 7, 1926
                                    16 rue Cortambert

Dear Sir and friend,
  I couldn't ask for anything better than to send my pamphlet to
Pierre Van der Meer, but I have only one copy left and the rough
drafts I have kept are incomplete. For the portrait, I will have sent
to him the one Manuel made of me. The one made by Martinie is
absurd. As soon as *Le Voyageur* appears, I will send it to him with
pleasure. I am very touched that Van der Meer should be interested
in me. I have known of him for a long time now, through Bloy's
journal.

Excuse me for writing such a short letter but I have so much work that I don't know how to handle it all. I hope you are quite well and that in your prayers you will remember your affectionately devoted

JULIEN GREEN

20

January 6, 1927
16 rue Cortambert

Dear Sir and friend,

I hope you will forgive my long silence, but my novel[1] has given me so much trouble that I have not been able to find the time to go to see you. It is finished now, happily, and although I still have a few corrections to make, I am going to send it to you today or tomorrow. You do not know how happy I will be to know how you feel about this book, and I beg you to feel perfectly at ease in telling me exactly what you think of it. I have done all I could to make it a good novel, and if it isn't then it can't be my fault. Don't be afraid then of hurting me. I want the truth from you.

Now, if it's all right with you, I will come to get my manuscript as soon as you finish reading it, and this will give me the chance to see you. If you could tell me the day I might come, I would be very much obliged. I could come Friday, the 14th, or Tuesday or Wednesday of the following week, after lunch.

Please accept, dear Sir and friend, my most devoted friendship.

JULIEN GREEN

1. *Adrienne Mesurat* (Pléiade I).

21

Pax
Meudon, January 11, 1927   in haste

My dear friend,
    I have just received your novel and am very anxious to read it.
As soon as I finish it I will write to you. In the meantime I send you,
along with my thanks, all my best wishes and my very affectionate
remembrance. I hope to see you soon.

JACQUES MARITAIN

    If you would like to see Father Lebbe again (he is leaving for
China), he will be here Friday, the 21st. He will say Mass at 8:00 in
our chapel and then stay the rest of the morning.

22

Pax
Meudon, January 15, 1927

My dear friend,
    I read your novel through at one sitting. I find it *very beautiful*,
with an interior power, a rectitude, and a profundity that are admirable. In brief, I am very enthusiastic. I take great joy in the fact
that it is coming out in the Roseau collection, and I am grateful to
you for this.
    God has given you great gifts. What moves me the most pro-
foundly is to see them bearing fruit in His light, and close to Him.
And indeed, with such spiritual gifts, how necessary it is for you to
cling to Him in prayer.
    I shall be very happy to see you and to chat with you. Can you
come Monday the 17th, the day after tomorrow, at 4:00? If not,
I won't be free again till Sunday the 23rd. In any case, please give
me a call about noon (Bellevue 357).
    Did I write that Father Lebbe will pass through here on Friday

the 21st? He will say Mass in our chapel at 8:00 and then stay through the morning. I would be very happy if you could come. Pray for us, my dear friend. Affectionately in Xto Jesu.

JACQUES MARITAIN

23

16 rue Cortambert XVIe

March 3, 1927

My dear friend,

I have just learned something that greatly surprised me and which I cannot keep from telling you immediately. It seems there is question in Roseau d'Or of giving me number *16* instead of number *15* as it had been agreed a long time ago.

At Plon they tell me this will make no difference at all since numbers 15 and 16 should appear at almost the same time and there will be a difference of only a few days between the two dates of publication. But since there is so little importance in the date I fail to see why there should be any changes in what was agreed upon and made public. As far as I am concerned, I would be truly upset if the publication of my novel were put off, even if only for a week, and I would like to remind you of the promise you were good enough to make to me. I know very well that you can do nothing about the slowness of the printer, but that's not what I mean. I ask simply that I be given number 15 in this year's series, as we agreed. It may seem a "foible" that I attach so much importance to a question that may be of no interest to others. The last time I had the pleasure of seeing you, you asked me if I considered it important that the book come out at the end of March. And I answered: yes, certainly, and once again I cannot tell you how much I desire that there be no delay that could in any way be avoided. And it's very simple, isn't it, to avoid changing the order of the numbers in a series, at least as far as the next three volumes are concerned. I would like to think that there is really no question of a change at all and that I have been misinformed, but if you could send me a word to reassure me, I would be most grateful. I ask your forgiveness for sending no more than this unpleasant letter, and I hope you will excuse me, but you cannot realize how much this whole affair bothers and upsets me; I couldn't sleep last night. I have complete confidence in whatever you decide and I beg you, my dear friend, to believe in my deepest affection.

JULIEN GREEN

24

March 3, 1927

Dear Sir and friend,

I wrote you in haste a short while ago and I beg you to excuse me if my letter has caused you the slightest displeasure. Since then I have had a conversation with Maurice Bourdel, and he has assured me that nothing would be changed in the order of publication of this second series of Roseau d'Or and that I would have number 15 as you had told me. Let's pretend, if you like, that I have written you nothing, and pardon me once again for this useless correspondence. I think of you often and with great affection.

JULIEN GREEN

25

Pax
Meudon, March 4, 1927

My dear friend,

I am deeply upset about your problem. Here is what happened. On the one hand, Massis[1] has almost finished his book, which is being printed as it comes in; and he is burning to appear in print as soon as possible. On the other hand, this book had been announced a long time ago as number 15, so that many bookstores subscribed to number 15 thinking it was *Défense de l'Occident*; to give Massis number 15 and you number 16 then would spare Plon a few commercial difficulties. When they mentioned this to me, I answered that the change in numbering did not seem to have any great importance, *on condition* that your book would be *in no way put off because of it*. It was decided in the last meeting at Plon (that is, Wednesday, the day before yesterday) that numbers 15 and 16 *should come out on the same day*. That means the beginning of April, and that the issue of Chroniques, which is horribly late (number 14), only at the end of March. If by chance Massis is late, I have asked that he get number 16 (so much the worse for Plon's commercial difficulties) and this morning I am again writing to M. Bourdel in this vein. I believe then that there is no reason to worry. Write me quickly if this reassures you; I would be so sad if Roseau d'Or caused you any pain. This whole affair has turned sour for me. I did all I could to arrange it for the best when it fell to me to do so, and I thought it was going so well.

I just received your second letter and I am overjoyed that everything has worked out and that M. Bourdel is keeping number 15 for you. This simplifies everything. It is a great relief for me.

My dear friend, believe in my deep affection.

JACQUES MARITAIN

1. Henri Massis, a fervent disciple of Charles Maurras, the leader of the ultra-right movement Action Française, had a falling out with Maritain, Mauriac, and Gide for the position he took in his *Manifeste des intellectuels français pour la défense de l'Occident et la paix en* Europe in favor of Mussolini's invasion of Ethiopia. ⟨As a reader of the manuscript of Massis' book *Défense de l'Occident*, Maritain was strongly critical of many of his friend's positions and statements.⟩

26

March 4, 1927

Dear Sir and friend,

Your letter just arrived and I don't know how to thank you. I was so afraid you would be irritated by the trouble I am causing you, and if you had been I would not have been surprised nor would my feelings have been hurt. The whole question of numbers must seem ridiculous to you, and finicky as well, but as you know, a scalded cat fears cold water, and I cannot get out of my mind the interminable delays in the publication of *Mont-Cinère*. Let me say in my defense, though, that since December I have been told time and again that I would appear *immediately after* Chroniques because Massis is not ready. Suddenly Massis is ready. Is that my fault? He himself said he did not expect to finish his book so soon.

Pardon me, dear friend, and thank you again for your great kindness. You have all the affection of

JULIEN GREEN

27

March 16, 1927

Dear friend,

The other day I told a number of Father Lebbe's stories to some friends, unbelievers for the most part, who appeared extraordinarily impressed by them. And one of them said to me: "Why doesn't Maritain put out a collection of these stories in Roseau d'Or? That would do much more good than . . ." (and here he mentioned several books from this collection which he considers, I think, too difficult, or, in any case, of little practical interest). I propose this idea because it appears to me excellent and perhaps of Providential origin. It seems to me that the story of the wheat could at least lead the reader to reflect, if not to convert. Imagine, for example, each of the collaborators at Roseau d'Or writing a story based on the documentation Father Lebbe would give him. Oh, imagine the story of the wheat told by Claudel! Don't you think it very much in his style?

I think of you with profound affection.

JULIEN GREEN

28

[Beginning of June 1927]

Dear friend,

You'll never know how deeply I was touched by the way in which you spoke with me yesterday evening, but there is something that distressed me very much. It is the fact that during the course of our conversation I lied to you on a very precise point. I can find no reason which could explain this lie, much less excuse it. It seems to me I must have done it out of carelessness and that afterward human respect kept me from telling you the truth. And then I was undoubtedly afraid that I would be led on too far and tell you things I don't want to tell you now. But here's what it was all about. You asked me if I intended to live alone and I said yes when I should have said no.

I want you to forgive me not only because you are a Christian but from the bottom of your heart so that nothing remain of the fault I have committed. I will not even try to give you an idea of the pain this has caused me. I think I can say that I never lie, and it is very disagreeable to think that I have hidden the truth from one of the persons I love most in this world, even if it happened only once. I write all this to you very quickly and very badly, but I want you to know right away what I have done and to ask God to pardon me.

I embrace you with all my heart.

JULIEN

29

Pax
Meudon, 10 rue du Parc

My dear Julien,

You didn't really lie to me, for I understood what you did not tell me. Now that I know you a little better, my dear friend, I love you more than before, and the sense of respect I feel for your soul has grown even greater. If there is any evil in you, an evil whose very thought weighs heavily on my heart, yet I know, and I could never doubt it for an instant, that the entire substance of your being is of such nobility that you yourself cannot know it—a nobility I wonder at with trembling before God Who made you. This I know forever.

Let me speak to you frankly: a conversation like the one we had, a letter like the one I received this morning, casts me down before God and makes me ask for death. Because God has led me to understand I *must* help souls like yours to work out the problems in which they find themselves involved. What good am I if I do not carry out this service? Incapable of helping you by my miserable words, what can I do except offer up for you the sufferings and death it should please God to send me? I make this offering with all my heart. For we are engaged in a great and terrible struggle. Whatever it may cost, however long it may take, we must try to clear these things up. I ask you to speak of this often with me, certainly not to trample indiscreetly on what is your personal concern, but in an effort to examine the problem in the light of truth, and by doing so, without our knowing how, to help certain souls.

St Francis[1] wept because Love is not loved. What makes everything so serious is that it is a question of our debt to Uncreated Love. The Gospel nowhere tells us to mutilate our hearts, but it counsels us to make ourselves eunuchs for the Kingdom of God. This is how I think the question must be posed.

I know some married couples who for the love of Christ have made a vow of continence, and whose mutual love has divinely deepened because of it.[2] Why could the same *separation* not be possible in other cases? Or must we put down the Cross of Christ and replace it with the cross of our own choice?

Pray for me, my dear friend, as I pray for you. I embrace you with all my heart.

JACQUES

1. Saint Francis of Assisi is a subject who has always interested Julien Green. In 1982 he wrote a book about the life of this saint, whose name he took at his baptism as a Catholic. (Published in French as *Frère François* (Paris: Le Seuil, 1983), it is available in English as *God's Fool: The* *Life and Times of Francis of Assisi*, trans. Peter Heinegg (New York & San Francisco: Harper & Row, 1985).)

2. This question is treated in Chapter 7 of Maritain's *Carnet de notes*, "Amour et amitié," pp. 301–54 ((*Notebooks*, "Love and Friendship," pp. 219–57)).

30

June 25, 1927

My dear friend,

I have been thinking for a long time about your letter which brought me great sorrow, as you might have expected. I do not ask for death, which will be sent to all of us at the moment God chooses. Should we not instead bless life and be grateful to Him Who has given it to us? I tell you this without losing sight of the deep respect I owe you, but since you are speaking frankly with me, let me speak in the same way with you. I confided a bit in you the other day because I did not want to leave you in error about me, but what can I tell you today that I have not already told you? You think I am living in sin. I do not think so because my conscience is untroubled, and you ought to know me well enough to realize that I am not negligent in examining it carefully and that I am even inclined to push scrupulosity much further than necessary.

Be assured, dear friend, that I am profoundly aware of the affection you have never ceased to show me, and know that you will always have my friendship.

JULIEN

31

Pax
Meudon, 10 rue du Parc   June 29, 1927

My dear friend,

I am so sorry to have caused you pain. Believe me, that is not what I intended. What did I intend? I had no end in view except to tell you very simply—with perhaps too much naïveté—what I felt in my soul. It seemed to me that I could not reply to your confidence without opening my heart to you with absolute sincerity. If I spoke to you of death, it is because a moment arrives in life when, after having spoken and acted as one can (so badly, alas), one realizes that there is no other way of helping those one loves than to sacrifice for them whatever God may wish. It is a call which He Himself makes one feel and which one can hardly resist. Do you think that I am passing judgment on you? I know too little about your life to permit myself the slightest appraisal of your conscience. But then, I will never judge you. I do not think you are living in sin. I know nothing about that. What I do know is the depth of your heart, and that you are inclined, as a matter of fact, to push scrupulosity too far, and that at no price would you wish to offend Jesus. And because of this very fact, what causes you pain causes me even deeper pain. I have a feeling that there exist for you in this fearful earthly life, perhaps because you have been called more than any other to catch a glimpse of the other side of the tapestry, certain very dark and dangerous problems. I would give anything to help you solve them.

May the holy light of the Gospel enlighten both of us, my dear Julien. May we never refuse whatever that light may show us. Pray for me and forgive me if my letter made you sad. I embrace you.

JACQUES

32

January 11, 1928

My dear Jacques,

You will receive my book[1] in a few days. I hope it pleases you. I beg you to tell me without any consideration for my feelings if you find it weak. That will not discourage me, I assure you, and your opinion is too precious for me to do without it. Read it some day when you have a little time, read it in six months or in a year, but read it, Jacques, and tell me what you think of it. I like you too much for you not to tell me the truth, the *cold, hard* truth. You told me once that God gambled with death. This wager is the subject of the book I have sent you, a terrible wager where the winner is always the same. I cannot keep from telling you something about this novella. This is not like me, as you know. I have the feeling it will not please many readers. You will see that the real subject is scarcely indicated and that the main character is not much more than a shadow. This is due to the mediocrity of the person who is telling the story, a story he doesn't understand very much himself; it is also due to the fact that I feel unworthy to speak about certain things. One critic told me with a thousand utterly superfluous precautions that the story limped. His expression gave me more pleasure than pain, and it's a bit ridiculous to say so, but in writing this to you my heart beats a bit faster.

I often ask myself what you think of me and of the trouble I take with minute details. (For example, the question of numbers 15 and 16 last year. I never explained to you why I was so insistent, thinking it wasn't worth the trouble.) My recriminations against Plon must seem to you absurd and this whole side of my character very petty, but if you only knew what violence I have to do to myself in order to bring myself to complain! I do not want to say that there is not much mediocrity in me, I know myself too well, but there is also despair over this mediocrity. I am so happy to know you, Jacques. Several times in thinking of you I have been kept from committing evil actions. Isn't this the most you can do? In any case, you have no friend who is more deeply attached to you than your

JULIEN

P.S. I know a Belgian lady, Madame Jeanne Mamberger, very sick, who is suffering greatly and is very much afraid of death. She is a very religious woman, but this doesn't keep her from the ultimate limits of despair. Would you think of her a little in your prayers?

And don't forget me.

J.

I don't know if *Les Clefs de la mort* will constitute the prologue of my novel.

1. *Les Clefs de la mort*, after appearing in the *Revue de Paris*, was published by Jacques Schiffrin in his Éditions de la Pléiade in 1928. (Plon, in 1930, republished it in a collected volume entitled *Le Voyageur sur la terre*. In addition to the title story and "Les Clefs de la mort," the volume contained "Christine," originally written in English and published in 1924, and "Léviathan," published in 1928. It appeared in English as *Christine and Other Stories* (New York: Harper and Brothers, 1929), with the "other stories" translated by Courtney Bruerton.

33

Pax
Meudon, January 15, 1928

My dear Julien,
I have just read your book and was profoundly moved. I have to make an effort to remind myself that this is a work of art (one which I find admirable): it belongs to a higher region. You have been told that there is a certain clumsiness in these pages. In reality one has the impression that your hand trembled a bit—with respect—when writing about such a subject, and there is nothing more beautiful. I find in addition that you have overcome with mastery a great number of difficulties. Your presentation is direct, full, tightly organized, free; it breathes like a living being; at each instant the reality of the soul and of the invisible realm rises to the light in magnificently assured turns of phrase, discovered from within, and far truer than all the "observations" of the world.

In these pages everything is pure; everything has its true nature. The mystery with which they are filled contains no obscurity other than that too great transparence of divine things which makes them dark for our poor owl eyes. The reality of Christ's grace and the arrows of the angel of darkness appear there with the exact weight that is due to each of them; the principal character remains hidden as it should, that is, the Love which moves all things is not even named, and passes into the heart.

I do not know if this book will please Gide as much as *Le Voyageur* did; it breaks certain bonds whose wounds Gide is very fond of. It seems to me that in general today some have the perfect means of telling a lie without betraying it, and others have worn-out means that tell the truth only to betray it. You have the means of expression that make the truth true; you bring to us that deliverance of truth which we have waited for so long. This is a great joy, and I thank you for it, my dear Julien.

Yes, God does gamble with death, and you show this terrible wager in its starkest reality. The overwhelming presence of death and of the Author of death in your book has moved me all the more for the fact that it arrives at the very moment when we are more than ever aware of the hideous violence of this ancient Homicide, and when we are trying, under terrible conditions, to snatch a precious soul from death and from him. Pray to save this soul from despair, Julien, and pray for us too. For our part we will pray with all our heart for that lady you spoke of in your letter. Let me know how she comes along.

You were wondering, Julien, what I thought of you and "the trouble you take with minute details." I have always considered this care an indication of the depth of your heart. For a certain kind of depth there is nothing that is minute. I can scarcely think of you without being filled with a feeling of respect and tenderness for this heart and for the heavy treasure, as St. Paul calls it, which it carries within itself.

I embrace you with deep affection.

JACQUES

Raïssa shares everything I feel about your book. She and I thank you tenderly for the lines you inscribed as a dedication.

34

[January 19, 1928]

My dear Jacques,

You will never know all the good your letter has done me. It restored my confidence and helped me work better at the book which I hope to give you, if it turns out to be worth it.[1] I do not have to tell you with what anxiety one begins a book, or into what discouragement one can fall. It is at such moments as this that it is good to feel oneself loved and understood as I am by you. I think often of the soul you spoke of to me in your letter and I remember her in my prayers. The lady for whom I asked your prayers is certainly doing better. Perhaps there is really nothing wrong with her; but she is neurasthenic in the most precise sense of the word, and that's worse than anything else. She needs an imposition of hands. My dear

Jacques, in ending this short letter I do not leave you; many times each day my thoughts turn to you with affection and gratitude for all I owe you. Could you, that is, you and your wife, have lunch with us some day when you are in Paris? This would make Anne and me so very happy. You have only to let us know two or three days in advance by telephone. Good-bye Jacques, and thank your wife for me.

I embrace you.

JULIEN

1. Green is referring to what will be published as *Léviathan*. After an initial publication in serial form in the *Revue de Paris*, it appeared in Plon's Roseau d'Or series in 1929. (*The Dark Journey*, Vyvyan Holland's translation, was published by Harper and Brothers in New York that same year.)

35

[March 2, 1928]

My dear Jacques,

I think of you so often and with so much affection. Every day I ask myself if you are not sad, but yesterday my sister told me that she saw you leaving a movie theater where *Le Cirque* was playing and that you looked happy. This gave me great joy. There are times when I want to take the first train for Meudon and go talk with you for a few minutes, but I know how little time you have to yourself. Think of me now and then, my dear Jacques; I need more and more that you do so.

I embrace you with all my heart.

JULIEN

36

16 rue Cortambert
[March 29, 1928]

My dear Jacques,

Your short note touched me so very much. I myself would have announced to you the good news from America,[1] if I had not understood that it must not be spoken of. The evening we went to Gaveau I was already aware of it all, and I had some difficulty hiding my joy. Now, I think, the affair has been definitely settled. If I am not mistaken all the difficulties have been resolved, and I thank God for it with all my heart.

I embrace you, my dear Jacques.

JULIEN

1. *The Closed Garden* (*Adrienne Me-*   the Month Club selection (for May 1928).
surat in English) was chosen as Book of

37

June 1, 1928

My dear Jacques,

The letters that Léon Bloy[1] wrote to you and your wife have made it possible for me to know you better and to love you all the more. I want you to know that I think of you often, every day and several times a day, and that what you say to me always has a great importance in my eyes. Your pages published in the *Mail* are very beautiful, very striking, but I regret that they don't reach a larger public. I hope you will take them up once again in a book. Those contradictions you mention in the beginning of the article give much cause for reflection, and you know, as I have told you, how much the words of Satan to our Savior terrify me. Oh, I want so much to love God! (For can one say one loves God when so many things, so many little things, separate one from Him, as is the case with me?) I am like the Pharisees who keep repeating: the Temple of God! And in all this I do not see how I can be saved.

My dear Jacques, you would give me such pleasure if you would come to lunch at my house one day next week. My sister is leaving for Switzerland where she intends to spend ten days, and I will be alone. Would Monday, Tuesday, or Wednesday suit you?

I hope to see you soon and I embrace you with all my heart.

JULIEN

I read Ghéon's book.[2] The whole biographical section seems excellent to me, but the beginning in story form is so poor and so very bookish! I don't know any more when he speaks of *a lady of worldly but wicked life*. What would Léon Bloy think of this *but*?!

1. Jacques and Raïssa Maritain discovered Léon Bloy in 1905. After reading *La Femme pauvre* and *Quatre ans de captivité à Cochons-sur-Marne*, they sent a money order to the writer, who thanked them and invited them to come to see him. Under his influence they converted, choosing him as their godfather. His *Lettres à ses filleuls*, with a Foreword by Jacques Maritain (Paris: Stock, 1928), are the letters he wrote to Maritain and to Pierre Van der Meer. "It is a painful thing to surrender to the public the secrets of a friendship that one thought was reserved for the sight of God alone. I admit that of themselves the godsons of Léon Bloy would never have dreamed of publishing a correspondence that was so infinitely precious to them, but of a completely private nature, if they had not been asked to do so by Mme Bloy. . . ."

2. Henri Ghéon, (a popular author of the early French Catholic Literary Revival and) an intimate friend of Gide's, was the author of theatrical plays like *Le Pauvre sous l'escalier*. Here Green is referring to *Le Comédien et la grâce*, a book of Ghéon's which appeared in the Roseau d'Or collection.

38

Chartreuse de la Valsainte
August 19, 1928

My dear Julien,

I have thought very much about you in this house where everything is for God alone. How I wish you would come here for a few days. It is such a joy finally to see Christianity really *lived*. It's a far cry from the "French Catholics"![1] . . . (But these are also French.) Believe in my faithful affection.

JAC

⟨1. Shortly after his conversion to Catholicism, Green published his *Pamphlet contre les catholiques de France* under the pseudonym Théophile Delaporte. This fervent attack on the bourgeois mentality of the majority of the French clergy and laity, Green insisted, was directed at himself first of all; for, he wrote, "I was furious to discover that I was not a saint." It was this *Pamphlet* which led Maritain to invite Green to Meudon and to begin a friendship that was to last almost fifty years. When Green decided to republish his *Pamphlet* in 1963, he asked Maritain to supply a Foreword. His old friend was delighted to do so, and in it expressed his admiration for the "hardness of those beautiful

Pascalian contours which contained a kind of trembling distress." He recognized in the author a soul of exceptional depth and foresaw in those pages the beginnings of a long and fruitful career, as well as the "fear" and the "watchful despair" with which this author would make his way along "the paths of this world and of literary glory.")

39

November 9, 1928
16 rue Cortambert

My dear Jacques,

The name *Léviathan* came to my mind last night, and this is what I have decided to call the novel I gave you. In the *Commentaries on the Book of Job* by Abbé de Sacy,[1] it is said, in fact, that Leviathan is the figure of the demon "who could be conquered by no man, but only the Redeemer of all men." Whether one realizes this or not is of only relative importance. The name Leviathan is beautiful, mysterious, and doubtless rather sinister; this is essential. If, by good luck, you accept my book, we can explain the title in the little notice that ordinarily accompanies copies in the Roseau d'Or series. I embrace you, my dear Jacques,

Very affectionately,
JULIEN

1. Louis-Isaac Lemaistre de Sacy, a recluse, and one of the spiritual directors of the "Messieurs" and religious of Port-Royal, wrote a translation of the Bible which is admired even today for the no- bility of its style. It was with him that Pascal had the famous conversation on Epictetus and Montaigne, in *Entretien*, reported by Nicolas Fontaine.

40

Pax
Meudon, November 14, 1928

My dear Julien,

I have just finished reading your book and I find it very beautiful. It is a work of singular power which tears at the heart and takes possession of it, as if it comes from very far away, full of mystery and a supernatural terror. It seems to me you have again played an astonishingly difficult match and have won. Leviathan, yes, the world that wants nothing to do with grace, that is entirely outside the light. I have never read anything that breathes such tender pity and such overwhelming sorrow. All the main characters end up in paroxysms of misery and take on gigantic proportions. And all this in the most mediocre of settings, with souls stripped completely bare. I admire how you work all this out from above, without connivance, without a moment's weakness, though your blood is shed at each instant. Impossible happiness. My very dear Julien, this book confirms me in the idea that there is only one issue for you: the heroically Christian life. And you must not put this off too long.

From the point of view *of the novel*, one might reproach your universe for ignoring the debate, the choice, that comes from the glimmerings of man's reason as well as the baitings of grace, and all the agitation of intelligence and of conscience which characterizes our human condition. Passions rise like the sun, alone filling the whole sky. But one might answer that the novelist is free to paint only one aspect of what is; and that this universe of darkness is none other than Leviathan.

Why should you think that I would hesitate to accept the book for Roseau d'Or? It portrays sin in the fashion I think it should be portrayed.

I embrace you.

JACQUES

When I see you I'll point out a few details that you can look over on the galleys. Why not make a drawing representing the façade of the restaurant or of the square?[1] I'll speak with you about this again.

⟨1. The main action of *Léviathan* centers in a restaurant whose proprietress exercises a sinister control over the lives of those who work in or frequent her establishment.⟩

41

Pax
Meudon, December 14, 1928

My dear Julien,

I have been thinking over what you said about *Le Livre blanc*[1] (which I hope to read some day anyway. What caused me the greatest pain in this whole affair is that Jean did not have the confidence to show it to me, when all the while he acted *as if* his confidence were complete). If I remember rightly, you thought it was (or could have been) a *courageous* book. In my opinion such courage is not there. "Testimonials" like this make the author *appear* courageous in the eyes of the world—that is to say, they are just the opposite of courage. They are signs of obedience to the spirit of the world; they slide down the slope of time, of its flattering and corrupt curiosity, which is insatiable. There is only one courage and that is to burn away in oneself every trace of sin, and to remain with Jesus, in a century which belongs completely to the Devil. *Elegi abjectus esse in domo Dei mei magis quam habitare in tabernaculis peccatorum.*[2]

Jean *will not admit to being tolerated.* If he speaks of what offends God in him, one is not to tolerate it; it is *intolerable.* If he speaks of his soul itself, of his very being, he is not to be tolerated, only to be loved. And if he carries his cross as Jesus asks him to do (and as He offers him the grace to carry it), one must respect him. But I am afraid that he is demanding for his evil the rights of citizenship in God's Kingdom, and that he wishes to call good evil and evil good.

I speak to you of these things, my dear Julien, because I feel with great sorrow all that there is of darkness in this *whiteness.* We have come to the time when the "Prince of the darkness of this world" disguises himself as an angel of light. His face chills the heart. A cursed period, the age of Leviathan, doubtless. However, the reign of Jesus will never be more radiant, except in the depths of souls, in humility, in unimaginable obscurity, impenetrable to Satan, where souls know the nature of love and its demands.

I embrace you with all my heart.

JACQUES

1. *Le Livre blanc* appeared without the author's name when it was published in 1928. It was attributed to Cocteau, who later acknowledged its paternity. (Mari-tain was deeply hurt that Cocteau did not consult him before publishing it.) ⟨2. Psalm 83:11.⟩

42

Pax
Meudon, Christmas 1928

Dear Julien,

I am a bit disturbed not to have any news about the ending of your novel.[1] Has it been written? Should I ask for a typed copy from Plon?

I thought of you last night. You know what affectionate best wishes we send to you and your sister. I embrace you.

JACQUES

⟨1. *Léviathan.*⟩

43

16 rue Cortambert XVIe
[January 4, 1929]

My dear Jacques,

I am still sick and feel completely worn out. My novel has cost me such effort that I believe I will need a rather long time to recover entirely. Today in spite of my weakness I want to write you to tell you that you are near me, but, please, do not hold it against me if I don't write to you. (I have the impression that you are angry with me for not having answered your letters, but you do not know what fatigue the slightest effort costs me!)

Perhaps it will take several days like these to make me realize in what great spiritual misery we live, and mine is extreme.

I embrace you with all my heart.

JULIEN

44

Pax
Paris, Tuesday   [1929]

Dear Julien,

Here are the corrections I propose. I underlined in pencil all that has been changed. It seems to me better this way. Call me and tell me what you think.

In paragraph 2, I am hesitating about a number of words. Tell me those you choose. I hope that in the last lines (the new ones) of this paragraph I have given a more exact expression to your thought.

I have also made a change in the second part of the section to be inserted. The first version seemed to me too brutal. If you think it proper, we could separate the two parts by an asterisk as I indicated here, which would show that these two parts correspond to two somewhat different points of view (the author—Roseau).

As far as signing it in any way whatever is concerned—this seems to me impossible. It would appear to take on an exceptional character, for this has never been done before; and what is more, I would not care to create a precedent. Besides, everything seems to me perfectly clear and explicit in itself.

Tell me if all this is acceptable.

Yours in all affection, my dear Julien.

JACQUES

I realize that I will get back to Meudon tonight no sooner than 9:30. You will have to telephone me then tonight about 10:00 or tomorrow about 9:00.

[Text included by Maritain in his letter]

Nothing is farther from *naturalism* than the novels of Julien

Green. In them "observation" of things has little importance. Their force comes from within; they rise from the depths of the soul, from the region where dreams take shape, where spirit and flesh know their bonds of despair.

This *Léviathan* is a prodigy of melancholy and violence. Passion (privation) and sorrow are there like objects carried to the paroxysm of their essential form. It is the nature of this book to make no concession to the confusion of the unformulated; it fixes in a spotlight of terrible intensity the work (the passages) of tragic misfortune.

The author has no intention other than to write a novel. His business is to tell in the best possible way the stories he invents. He makes no pretense of supporting any thesis or bearing any kind of testimony.

*

The meaning of a book such as this, though foreign to the intention of M. Julien Green, takes on, it is true, only more objective value. Roseau d'Or, as has been maintained from the beginning, is not a confessional collection and has never claimed to make of religion (which is too elevated and too free for that) the label or the distinctive brand of a literary movement. It aims at publishing only works having a spiritual dimension, and does not publish *Léviathan* as a book to be classified as what is customarily called a "Catholic novel"; what it sees above all in such a work is a sign of the secret terror which fills that universe of the passions which Christians call the *world*. It is also an example of an art powerful enough to describe evil and treat the blackest of subjects as much without hypocrisy as without complicity.

45

Pax
Meudon, Holy Thursday [1929]

My dear Julien,

I wanted to write to thank you for the copy of *Léviathan* you sent and to say how much Raïssa and I were touched by the lines you inscribed in this lovely copy. During all these days I have been over-whelmed with fatigue, and I am only now beginning to breathe easily once again.

I hope we will see each other soon. I will be away during Easter week. Then I will telephone you.

One of my friends asked me to tell you that M. Pierre Vigon, 42, rue Giofreddo, Nice, has sent a manuscript to the *Revue hebdoma-daire* (it is a matter, I believe, of a literary prize), and they would be very grateful if you could see to the competent reading of the manu-script. They tell me that this M. Pierre Vigon is in a quite awful situation and that he is ready to accept even a position of salesman in a bookstore. If you hear about any such opening, would you please let me know?

To your sister and to you we send our best wishes. You know, don't you, how often I think of you? I embrace you with all my heart.

JACQUES

46

16 rue Cortambert XVIe
[1929]

My dear Jacques,

Have you returned? We must get together. Excuse me for not answering your letter which brought me such great pleasure. Our dear Jean has just finished a book of whose beauty I have no way of giving you an idea.[1] This is what the rest home produced. Hurry and read it. I don't know how you will be able to resist it.

You are never far from my heart, my dear Jacques, and I embrace you very affectionately.

JULIEN

1. In 1928 Cocteau underwent treatment for opium addiction in a clinic at Saint-Cloud. There he received a visit from Julien Green and entrusted to him the typed copy of his novel *Les Enfants* *terribles*, which he had just finished. After a first enthusiastic reading, Green considerably moderated his appreciation, but without going as far in his reservations as the Surrealists did.

47

Pax
Meudon, May 27, 1929

My dear Julien,

I would like to see you. But when? At this time of the year I am abominably overworked. The only time I see free is Saturday, June 8th. Could you come to Meudon that day about 9:00 in the evening? That seems to me the best time. It's not so hot at that time of day. Perhaps we'll be able to get together before that (as it happened last year about the same time, because of music). We will without a doubt be going to the Opera on the 30th for Auric's ballet,[1] and on the 4th and the 7th for the Ballets Russes.

I saw Jean and read *Les Enfants terribles*. Antigone delivered to the Furies. It is filled with wonderful poetry and tragedy and, as you said, the fantastic and the real mesh miraculously. But the human background of it all inspires fear, as I told Jean. What commerce with the powers of darkness! Jean is an Orpheus who moves through the streets of death, and one can see only eternal horrors moving about on all sides. The heart trembles to think that it is from this that a masterpiece was born.

I'll see you soon, my dear Julien.

I embrace you with all my heart.

JACQUES

⟨1. Georges Auric, a friend of Maritain's, was a member of the famous group of musical innovators "Les Six." During the 1920s Auric frequented the circle of Diaghilev and the Ballets Russes.⟩

48

Pax
Meudon, Saturday   [September 1929]

Dear Julien,

Yes, I am back at Meudon and would love to see you. It is impossible during these days. All my time is taken up by the retreat

that Father Garrigou-Lagrange preaches here each year. This retreat is always a source of great worry for us, for the whole responsibility falls on our shoulders; but we will be so glad to have Father
Charles ⟨Henrion⟩ with us. I will be away in October to get some
work done. But I hope to see you before I leave. I will telephone.
(Our number is Bellevue 357.) On the way back from Austria I
passed through Konnersreuth, where I saw Theresa Neumann[1] and
was present at one of the painful ecstacies in which she suffers with
Christ. She is a very simple peasant girl, a child (not in age, she is
about thirty years old), admirably free from all self-interest. I will
never forget the purity of her eyes, illuminated by the vivacity of
love.

I'll see you soon, dear Julien, perhaps *Wednesday*. I will confirm
by telephone. Raïssa and I both send our affection. I embrace you.

JACQUES

1. Theresa Neumann, a famous German stigmatic. Hitler did not dare to touch this Bavarian visionary, who predicted in 1929 that the war between Germany and France would be terrible for her homeland.

49

Pax
Meudon, 10 rue du Parc   Christmas 1929

I think you must have forgotten me, my dear Julien, for I have
been waiting a long time now for you to telephone. I wish you a
happy Christmas and embrace you with all my heart.

JACQUES

50

Pax
Meudon, 10 rue du Parc   February 14, 1930

My dear Julien,

Do you remember that some months ago I spoke to you of a
Prière pour Sodome written by Massignon[1] and that you said you

would be interested in reading it? I saw Massignon recently and asked him for a copy for you that I have sent on. I had greatly encouraged Massignon to publish these pages, where under a mass of scientific erudition there burns a very great and very generous love.

When are you leaving for London? I don't know if I'll be able to see you before that. I am crushed under the burden of preparing my two conferences. But let me know what you are doing.

I embrace you with all my heart.

JACQUES

Massignon's address (should you wish to write to him) is 21 rue Monsieur.

March 28. I have waited to send you this letter till we should both be back from England. (I was able to see the Italian exposition!) I have just returned, very pleased with my trip. What an astounding impression passing abruptly from Paris to Dublin and from Dublin to London. Alas, now I have an enormous amount of work to catch up on. As soon as I have a little free time, I'll give you a call. I would so much like to see you.

Is there still time to speak to you about a manuscript submitted for the prize of the *Revue hebdomadaire*? If possible, I would like you to read *Georges Izard's* novel.

1. A Catholic writer specializing in Arabic studies, Louis Massignon was a friend of Claudel's and Maritain's, and one of the first priests who married with the permission of Rome. A conference of his which considered gardens from a natural and a mystical point of view awakened profound echoes in Julien Green (see his *Journal inédit*).

51

Pax
Meudon, 10 rue du Parc   June 2, 1930

My dear Julien,

What has become of you? I have been sick, overwhelmed by the flu during almost the entire month of May. I have been trying to catch up on all the back work for some ten days now. But I would so much like to see you before you leave on vacation. Let me hear from you.

I embrace you.

JACQUES

52

16 rue Cortambert, XVIe
[September 10, 1931]

Dear Jacques,

You musn't hold it against me that I don't write you more frequently. You know that letter writing has never been my forte! But I have been thinking of you, and I am upset to find out that you were worried. Let's get together as soon as you return.

I traveled a bit this summer and worked quite a bit too. My book[1] gave me some difficult moments, and it is far from finished.

I embrace you, my dear Jacques, very affectionately.

Your

JULIEN

1. *Épaves,* after appearing serially in the *Revue de Paris,* was published by Plon in 1932 (Pléiade III). (Vyvyan Holland's translation, *The Strange River,* was published by Harper and Brothers that same year.)

53

16 rue Cortambert, XVIe
[September 25, 1931]

Dear Jacques,

I wanted to call you but your name is not in the directory. May I see you if you are at Meudon? Perhaps you will be coming to Paris some day next week. I give you with joy any afternoon you want.

I think quite a bit about you and your wife and send you my affection.

JULIEN

54

Pax
Bagnoles-de-l'Orne, April 27, 1932

My very dear Julien,

I was very sorry not to be able to get in touch with you and go to see you before vacation. I have been jostled from every direction. And yet how happy I would have been to speak with you about so many things!

I suppose you are traveling right now. Raïssa has to spend a second season here. She is bearing up under the treatment better than last year.

You know, I suppose, that "Roseau d'Or" has come to an end at Plon, and that a new collection—"les Iles"—will be its continuation at Desclée De Brouwer. Is it necessary to tell you that I would be very happy to have you collaborate on it? If you are committed to Plon because of your novels, there are always the issues of the Chroniques, which I have to develop somewhat and in which you could publish some novellas or essays.

We will speak of that when we return. This note is to let you know how faithfully I keep you in mind. Raïssa sends her affectionate remembrance to you and to your sister.

I embrace you.

JACQUES

What do you think of that villa called *Désiré* whose picture I sent you?

55

September 19, [1932]
28 avenue du Président-Wilson (XVIᵉ)

My dear Jacques,

On returning from my trip I found your card. Thank you for thinking of me. You know I am never far from you, even when we don't see each other for months! The next time you come to Paris let me know. It will make me so happy to see you.

Affectionately,

JULIEN

56

Pax

Meudon, Epiphany   [1933]

Dear Julien,

I have to begin right away to prepare the *May* issue of *Chroniques* of "Roseau." I would be very happy if it contained a novella by you. Be kind enough to tell me quickly if this is possible. (I would need the manuscript by the end of this month.)

For the moment I have plunged into a work on metaphysics[1] which takes up all my time. As soon as I have gotten out from under it (soon, I hope!), I'll let you know. We would be happy for you to come to dinner some evening with your sister and Bérard.[2]

I think about you very much, my dear Julien. My love to your sister. I embrace you.

JACQUES

P.S. Raïssa is sending you the book she translated[3] to replace the one that got lost.

⟨1. Probably *Sept leçons sur l'être et les premiers principes de la raison spe-culative* (Paris: Téqui, 1934), which is available in English as *Preface to Meta-physics: Seven Lectures on Being* (New York & London: Sheed & Ward, 1939).⟩

2. Christian Bérard, a painter and decorator, was a friend of Maritain's, Jouvet's, Cocteau's, and Green's. He illus-trated *Si j'étais vous* (see 64.1), and pro-

duced numerous sets for Louis Jouvet and the Ballets Russes. He died of a heart attack in the Théâtre Marigny during a rehearsal.

⟨3. Raïssa had translated John of St.

Thomas' Latin treatise on the gifts of the Holy Spirit: *Les Dons du Saint Esprit* (Juvisy: Cerf, 1930). This edition had a Foreword by Reginald Garrigou-Lagrange, O.P.⟩

57

December 29, 1934

Thank you, my dear Jacques. Just this moment I received *Saint Dominique* which I promised myself to read in the coming days.

I thought of you from the depths of my heart on Christmas day and of Raïssa too. Don't forget me either.

I embrace you affectionately.

JULIEN

All my best wishes.

La Piété Vaïshnava[1] didn't teach me much, but *Procession*[2] moved me deeply, and I was happy to read the signature!

I'm curious to know what you think of Ramakrishna and of his gospel. Have you seen *Le Visage du silence*? (This book is by Dhan Gopal Mukergi, published by Attinger. You'll like it, I think.)

1. Green's reading of this book on Buddhist mysticism is evidence of his interest in Buddhism at this time; it resulted in his writing *Varouna* (see Letter 76).

2. *Procession*, a piano piece by Arthur Lourié (see 71.2), is dedicated to Julien Green.

58

August 31, 1935

Dear Jacques,

Excuse me for not yet having answered your letter. I received it in the country where I count on spending another ten days or so. If you are in Paris around September 15th, I must see you. I have thought about you often, affectionately—that goes without saying.

Villeneuve[1] wrote me again. He tells me he is very sick, but they hope to save him. Poor boy! His letter, with some incoherence, is full of soul, and he seems to have a feeling for spiritual things, as far as I can judge. He wants to live, but he is ready to take his departure if he has to, for he is very brave. If you have the time, tell me what you are up to, my dear Jacques. I get angry with myself for never writing you, and for seeing you so rarely, but as you see, I don't do much about improving.

All my affection to you and to Raïssa.

JULIEN

1. Paul de Villeneuve, the nephew of   18.1), was a good friend of Julien
Pierre Van der Meer de Walcheren (see   Green's.

59

March 15, 1939

My dear Jacques,

I spent more than two hours with Father Klein whose great charity made a profound impression on me. Yet I'm afraid that he is mistaken about me and that he has a tendency to see only the good side of souls, because he loves them. I told him only a very few things about myself and I would be really distressed if he should believe he has to do with a more than ordinary person. I suspect that you must have spoken well of me to him. Aside from a few gifts (which come to me from God and of which I have made only very mediocre use), I have nothing at all to set me apart from the throng; if you imagine that these are only words, you are going to expose yourself to grave disappointments concerning your friend Julien!

I experienced a terrible anguish the whole time I spent with this good priest. Even with you I was already ill at ease. There was someone who was displeased by these visits. How can I describe what took place within me, or rather around me? I moved in a circle of fear and anger. All this made me sick and I still suffer from it today, but I want to get this little note off to you and to tell you of my gratitude. I do not know if I would be able to put my total confidence in Father Klein, even though I have the greatest respect for his knowledge and for the very beautiful qualities of his soul. He will help me with his prayers, I am sure. My heart is too heavy to write you more than this, but I embrace you with all my heart.

JULIEN

Those were some stupid things I said to you yesterday about the Book of Job!

60

Meudon
March 16, 1939

My very dear Julien,

I do not believe that Father Klein is mistaken about you and that he looks at you in too good a light. I think that what distinguishes you from other men, apart from those "few gifts" of which you speak, is precisely the crushing awareness you have of the presence and of the absolute importance of your soul, and it is perhaps for this reason that you feel your soul to be the object of such a violent struggle.

The malaise and anguish you felt Monday was felt as well by us, that day and the next. A weight of unspeakable sadness, a hand of unheard-of heaviness weighing on the heart. Could it be that we too were thus participating in what was going on within you rather than around you? Dear Julien, I'm afraid that despite his goodness and his great desire to serve souls, Father Klein has disappointed you. I wonder if, given the superhuman, infinite value of what you expect, a conversation with any priest could satisfy you. I wonder if you do not find yourself in reality led to make a choice between two things: either, driven by a hunger for the sacraments, to go find anyone, the very first priest encountered in a church; or else, driven by the hunger for wisdom, to go spend a few days in a holy and protected place, in a world of prayer like that of the Chartreuse de Valsainte of which I spoke to you[1] and where, if there is someone whom this visit displeases, he would be forced to stop at the door.

Goodbye, Julien. We love you more than ever. I embrace you with all my heart.

JACQUES

1. Although Maritain had recommended a visit there as early as 1928 (see Letter 38), Green did not go until 1981. (In *L'Arc en ciel* (Paris: Le Seuil, 1988), the thirteenth volume of his *Journal*, Green writes at length about this Carthusian monastery, located in the Bernese Oberland, near Gruyère, Switzerland.)

61

March 23, 1939

Dear Jacques,

I have been sick these last few days and I have not been able to answer you as quickly as I would have liked. Your letter brought me great comfort. Don't think that Father Klein disappointed me. It is true that I almost always expect a miracle—but I also know that Father Klein could not have spoken to me other than as he did. I noticed that those words which count most for me are those which are pronounced *as if inadvertently* by certain people very advanced in the spiritual order. Father Klein had made it a point to convince me, and this fact gave rise to that fundamental misunderstanding of which, I am sure, he was not even aware. I am much too simple a person to be understood easily by everyone. The very presence of a religious has a stronger effect on me than the most clever reasoning. For this reason I think that your advice about Valsainte is excellent. The difficulty is to leave Paris at the moment when my book is going to come out,[1] when I have to be here to correct the proofs. But I am far from despairing. If this thing must be done, it will be done.

I cannot write you any more today, but I count on seeing you soon, both you and Raïssa. I embrace you.

JULIEN

1. *Derniers beaux jours (1935–1939),* the second volume of Green's *Journal,* was published by Plon in 1939 (Pléiade IV).

62

[undated]

My dearest Jacques,

These last weeks have been very trying for us all, and I believe I have had my full share of the general anxiety. But in moments even more difficult than the present, we can always take refuge in prayer, and this is an immense grace.

I must tell you though that since our last meeting I have known some periods of very great distress that I would never mention if I did not know that you and Raïssa love me very much. Like the blind man in the Gospels, I had asked God to make me see, and to make me see before Easter. This was perhaps a rather childish prayer, or perhaps I didn't ask in the way I should have. It would not take much more to make my faith entire, absolute, but if the soul is still darkened by sin, how could its faith be anything but imperfect? However, there is in the depths of my soul an unshakable confidence in the goodness of God. I know that one day He will make use of me for the good of others, in a most humble manner, but before that time, what trials! I am not writing these words without having thought them over carefully. If you were here, I would confide to you what I have never been able to say to another, and I would tell it to you because you are in a way my director! What permits me to speak to you today with a little less reticence than is my wont is the fact that these are exceptional times. For my part, I believe we are in very grave danger; nevertheless there is in my heart a peace that nothing can trouble anymore. I don't mean that I will have no more periods of sadness and discouragement, but now I know that there is a refuge and it is within ourselves.[1]

I must now mention to you an extremely serious problem that has arisen in my life. Do you remember our conversation about the religious of the Isle of Wight . . .[2]

1. Through Raïssa, Green made the acquaintance of Alex-Ceslas Rzewuski, a Polish Dominican who brought him back to the Church. Father Rzewuski is the author of *A travers l'invisible cristal* (1976) and *L'Instant* (1981), both of which were published by Plon.

2. An unfinished letter put by Green in Maritain's hand when he visited him a few days later on April 22. Green dates his letter April 20.

63

[April 25, 1939]

Dear Jacques,

I am writing you this note before leaving to tell you that I received Communion this morning after a conversation I had yesterday with Father Rzewuski.

I received Communion as much out of obedience as out of love, and on the assurance of Father Rzewuski that it is not necessary to believe all that the Church teaches in order to approach the Holy Table. I am still very troubled, but much less, and I have confidence. My only fear is that in going too fast I may find myself someday faced with an insoluble problem, humanly insoluble, and about which I will speak with you again.

Need I tell you that I am happy in spite of what remains of my disquietude? You know everything I am thinking, I am sure.

JULIEN

64

September 12, 1939

My dear Jacques,

These last weeks have been painful for us all, and I have thought often of you and Raïssa. Are you still at Meudon? You are never far from my thoughts, but it seems to me that events have only brought our hearts closer together. If you could just drop me a line to give me news about you, you would bring me great joy.

I am writing you this evening to ask for some information that you alone can give me. I have several decisions to make, one of which at least is very important. Do you know of a monastery in this country where I could make a retreat? Or in Canada, perhaps? Excuse me for not speaking to you at greater length of a project which would require a great deal of explaining but I am pressed for time and must mail this letter immediately if it is to leave on the next plane. I intend to write you again in a few days.

My address is still Care of James M. Butler, Box 56, Suffolk, Virginia, U.S.A.[1]

Your last letter touched me deeply; it came to me at a moment when I had great need to hear the sound of your voice. This country is for me the country of solitude, but this is doubtless necessary.

Affectionately yours and Raïssa's.

JULIEN

Remember me, please, to Miss Vera.

1. Jim (James) Butler was a fellow-student of Green's at the University of Virginia—Green studied there from September 1919 to July 1922—and one of his first readers. Green admits, in the Preface to his *L'Apprenti psychiatre* (Paris: Livre de Poche, 1976–1977), that he recounted to Butler the subject of *Si j'étais vous* in 1921.

65

The Rectory at Avoise

Sarthe   September 27, 1939

My very dear Julien,

How happy I am to receive your letter. Never before has friendship seemed to me, at times such as these, like something strong and
divine—this at least totalitarian bombs will never be able to destroy. Our heart is united with yours in a most profound way.

It is distressing that in the New World there are so to speak no
contemplative religious orders. Some Carmelites, yes, and other
communities of women. But of religious orders for men, I think
that in the United States there are certainly a few Trappists; however, I would not recommend them to you for a retreat. The only
community about which I have some good information is in Canada,
the Benedictines of Saint-Benoît du Lac at Sherbrooke, in the Province of Quebec. I know that one goes there by way of Montreal. I
have never gone there myself, but I remember having received two
years ago a good letter, an extremely touching one, from the Father
Abbot. You could go there on my recommendation. It is the only
place I know of where one can make a retreat. But I still know
nothing of them from personal experience.

We have left Fontgombaud[1] in order to be closer to Paris. Classes
start at the Institut Catholique on November 3rd, and I will go
there from here to give my lectures. It is not beyond the realm of
possibility that later I might be sent on a mission to America.

Dear Julien, Raïssa and I embrace you affectionately and Vera
asks to be remembered to you.

JACQUES

We think Anne is still in France. Raïssa will write to her.

Have you received *Lettres de nuit*, the collection of Raïssa's
poems? It was sent to you from Fontgombaud at the end of August. . . .

⟨1. A Benedictine monastery in the Loire valley.⟩

66

The Rectory at Avoise
Sarthe   September 29, 1939

Very dear Julien,
Yesterday I sent you an airmail letter, but I wonder if the mail
service by air is working very well. The word is to tell you that the
only place in my opinion where one can go for a retreat is Saint-
Benoît du Lac, at Sherbrooke, in the Province of Quebec. I have
not been there myself, but I have been in contact by letter with the
Father Abbot. You must go there by way of Montreal.
All of this, and other things, I put in yesterday's letter. But per-
haps this one will arrive first?
Dear Julien, we think of you with great tenderness, Raïssa and I.
Believe in our profound friendship.

JACQUES

67

Suffolk, October 10, 1939
My dearest Jacques,
I don't think you can realize what joy your letter gave me. What
moved me almost as much as the content of the letter was the haste
with which you wrote back. I see in this the best proof of a friendship which is extremely precious to me and for which I thank God.
When I wrote you I found myself in a state of moral distress such
as I have never known before, and it was truly a cry for help that I
cast in your direction. And I was sure I had not called out in vain. A
few days before, I had gone to ask advice of a religious in a Benedictine priory in New York; he strongly urged me to make a retreat
with the Trappists of Cumberland, Rhode Island. But something
kept me from going there. I preferred to come here to Virginia
where I found, in the absence of someone to direct me, a Catholic

chapel about which I will tell you some day. There I have passed some unforgettable moments at the feet of Our Lord.

I know Sherbrooke[1] from having passed through it this summer but not the monastery you pointed out. I will certainly write to the Father Abbot and am very grateful to you for having given me his address.

Yesterday, feeling troubled once again, as unfortunately happens to me very often now, I wrote a letter to Father Rzewuski which he is going to find rather incoherent, I'm afraid. All that is happening in the world at present breaks my heart, and this suffering is all the greater in that I seem unable to find out what Our Lord wants me to do; but He has already accorded me such great graces that I have no doubt He will one day make His will known to me in a very formal way.

Anne will join me the day after tomorrow. I think of you and Raïssa with great affection and beg of you to remember me in your prayers. I do not know what fate is reserved for all of us, but I believe Our Lord wants to have us pass through a sort of Dark Night[2] in order that we may come to Him, and this Night is beginning.

Send me news of yourself, my dear Jacques. My address in America is still the same (Care of James M. Butler, Box 56, Suffolk, Va.). I think of you all with a sad and heavy heart. I read Raïssa's book (which I already knew in part) and found it very beautiful.

Remember me, please, to Miss Vera. I embrace you and Raïssa affectionately.

JULIEN

October 17. I kept this letter, wishing to add a word. I am in New York for a few days with Anne, who sends her love. She will probably stay here a rather long time, but not I. I miss France too much. I expect to come back at the beginning of next year.

1. Julien Green has always had friends at the University of Sherbrooke where numerous theses have been written about his work. Among those that have been published, the most notable were done by Charles Bolduc and Suzanne Toulet.

2. An expression from St. John of the Cross.

68

Avoise
Sarthe   October 23, 1939

Very dear Julien,

Did you receive the letter I wrote you (or rather the letters, for there was one by air and one by surface mail) in reply to yours, and did you find what you were looking for? Robert de Saint Jean[1] wrote me on his arrival in France. I was very touched by his letter. I answered him at avenue de La Bourdonnais, not having his military address. I hope you have good news about him. And about Anne. (But perhaps she is there with you?)

And here is a request: I will probably go to America in December for the month of classes I promised at Toronto (January 1940[2]). After that I will doubtless give a few conferences in the United States as in previous years. But this time Raïssa and Vera would like to come with me, preferring the risks of a crossing amidst the submarine warfare to a long separation. It's a subject of great anxiety for me, not only because of the dangers, but also because of the rigors of the Canadian winter, which I fear very much because of their health. If it turns out that they do come with me, I would like them to pass the winter in a milder climate. And it is on this subject that I would like your advice. Where do you think they could live? Virginia? Texas? Perhaps in a religious community where French is spoken? Near Chicago we know a college directed by a woman of great value, Sister Madeleva, who would receive them perhaps.[3] But the climate is very harsh there. At any rate, if you can furnish me some advice, thank you in advance.

So now I can hope to see you in a few weeks, either by your coming to visit me in Toronto where I would be happy to introduce you to my friend Father Bondy, or by my going to see you if I should travel in the United States. This would be a very great joy for me.

You know, dear Julien, with what great affection we think of you. I embrace you with all my heart.

JACQUES

⟨1. Robert de Saint Jean, a friend of Green's of long standing, is frequently mentioned in his *Journal*. He is the author of a study of Green in the series "Ecrivains de toujours": *Julien Green par lui-même* (Paris: Le Seuil, 1967).)

2. On January 4, 1940, the Maritains set sail from Marseilles for the United States. Five years went by before their return.

3. Maritain is referring to Saint Mary's College in South Bend, Indiana. It is near the University of Notre Dame where, in 1938, he had participated in a colloquium on political and social philosophy.

69

Suffolk, November 23, 1939

My dearest Jacques,

Your letter finally arrived after a long delay, and I am hastening to answer by air mail, even though I fear it may be useless, and that you have already departed. I have been able to get no information on religious communities in the South. There should be some in New Orleans, but how far from Toronto! I should have, I hope, some precise information a little later. (I have the address of someone I should write to.) The simplest, when you arrive with Raïssa, would be to send a word by air mail to my sister Anne (Care of James M. Butler, Box 56, Suffolk, Va.). She will have the information you want. Don't let Raïssa and Miss Vera spend a winter north of Washington. They would suffer too much. In the South they will find, if there are no convents handy, charming little villages like Petersburg, Virginia, or Fredericksburg (same state) where they could spend several weeks. They would do well not to go to a hotel, but to find lodging with a local resident (Tourist Rooms). These Tourist Rooms are by far the best in America, as far as comfort goes. If Anne is there, and I am almost sure she will be, she can give them excellent advice and will be delighted to see them. I don't advise Suffolk, which I really don't like.

Alas, I fear I may not be able to see you in this country! I must go back. I feel too keenly that my place is in France and that I don't have the right to remain here.[1] Our Lord will guide me; I believe this firmly, my dear Jacques. This letter is not as long as I would wish it, but I have to get it off right away. Remember me, please, to Miss Vera. I embrace you and Raïssa affectionately.

JULIEN

P.S. The pastor of our parish gave me the following address:
Convent of Benedictine Sisters
Bristow
Virginia.
He recommended this convent in particular, where, he assures me, one is lodged very comfortably. If I have understood correctly, there is a sort of hotel which belongs to the convent, a little outside the city. The climate is good, very dry.

I will write you a long letter which my sister can give you or send you from Suffolk, for I'm afraid I no longer have the time to get it off myself.

1. Julien Green was in the United States from April to December 1939; in July of 1940, after leaving Paris and crossing Spain, he sailed from Lisbon to return to his homeland, (where he remained until September 1945 when he returned to France).

70

New York
30 Fifth Avenue

July 15, 1940

Dear Julien,
I learn from the evening newspapers that you have just arrived in New York.[1] How anxious we are to see you. Telephone as soon as possible and come.

I embrace you.

JACQUES
ORchard 4–2972

1. An article in *The New York Times* of July 16, 1940, announced the arrival the day before, aboard the *Excambion*, of exiles coming from Europe: the French composer Darius Milhaud and Julian Green, using the English spelling of his given name. The article was accompanied by a number of photographs.

71

August 8, 1940
c/o Mrs. George W. Williams
15 Blythewood Road
Baltimore, Maryland

Dearest Jacques,

I would prefer not to have to ask you a favor in the first letter I write you from here,[1] but you will excuse me, I'm sure. Could you see to it that the little note I have included gets to Father Couturier? I no longer have his address in New York.

A letter from Anne tells me that she thinks she will soon get from the Kommandantur permission to go to Paris (oh! to have to write such a sentence!) *She saw Father Carré* who should be at Pau, or very near Pau, and who told her that he would do everything in his power to help us *all*. (Take your share of the word *all*!) I don't think that it is a question here of spiritual help alone and that in case of need we could depend on our friend for certain commissions, provided they are not dangerous and would not cause him difficulties.

I have succeeded in getting into my sister's hands half of what I had deposited in a bank in occupied France. So this type of operation is still possible. I mention this to you because you may find it useful. My sister says also that many Parisians are returning home. She does quite a bit of work for refugees. According to what she gives me to understand, many unfortunate people come to her; that's because they know how good and generous she is.

What news do you have of Lourié?[2]

I will write again in a few days.

Affectionately,
JULIEN

How can I get the address of Father Carré?

⟨1. Julien Green spent the war years in the United States. For a time he lived with his cousin, the Mrs. Williams mentioned in the heading to this letter, in Baltimore. During this time he gave conferences, taught courses in Creative Writing at Goucher College, and published articles, his book *Memories of Happy Days* (New York: Harper and Brothers, 1942) and translations of the works of Charles Péguy: with his sister Anne, *Basic Verities* (New York: Pantheon, 1943; see 82.1) and *Men and Saints* (New York: Pantheon, 1944); and, alone, *God Speaks* (New York: Pantheon, 1942).) In 1942 he was drafted into the American Army and worked at the Office of War Information. He returned to Paris at the first possible moment after the end of the war.)

2. Arthur Lourié was a Russian musician who became an American citizen.

In addition to the already mentioned *Procession* (see 57.2), he composed two operas, *Le Festin pendant la peste*, based on a little book by Pushkin, and *Le Nègre de Pierre le Grand*, chamber music, quartets, lieder, ballets, and religious music. After Raïssa's death, Maritain put his house at 26 Linden Lane, Princeton, New Jersey, at the disposal of Arthur and Ella Lourié.

72

Baltimore, August 12, 1940

Dear Jacques,

It would be a joy for me to give you a book for your collection, but what kind of a book do you want and what conditions would they offer? Your letter made me recall the one you wrote me in 1926 to ask me for a novel.[1] Could we have imagined then that fourteen years later we would be in exile!

I think often of you and yours. Unfortunately I cannot come to New York at present, but I hope to see you this fall. Remember me; I need this very much.

Very affectionately,

JULIEN

1. Cf. Letters 8 and 10.

73

New York
30 Fifth Avenue

August 31, 1940

Dear Julien,

I have had so much work these last few days that I have been unable to answer sooner. You gave me great joy in agreeing to collaborate on the collection I mentioned to you.[1] Yes, we are going to start up again in exile. All that we find out here about France (at least about official France) is overwhelmingly sad.

What kind of a book would you offer for the series (whose name we have not even found yet)? Absolutely anything you wish: novel, short story, essay, meditations. If you could write a book on the Bible, what it means for us, how it should be read, how beautiful that would be.[2] As far as the conditions are concerned, I think they will be the usual ones here; I have not yet spoken to the editor. (I think that in general American editors give 10% on the first 1,000, with a progressive increase after that?)

Would you mind asking Robert de Saint Jean for me if he would like to write a life of Chateaubriand for this same series? Not a romanticized life, naturally. An historical and literary study as complete as possible, and one which would especially concern the soul of Chateaubriand. It seems to me that the subject would interest him and that it would be important for the American public.

Do you have any news from Anne? We got some letters from Éveline,[3] who was at Toulouse. No doubt she is now back in Paris. No direct news about my mother. Lourié left Paris on foot, on the eve of the arrival there of the Germans. He is at Vichy (40 avenue Victoria). Alas! He left all his manuscripts in Paris. With the shameful anti-Semitic campaign now developing in France, even in the unoccupied zone, we are troubled with a growing anxiety about his welfare. I wish he would come here. I am trying all kinds of possibilities to bring this about.

I think we will stay in New York till January (but on September 15th we will have to get another apartment). Columbia University has offered me the post of Visiting Professor for the first semester and Princeton for the second. I will have to live in Princeton then after January, which I hardly find enchanting. On September 16th I am supposed to give a conference in Philadelphia, for the bicentenary of the University of Pennsylvania. I have been given the subject "Trends in Religious Thought."

I hope we see each other in New York this fall. We think of you with all our heart.

Very affectionately yours, my dear Julien.

JACQUES

Give my thanks to Robert [de Saint Jean] for his letter. Brodin[4] wrote that he will be happy to help him. I have received no reply from Bryn Mawr.

I am very happy that Anne saw Father Carré. I do not know his address, but Anne could get it from the Dominicans of Saint-Maximin (École théologique, Saint-Maximin, Var). If she has not already returned to Paris, could she perhaps go to Vichy to see Lourié and arrange with him to save his manuscripts? Tell her of our deep affection.

1. Golden Measure books, which replaced the collections Roseau d'Or and Les Iles, was published by Longmans, Green and Co., ⟨and edited by Jacques Maritain and Julie Kernan⟩.

⟨2. Green tried to write such a book, but soon abandoned the project. In his *Journal* (January 23, 1941, *Devant la porte sombre*, Pléiade IV) he wrote: "I am trying to write an essay for Maritain on the reading of the Bible, but I am beset with such difficulties that I lose courage even before confronting them.

Before throwing oneself into the abyss, one must know how to fly.")

3. Éveline Garnier, Maritain's niece, was the author of the memoirs of her family, "Souvenirs sur mon oncle," which appear in *Cahiers Jacques Maritain*, 2 (April 1981), 9–20.

4. Pierre Brodin, a professor and literary critic, and husband of Dorothy Rothschild, one of Maritain's godchildren, is the author of a book on Green: *Julien Green* (Paris: Presses Universitaires, 1957).

74

Baltimore, September 18, 1940

Dear Jacques,

I should have answered you long ago, but I have been so preoccupied, and feeling so bad to boot, that my correspondence has suffered a bit. One of my sisters is in London with her husband at the moment;[1] you can imagine with what feelings I read the news from England each day! What is there left to fill up the cup? Will everything continue to fall before that man? Still London seems to be holding out.

I would very much like to write a little book on the Bible. I would call it: A Layman Reads his Bible, but keep this title to yourself, please; it is convenient, sums up quite well what I want to say, and you know how hard I find it to give titles to my books! Isn't the editor offering an advance? I'm sorry to have to insist on this point, but the circumstances make it necessary.

Do you, by chance, have my little Pamphlet? Not that I want to borrow it from you, but I believe that if you don't have it, there is a good chance this book—my first book—may disappear even more quickly than it would otherwise, for I have no copy here, and God knows what will happen to our books in Paris.

Would you have a book to lend me? I promise to take very good care of it. For example, one of the little books in the collection "The Spiritual Life." All my books on mysticism are in France, and I can't tell you how much I miss certain of them.

Anne is still at Pau. She often sees Father Carré.

I think with affection of all three of you, dear Jacques. The sufferings of your country, which is in a way mine too, make you doubly dear to your friend

JULIEN

1. Éléonore, Green's oldest sister, had lived in Trieste, with her husband, Kenneth Joll, and their son, Patrick. They later moved to Genoa. When Italy entered the war, they moved to London.

Patrick, a painter, returned to Italy after the war and died near Florence in 1968 (November 13, 1968, *Ce qui reste de jour*, Pléiade IV).

75

January 29, 1941

My dearest Jacques,

I read your beautiful book on France[1] with all the emotion that such a subject treated by an author like you can arouse. How many times tears came to my eyes in thinking of all the mistakes that could have been avoided, and whose logical but tragic sequence you make us see with such lucidity. This book will be a painful souvenir of our exile, yet I will place it among those dearest to me because it comes from you and speaks to me of a country I love with all my heart. I think that in writing *A travers le désastre* you have well served the cause of France.

I have begun my book on the Bible, but from the very first I have been assailed with doubts about how interesting what I have to say will prove to be. But I am going to try. Before becoming too committed, however, I will have to get a start to see if I need two hundred pages, or if I have enough material to fill them. In other words, I don't want to throw myself into the void without being sure that I can fly! If there were question of some other book, I would hesitate less, but I have no desire to put our editor to the trouble of printing platitudes. Wasn't it Hello[2] who used to say something like—I am quoting from memory, and with good reason—that silence circles blushingly about the words of Scripture?

I lost Milhaud's address. Do you have it? Is he getting by? He was so kind to us during the July crossing.

As for me, I am on the point of accepting a position as professor (for two or three months) at Goucher College. I will have to explain to twelve or fifteen American girls how one goes about writing a novel!

Anne and I are responsible for some French prisoners in Germany. We are shamelessly "tapping" our richest friends, and with excellent results, I must say, but much more money is necessary to keep these unfortunates from dying of hunger and cold. The Red Cross of Geneva insists that the packages (food and clothing) sent over there are put into the hands of those they are destined for in the presence of a French delegate; the recipients sign receipts of which we have seen copies. Do you know anyone in your circle who would be willing to give $9.50 to begin with and then $5.00 a month to save the life of a Frenchman? Or less. If they couldn't afford that much, a foundation could be set up. We would furnish all the necessary information and guarantees.

Give all my affection to Raïssa and remember me, please, to Miss Vera. I hope you receive good news from France, or at least reassuring news.

I embrace you, my dear Jacques.

JULIEN

1. *A travers le désastre* (New York: La Maison Française, 1941) was smuggled into France and distributed clandestinely. ⟨It appeared in English under the title *France, My Country Through the Disaster*, Golden Measure Books 1 (New York & Toronto: Longmans, Green and Co., 1941).⟩

2. Ernest Hello, a friend of Bloy's, was the author of essays (*L'Homme* [Paris: Palmé, 1872]) and of a remarkable work entitled *Physionomies de saints* (Paris: Palmé, 1875).

76

May 11, 1941

My dearest Jacques,

I don't know whether or not La Maison Française has sent you my book, but if it has not, let me know, please, and I will have them send you a copy of the novel I want to speak to you about today, for I thought of you many times while writing it.

At the time I started it, in June 1938, I was still under the influence of numerous readings which would have done me irreparable harm if Our Lord hadn't taken it upon Himself to turn them to the good. The daydreams of Hindu philosophy proposed, it seemed to me at the time, the most reasonable explanation of human destiny, and I was ready to believe in metempsychosis.

This was the starting point of *Varouna*,[1] which came to my mind as a story of reincarnation. What I was completely ignorant of at the time was the extent to which grace was at work in me at the very moment when I believed myself far from the Church; so that, in an heretical setting, the account which forms the first part of my book seems to me to have no other than a Christian sense.

When I arrived at the third part, I had already been converted for several months; consequently the tone of this little novel is not only Christian, but Catholic. It is the story of a writer who is on the eve of his return to the Church but who has no inkling of the fact; you might call it a study of pre-conversion.

When I finished this book, whose fundamental idea now seemed to me quite questionable (in spite of the Catholic tendency I just pointed out), I constrained myself, if I may put it this way, to have it baptized, explaining in a Preface, which I had to rewrite six or seven times, that modern ideas about metempsychosis are due to an error which makes us attribute to an individual memories which belong to humanity. There cannot be in me the memory of an individual anterior existence, but I share with the human race, which is beginning to grow old, a kind of common fund of immemorial recollections. I have explained all this a little more at length in a page of my journal which I will give you to read.[2] What I am telling you today is only to put you on your guard against articles, like the one in this morning's *Times*, which present *Varouna* in a false light. Perhaps I told you that I had Father Carré read this novel, asking him to point out what appeared to him most shocking from the point of view of the Faith. You weren't there, as a matter of fact, and of whom else would I ask such a service? The Preface was the subject of long conversations between Father and me. Perhaps, after all, the theme of this book is only a sort of commentary on the Christian idea of the solidarity of souls. In the place of the quote from Villiers de l'Isle-Adam, which I found in Termier's book *A la gloire de la terre* (Termier[3] himself borrowed it from Bloy; here's a quote that did quite a bit of traveling!), instead of this so sad and beautiful sentence, then, I could have cited that of Bloy—and I'm sure you're going to love this sentence: "A certain movement of grace which saves me from a serious danger may well have been determined by a certain act of love accomplished this morning or even a hundred years ago (my underlining) by some very obscure person whose soul corresponded mysteriously to mine, and who thus receives his reward. . . ." What is this correspondence, if not an aspect of the Communion of Saints?

(I notice in copying this quotation that you made use of it in your book on *La Situation de la poésie*![4])

There you have it. I have many other things I might tell you about this matter. It is not that I have any illusions about the importance of my book, but I consider it very important that you and Raïssa understand. Some day I will recount my conversion because I think I have a duty to do so, and this will be a way of confessing my faith. Perhaps you don't realize what an important role you played in my return to the Church. Words you don't even remember, I'm sure, had a very determining influence on me (like what you told me in 1939 about Aristotle and Plato concerning precisely the problem of metempsychosis). I cannot thank you enough for all you have done unless it be in begging God to bless you.

Very affectionately,
JULIEN

P.S. The other evening I used the following sentence (in my conference on the Bible) concerning the Douai version: "I shall not examine the Douai version with you, as it has had little influence on the English language."[5] Is that what you would advise me to say? I hope so. I told Raïssa at first that I would not speak of the Douai version, then I did as if I had said yes, as happens to me often.

1. *Varouna*, which had been published by Plon in 1941, was republished in French in New York by La Maison Française in 1941. (An English translation by James Whitall, *Then Shall the Dust Return*, was also published in 1941, by Harper and Brothers in New York.)

2. February 28, 1941, *Devant la porte sombre*, Pléiade IV.

3. Pierre Termier was a geologist and friend of Bloy's, who once said to him: "You are called Termier in order to pay my bills at the end of the term." Termier did so without protest.

4. This volume, originally published in Paris by Desclée De Brouwer in 1938, has been translated by Marshall Suther: *The Situation of Poetry: Four Essays on the Relations Between Poetry, Mysticism, Magic, and Knowledge* (New York: Philosophical Library, 1955).)

5. The Protestant Bible in the King James Version of 1611 gave its cadences to English prose, but a comparison of texts reveals many felicitous expressions borrowed from the Catholic Douai version of 1582.

77

Princeton
May 13, 1941

Very dear Julien,

Raïssa and I send our heartfelt thanks for your letter. This is no more than a hasty word to tell you that *Varouna* has not yet arrived, and that we have not read the article in the *Times*. Be sure, Julien, that we will be able to recognize the meaning of your book. I will write at greater length when I have read it. It is a joy to think that you intend to describe your way to God; such a book would do an immense amount of good.

Great news! Arthur [Lourié] arrived yesterday on the *Excambion*. You can imagine what it was for me to wait for him at the port and finally to see him. He lives at the same address as we do. I hope he sees you soon.

Tell Anne of our affection for her. I embrace you.

JACQUES

78

New York City
30 Fifth Avenue   October 4, 1941

Very dear Julien,

I am late in thanking you for *Varouna* and in telling you how deeply the book moved me. The fact is that I find myself caught up in a whirlwind of work which has set my correspondence back indefinitely. However late this may be, I would not want my silence to make you think I was indifferent to your work.

As far as the meaning of the book is concerned, I think that the Preface leaves no room for doubt. The mystery with which you are grappling is in reality far more profound and far more strangely human than metempsychosis. You express as well as possible all that can be said on the subject in the last two paragraphs of your Preface.

It is the story of Pierre Lombard and Jeanne's diary which made the deepest impression on me. The first part of the book seemed to me less "inspired" and more "willed," with less latitude as far as its interior substance is concerned and at the same time more sustained in style; it seems to me, if I may be so bold as to say so, too well written. The other two parts are haunting. I believe you have truly confided to this book more of your secret self than to any other, and this is another thing that touched me so deeply as I read it. You have given living reality here to that idea we spoke of one day in Paris, that in the life of the world there is a solidarity of souls and a re-versibility which corresponds in some degree to the Communion of Saints. And you have touched on all the great themes of destiny and fate in a dimension completely different from the "determinism" of the philosophers, which does not get below the surface. Meditating on the foreknowledge of futures, I have come to believe that in the universe of men there exist certain *inclinations* that determine "sit-uations" in which, when they are similar, the men who find them-selves there act in a similar manner, in such a way that by having a sense of these "inclinations," one can have an intuition of what they'll do; and it seems to me that your book can be interpreted in an analogous way, with such moral situations turning up repeatedly in the passage of time. And the chain, as you indicate so luminously, can be broken only by a free act of love. The figure of Hélène Lom-bard and her action on Jeanne have a central importance here. At the same time the mystery and the pain of literary creation takes on a depth that ordinarily goes unnoticed.

Each of your books, my dear Julien, is an act of courage, and this one, which is concealed under the appearance of three short stories, goes very far. Raïssa loves this book as I do, and insists that I tell you so.

Tell us about yourself, my dear Julien. I hear you have published a very beautiful article in *Harper's Magazine*.[1] I found out too late to get a copy. Could you send me one? I'll be sure to return it. We are still overwhelmed with work. All we hear from our friends who arrive from France breaks our hearts, and at the same time strength-ens our hope in this abandoned people. Do you know that Chagall[2] is here, and Zadkine[3] too? Lourié arrived before they did and wants very much to see you.

I hope to see you soon. Give our faithful love to Anne. I embrace you.

JACQUES

1. "An Experiment in English," *Har-per's Magazine*, 183 (September 1941), 397–405.

⟨2. Marc Chagall was a very close friend of the Maritains, especially of Raïssa, who, like him, was of Russian

Jewish origin.⟩

⟨3. Ossep Zadkine was a Cubist sculp-tor of Russian origin who emigrated to France. During the war he fled to the United States to escape the Nazis.⟩

79

Barbizon Plaza Hotel
New York
December 3, 1941

Dearest Jacques,

I read your book[1] with deep emotion, and it seems to me that I would never finish citing to you all the passages that struck me. The page on the "wisdom" of sinners has an admirable force and clarity, but I think I would prize above all the rest the last two pages of the book, which are truly magnificent. On page 41 there is enough, with the aid of grace, to redress a whole life of mistakes. We never know exactly what we do in writing a book. Perhaps God will make use of the page I am speaking of to save hundreds of souls today or in a century from now. If it's all right with you, I'll quote it in my journal; this will be the best way to thank you for having written it.

My memory, which is a bit slow, as you may have noticed, has finally consented to give up to me the name of the English mystic I spoke a few words about to you yesterday: Richard Rolle of Hampole.[2]

What happiness to think that you exist, my dear Jacques! You can do us all so much good!

I embrace you and Raïssa affectionately. My best wishes to Miss Vera, who, I hope, is feeling better.

JULIEN

⟨1. Maritain's *Crépuscule de la civilisation* (Montreal: Éditions de l'Arbre, 1941) was published in the United States as *The Twilight of Civilization* (trans. Lionel Landry [New York: Sheed & Ward, 1943]).⟩

⟨2. Richard Rolle was a medieval English hermit and wandering mystic whose writings on the spiritual life, especially his *De incendio amoris*, were very popular in medieval England. He also translated parts of the Scriptures into English.⟩

80

January 6, 1942

Dearest Jacques,

A word in haste to tell you that I have to come to New York on the 8th and that I would be happy to see you, all three of you, if you can spare me a moment, but as you are very busy, I beg of you not to change your projects in any way. I will leave again the next day after speaking at the Plaza.[1] No need to tell you how much I think of you and with what feelings of affection.

I embrace you.

JULIEN

P.S. As soon as I arrive in New York, about 1:00, I will give you a call.

1. Julien Green along with Jacques Maritain belonged to a committee to help French prisoners of war through the Red Cross. He was invited to New York to speak on their behalf. Other members of the committee were Eve Curie, Antoine de Saint-Exupéry, Charles Boyer, and Madeleine Caroll.

81

April 30, 1942

My dear Jacques,

A few days after having seen you, I returned to Stechert's, a bookstore on 10th Avenue, and as the *Isaïe* about which I spoke was still there, I bought it; they had put it on display (seeing that I was interested in it) and I was afraid it would get away from us, but I consider it as our undivided common property!

At first it was the price that made me hesitate; however, another reason kept me from buying it: I was afraid that the notes on the famous seventh chapter would give me no more than an *embarrassed explication* of one of the most important verses of all Scripture. It is this verse, in fact, which kept me for so long a time on the threshold of the Church and which was the object of my first conversation with Father Rzewuski. (I believe that, etymologically, a scruple is a tiny pebble that can keep one from running, and even from walking.) The discussion of the word *almah* by Father Condamin is completely satisfying, but the fact that there is παρθένος in the Septuagint translation remains in my eyes the most convincing argument. As far as the entire translation of the prophecy by Father Condamin[1] is concerned, it is neither better nor worse than the others we know. The notes are not as copious as I would have liked; they presuppose some knowledge of Hebrew on the part of the reader.

I am more and more convinced that all our principles of translation must be revised with regard to the Bible. We have made of the Bible a book that is uniformly solemn. A shadow of boredom is spread over the most beautiful pages in the world. We can blame only the timidity of the translators who make the kings, the saints, the great visionaries, and the military chieftains of the Old Testament all speak like ministers of the Protestant church.

I embrace you, my dear Jacques.

Affectionately,

JULIEN

1. Albert Condamin, S.J., the translator of Isaiah (*Isaïe* [Paris: Lecoffre, 1905]), was a Biblical exegete and professor at the Institut Catholique and at St. Mary's College, Canterbury.

82

August 20, 1942

Dearest Jacques,

Here is the text of the passage about you in the pages I wrote on Péguy.[1] After giving the names of all those with whom Péguy quarreled, I wrote the following:

He quarrelled even with Jacques Maritain. To us who know the great Catholic philosopher, this seems almost incredible. Whenever an important issue was at stake, Maritain has shown an indomitable firmness of spirit and I venture to say that, if Péguy were to return to life in our distracted world of 1942, he could not be prouder of any other friend of his; but, whatever may be our reasons for admiring Maritain, it is his kindliness and humanity which have endeared him to so many. I have been told, however, on best authority, that he and Charles Péguy were reconciled in later years. On their quarrel I shall say nothing, except that it seems to me to have been unduly emphasized by writers who were not present when the events they describe actually occurred.

In the first version of my Preface, the passage in question was shorter; I wanted to develop it, only too happy for the chance to pay homage to someone I admire as much as I love, and to whom I owe so much.

Thought a lot of our evening together yesterday. Dear Jacques, I thank God for having permitted me to know you.

Affectionately,

JULIEN

1. Anne and Julien Green were the principal translators into English of Charles Péguy. The book referred to here is *Basic Verities* (see 71.1). At the request of Kurt Wolff, the editor of Musil, Trakl, and Kafka, among others, in exile in New York from Nazi Germany, Julien Green undertook this translation to help the new publishing house which Wolff had founded in America.

83

[postmarked July 14, 1943, New York]

Dearest Jacques

My most affectionate thoughts fly to you in this great trial.[1] I know very well what your sorrow must be, and I pray with all my heart that Our Lord, Who loves you so much, will bring you consolation.

I embrace you affectionately.

JULIEN

1. Geneviève Favre, Jacques Maritain's mother, had just died in Paris. See 84.1.

84

New York City
30 Fifth Avenue   July 18, 1943

My dear Julien,

Thank you for your letter and for your fraternal prayers. Your friendship and Anne's too makes you understand so well and so deeply all that one can suffer. I had hoped so much to see my mother once again, and she had hoped so much to see me![1] She did not even receive the telegram I sent her by way of Switzerland, when I found out—too late—about her sickness. Pray for us, dear Julien, and think too of Éveline,[2] who bears all alone the weight of this sorrow.

I embrace you.

JACQUES

1. Geneviève Favre-Maritain, Jacques' mother, died in Paris on January 9, 1943. Separated by events, they had not seen each other since the war began. She was the daughter of Jules Favre.
2. Éveline Garnier, the granddaughter of Geneviève Favre-Maritain and Jacques' niece; see 73.3.

85

March 25, 1944

My dear Jacques,

I would have sent this check on our behalf many days ago if I did not have something to ask of you, and it is because I know you are very busy that I hesitate. There is another reason why I hesitate, as you will see, but don't let this preamble frighten you! Here is the problem. Needing my pamphlet to make some corrections in it, I looked through my papers for the copy I had made of this little book. I looked for it alone at first, then with the help of my sister, and now I am sure that in some way or other the copy in question got lost. I regret this because it took a great amount of time, and now I seem to have less and less time! You can guess what I am going to ask you. Would you lend me the copy I made for you?

What made me hesitate a bit to ask this favor of you is that it would only remind you of the Foreword you wanted to write for my book, whereas I would have much preferred that you forget about it until the day when you have more time to yourself. Believe me, there is no ulterior motive whatsoever in the request I am making today! And if by chance you can no longer find these pages (I lost my copy because I have no place to organize my papers), let neither of us think any more about it.

I miss all three of you very much. It gave me such great pleasure to see you. Do the "conversations" still go on? I hope some day to be able to listen to one again, and I hope too, very firmly, that in a not too distant future we will get together in Paris or Meudon to begin those meetings once again.

I embrace you.

JULIEN

86

New York City
30 Fifth Avenue   April 2, 1944

My very dear Julien,

I thank you with all my heart for your letter and for the great charity which keeps you from holding against me my lateness in writing the Foreword to your pamphlet. I am heartsick over this. I am returning these precious pages, but on one condition, my dear Julien, and that is that you send them back to me as soon as you no longer need them. No work can be dearer to me than to write the Foreword to a book which I admire so much and which is at the origin of our friendship. It makes me wild to think that the few days of tranquillity and concentration needed for this are constantly stolen from me by the miserable work imposed by exterior activities and by duties of office[1] that I detest. I want to write this Foreword and I will write it. Don't deprive me of this joy.

We miss you very much, my dear Julien. It was like an oasis to see you and to speak with you of all we love. There have been no more "conversations." We hope that they will take up once again and that one day we will be able to take advantage of your passing through New York.

Yes, we will be together again in Paris or Meudon, in a not too distant future to begin those meetings once again. But what will we find again in Paris or Meudon?

Pray for us. I embrace you.

JACQUES

⟨1. For the years 1943 and 1944 Maritain was President of the École Libre des Hautes Études, the Free French University in exile, in New York.⟩

87

April 25, 1944

My dear Jacques,

Forgive me for not having told you sooner how much your letter moved me; this is what I expected from you. I will return your typed copy of the pamphlet, or I will send you instead another more carefully made copy. In the one you sent me, two pages are missing (the first two), but that has no importance whatsoever, since it will be easy for me to recopy them at Columbia the next time I am in New York.[1] I tell you this so that you may not be surprised at not finding these two pages in the copy I will be sending you.

I also received this morning a copy of your book.[2] I thank you very much for sending it to me and I will read it this summer, when I finish my work for Mills College.[3]

I miss you and Raïssa very much. My sister does too. Doubtless you do not realize all that you give us, as you do to all your friends. We think of you with deep affection. Think of us too, dear Jacques, and pray for us.

I embrace you.

JULIEN

1. According to the postmark, the letter was sent from Baltimore.
2. Perhaps *Principes d'une politique* *humaniste*, or *De Bergson à Thomas d'Aquin*, both published in New York in 1944 by La Maison Française.

⟨3. During the spring semester of 1944 Julien Green delivered a series of con- ferences on literature at Mills College in New York.⟩

88

November 1, 1944

My dear Jacques

Father Couturier tells me that you are going to leave for France[1] in a few days and I have just enough time to wish you *bon voyage*. Need I tell you how much I envy you? But we will see each other again over there, or perhaps here, if you are not too long in coming back. I think of you and of Raïssa and Vera with deep affection and I embrace you.

JULIEN

⟨1. In late 1942 General Charles de Gaulle had invited Maritain to serve on the National Committee of Free France, but Maritain declined. In the fall of 1944 Maritain received another call from the Free French government urging him to return to France for consultation in the interest of his country. Having many personal affairs to take care of, Maritain accepted the invitation. On November 10th he received an *ordre de mission* and left for France on an American military plane. It was during the course of this visit that Charles de Gaulle and Georges Bidault persuaded him to accept the post of French Ambassador to the Vatican. See Doering, *Maritain and the French Catholic Intellectuals*, pp. 202f. Maritain returned to New York on January 1, 1945.⟩

89

January 9, 1945

My dear Jacques,

I am happy to learn that you are back and I am going to try to see you in New York this month or in the beginning of February. Do you realize that more than a year has passed since we last saw one another? I have many things to tell you and more to ask you, because you can be of great help to me with your advice. Need I tell you that I think of you often? You are never far from those who love you.

Your letter to the *New York Herald* moved us deeply.[1] I had not read the scandalous declarations of Mr. Crawford. What good fortune that you were there to point them out—and to destroy them! I am sending you the two pages I devoted to you in a conference I gave last month in New York.[2] I hope I have said nothing to displease you. I wanted to say publicly all the friendship and admiration I have for you, but its expression falls far short of the truth.

May I ask you to give Lourié the note for him that I slipped into your envelope? The piece of his they played the other night seemed to me admirable.[3] I expected a lot of Lourié, but not that much. What richness and what freedom, and how happy we ought to be to think that such great gifts have not been given him in vain and that he has been able to draw from them all they make possible! Here is a man who has not buried his talents.

I am anxious to hear you speak of France, of what you saw there, of all our friends. And I have plans I will tell you about. And you will be of great help in telling me how I can be most useful to my two countries.

All my affection to all three of you.

I embrace you with all my heart.

JULIEN

⟨1. Maritain's article "In Defense of France" (*The New York Herald Tribune*, January 8, 1945) was a protest against an address given by a Mr. F. C. Crawford before the Chamber of Commerce of the State of New York, which, in Maritain's opinion, gave a distorted view of the situation in France because Mr. Crawford's only sources of information were sympathizers with the Pétain regime and former collaborators. It was reprinted in the collection of Maritain's wartime articles and addresses *Pour la justice* (New York: La Maison Française, 1945), pp. 344–47.⟩

⟨2. This conference has been published in Pléiade III. It contains reminiscences of his literary associations around 1925. In the text there are several very laudatory pages dedicated to Jacques Maritain.⟩

3. This refers to a suite made from Lourié's *Le Festin pendant la peste*.

90

New York City
30 Fifth Avenue   January 16, 1945

Dearest Julien,

How can I tell you how much I was touched by your letter and the pages of your conference where you speak of me? Would that I looked something like this portrait traced with an affection so tender and so penetrating! No, you have certainly said nothing to offend me. It all makes me a bit confused. But it is a great comfort for me and a great consolation to know I am seen in this way in the eyes of a friend like you, even if he is too indulgent. Thank you from the bottom of my heart, my dear Julien.

I am anxious to see you and to tell you of Paris. What I noticed especially are the vestiges of all the horror that Frenchmen have seen and touched, and my soul is wounded by it all. It is mostly the sad and dark things that I can tell you of. And along with that the joy of seeing once again so many friends (those at least who were not deported) and of receiving such an admirably fraternal welcome. Many asked for news of you, and if you are thinking of returning soon.

Our radio wasn't working well, and we were unable to hear the orchestral suite played in Boston. But I already knew the piano version of *Festin*, and I am not surprised that you liked this great work, which we will soon be able to hear in New York. They tell me that the audience was enthusiastic and that Lourié continues to receive expressions of admiration. Finally, this time his success is decisive. It is a great joy for me.

I have been a friend for some months now of Mr. Howland Shaw, who was Assistant Secretary of State until the recent shake up. He is a convert and an admirable Christian, who devotes himself with great intelligence, and great liberty of spirit, to making the Gospel penetrate the social life of this country. He spends a great deal of his time with young people in prison. Here is his address: 2723 N Street, N.W., Washington 7, D.C. Tel.: Michigan 2152. Write him. If you can't go to see him in Washington, he will be happy to go to see you in Baltimore.

I hope that you will soon come to New York and that Anne will come with you. Let me know a few days in advance so that we can arrange to see you at leisure.

All three of us want to tell you of our profound affection for you and for Anne. I embrace you with all my heart.

JACQUES

91

January 30, 1945

My dear Jacques

Thanks for writing to reassure me. I can never tell you enough how much you mean to all of us.

Robert tells me your name has been proposed as French Ambassador to the Vatican,[1] and you can imagine how happy I am both for you and for the country you will represent.[2] With all my heart I hope this comes about quickly.

I expect to be in New York between the 10th and the 14th. Could you see me on the 10th or the 13th? I would be so happy. I am to have lunch tomorrow with Mr. Howland Shaw and I thank you so much for giving me his address.

I hope to see you soon, dear Jacques.

I embrace you.

JULIEN

1. General de Gaulle and his Minister of Foreign Affairs, Georges Bidault, wanted Jacques Maritain as French Ambassador to the Holy See, a position that was more important at that time than that of Ambassador to the Italian government. It was at the insistence of the provisionary government that Maritain ended up accepting the post.

2. Julien Green is an American and, consequently, it was not his country that Maritain represented in Rome.

92

New York
February 17, 1945

My dear Julien,

Your article is admirable.[1] It moved me deeply and will do great good in France. I would suggest only that you eliminate one phase (four words) which would risk hurting the wife and friends of Claude Bourdet (for rest assured that each will recognize his own).

What a joy it was for us to see you and Anne, and what sadness to leave you. Pray for us. I embrace you.

JACQUES

⟨1. Maritain is probably referring to the article entitled "Nouvelles de France ..." which Green was preparing for publica- tion in the Paris newspaper *Le Figaro* (March 31, 1945). It appears in Pléiade II, in Appendix II.⟩

93

Paris, October 18, 1945

Dear Jacques,

As you see, everything works out! What a joy to be here! But how I would like to see you here too, you, Raïssa, and Vera! We all miss you but no one more so than Anne and I.

We arrived fifteen days ago and we are hanging on as best we can, having no apartment. For the moment we are living with some friends (73 *bis*, Faubourg Saint-Honoré) who are exceptionally kind to us, but this can't go on forever and if we cannot find anything, it may be that we will have to pack our bags once again and leave. But I think our friends will help us, especially those we have in the invisible world.

Paris has never been more beautiful. How many times have I stopped right in the middle of the street, dazzled as if by some vision, before these marvelous *ensembles*! Couldn't we pull at our Ambassador's sleeve, begging him: "Come home, come home!"? That's what I would do right now if I were at the Palazzo Taverna. . . .[1]

Anne, who is with me, sends her affectionate remembrance to all three of you, and I, for my part, embrace you with all my heart.

JULIEN

1. The Palazzo Taverna is the residence of the French Ambassador to the Vatican.

94

The French Embassy
to the Holy See   October 27, 1945

My dear Julien,

I received your letter the moment I was closing my suitcase for Paris. I have just enough time to tell you that my mother's apartment, 149 rue de Rennes, Paris 6ᵉ, which is now rented in my name, might well serve as a refuge for you. It would give me great joy that you and Anne should live there!

Some of the furnishings are still in storage, but I think that would be only a slight inconvenience for you. The keys are in the hands of Mlle Thérèse Bonnard, who for many years kept up my aging mother's house and who cared for her with admirable devotion during her final sickness. Thérèse lives in the house. She works elsewhere during the day. It would be best for you to write to her to settle on a time when you could visit the apartment with her to see if it suits you. Show her this letter and tell her that Raïssa and I think of her with great affection.

Write me soon and tell me if this all works out well and if you will do me the honor of being my guests. Perhaps in this way we may be able to bring you as far as the Palazzo Taverna.

I'll write a longer letter shortly. All three of us embrace you and Anne with all our hearts.

JACQUES

Here is Éveline's address: 17 rue Rousselet (Suffern 32–38). Telephone early in the morning. She will be so happy to see you and will be able to guide you to the apartment on the rue de Rennes. . . .

95

> November 13, 1945
> 73 *bis* Faubourg Saint-Honoré,
> Paris, VIIIᵉ

My dear Jacques,

We were deeply touched by your letter and by so generous an offer. That is so like you. Mlle Garnier had the great kindness to show us the apartment herself which we visited with great emotion because of all we found there of your mother and of yourself, not to mention the memory of Péguy, so very much alive within those walls; it was the exact decor we would have expected. There is no

need to tell you that we would be thrilled to accept your invitation
if it should happen that we are unable to obtain the apartment we
have had in mind now for a month and about which we are now
negotiating with a friend of my sister's. We have received a proposi-
tion for a lease which we have accepted. The owner is a certain
Mme de Boigne, who, it seems, wants us very much as renters because of the new laws which would oblige her to house refugees if
the lodgings in question remained empty! The apartment is in fact
quite agreeable, small, and consequently easy to heat, very sunny
even though it is on the second floor with all the windows opening
on the courtyard. And do you know where the apartment is? Number 50 rue Cortambert. That ought to tell you something. In any
case I will be pleased to be near those nuns,[1] the daughters of Blessed
Julien Eymard, whom you know and who chant so well. Anne is
persuaded that this apartment has been destined for us by Providence
and that we owe it in great measure to the prayers of Father Couturier, who must have literally moved heaven and earth to obtain
it for us. If, however, at the very last moment they tell us we can't
live there, we will not be too disappointed because we can then go
to the rue de Rennes. And how can we thank you, my dear Jacques?
Do you know that when your letter arrived I had just said to Anne:
"If we can't live in Paris, I'll go live in Rome." Anne would have
gone to live with friends, but for my part, I was determined to
leave. It would have caused me too much pain to find myself in
Paris and not feel at home there. Yesterday we went to see our
furniture, which friends had stored in a garage (a few steps from
the Majestic!) in 1940. I was afraid this would be a difficult trial,
but it did me some good. By candlelight I saw all those things I had
been so attached to by weakness but which I had done without for
so long. Everything is in good condition, but what melancholy there
was in that enormous pile of furniture, and how many memories
came back to me! I stood there overwhelmed for several minutes,
but I think that was good for me. This is the kind of thing that God
brings about. I put in my pocket a few photographs of the family
and two letters from friends that were lying on a console, all cov-

ered with dust, and that's all I took with me. I realized in a second that it is best to be detached from everything. Perhaps I would have thought otherwise if I had had the promise of an empty apartment (I know myself quite well!), but the apartment we hope to live in is furnished. . . .

I have been speaking too much of myself, but I think very much about you, Raïssa, and Vera. I ask myself if Rome pleases you, if you are happy there, if you are going to come back to us. Would I be twisting the knife in a wound if I told you that Paris is marvelously beautiful right now?

You are always near us, dear Jacques, and you, too, dear Raïssa and Vera. Think of us. With all my heart I embrace you.

JULIEN

1. Green renounced Protestantism on April 29, 1916, in the crypt of the chapel of the Servants of the Blessed Sacrament, the White Sisters of the rue Cortambert, whose neighbor he was. Hence, he would be living on that street for the second time.

96

50 rue Cortambert[1]

My dear Jacques,

What happiness to know you are here! One word from you and I will run to see you, unless you would be so kind as to give us the joy of coming to see us.

I embrace you with all my heart.

JULIEN

1. This letter is probably from the summer of 1946. The envelope, which was saved, bears the address: S. E. (His Excellency) Monsieur Jacques Maritain, French Ambassador to the Vatican, Hotel Lancaster, 7 rue de Berri, Paris; but the postmark is not legible. Julien and Anne Green must have moved to 50 rue Cortambert during the winter of 1945 (see Letter 95 and the heading of Letter 97). In March of 1947 (see the heading of Letter 100) they are already at 52 bis, rue de Varenne.

97

Paris, November 22, 1946
50 rue Cortambert

My dearest Jacques,

Raïssa sent me the text of the Foreword you wrote for my pamphlet and which will remain among my papers, since it doesn't seem that it will be published. How can I tell you what I think of these pages? They delighted me as much as they saddened me, for I would never have dreamed of a more intelligent introduction or one that did more honor to my little book. Furnished with such a passport, the pamphlet would pass that frontier which still separates it from those for whom it was destined, I mean those Catholics who are a bit too much at ease in their Catholicism and whom there is question of shaking up in 1946 as I wanted to shake them up in 1924. But don't think I have forgotten what you told me the last time I saw you. Your reasons are excellent, and all I can do is renounce, as best I can, this admirable Foreword. As for republishing this book with an introduction by the author, I would never have thought of that if Albert Béguin[1] and Father Carré had not insisted on it. Father Couturier told me he would reread the pamphlet and tell me how he feels. I'll have to reread it too, for it's been many years since I've looked at it (I recopied it in 1940). What bothers me a bit is that this re-edition is presented to me as a kind of duty, and I would want particularly that it not be in reality a culpable mistake. At any rate, if I write this introduction, I will have you read it, and if you think it can dissipate those misunderstandings that the pamphlet might cause, I will take under consideration a new edition of this book. You know, this pamphlet seems far away from me today, but if it can do some good, even to only two or three persons, then I think it should be reprinted.

I think of you often, my dear Jacques. You are even nearer to me than in the past, and I love you as much as I admire you. Be sure to tell Raïssa and Vera of our affection.

I embrace you.

JULIEN

My book was sent to you, of course, in *July* and in its original edition.[2] What happens to books between Paris and Rome? Another copy was sent to you a couple of weeks ago. You will find there memories of our conversations in New York.

⟨1. Albert Béguin was a French literary critic and friend of Maritain's who frequented the Cercles Thomistes at Meudon. He did literary studies of many of Maritain's friends: Péguy, Bloy, Bernanos, and Bergson. In October 1950 he succeeded the deceased Emmanuel Mounier as director of the Personalist review *Esprit* (see 51A.2). He died in 1957. The December 1958 issue of *Esprit* is devoted to his memory.⟩

2. Green is referring to the third volume of his *Journal*, which Plon published in 1946: *Devant la porte sombre* (Pléiade IV).

98

The French Embassy
to the Holy See   January 7, 1947

My dear Julien,

I have been putting off writing you until I finished, in the midst of all the disturbances which fall on me like rain, the reading of your *Journal*. In its great reserve, this is an extraordinarily moving book, which has touched me in a very particular fashion, because it made me relive those years in America when our anguish was unremitting and when nevertheless my heart became strangely attached to that country and its people. I was happy to find there the echo of several of your conversations with Raïssa and me. There are many profound things in your book, and your marvelous love of Paris, and that image of your soul which shines through, as if in spite of you, with so much mystery and truth. Thank you, dear Julien, for having sent us this beautiful book of which we now have two copies (one sent by Plon, the other signed by you, not to mention the original edition which got lost).

What you write me about my Foreword to your pamphlet gives me the joy of seeing that you love those pages, and renews my perplexity over the question of their publication. What did Father Couturier tell you and what do you think after having reread the pamphlet? If you decide not to publish the pamphlet, the scruples I confided to you will have full satisfaction. But if you decide to put out a new edition with an introduction by the author, the very affectionate and touching way in which you speak about my Foreword makes me think it best that it appear along with your introduction. If there is a new edition, I would very much regret its absence. Write me, Julien, about what choice you make.

Is it necessary for me to say with what profound affection we think of Anne and of you? Our heart is very close to yours. Raïssa, Vera, and I send both of you our fervent best wishes for the New Year.

I embrace you.

JACQUES

99

The French Embassy
to the Holy See   Rome, February 20, 1947

My dear Julien,

M. d'Angelo, general director of Universalia, asks to be introduced to you, and I accede most willingly to his wishes.

Universalia is a Catholic organization recently created in Rome, which makes every effort to promote literature and the arts, and which, in addition to publishing a review of literature and the fine arts, has produced several films. Perhaps you know of the most recent one: *Un giorno nella vita*; after having had great success here, it is running in Paris at this time.

Universalia has proposed to adapt *Minuit* for the cinema, and M. d'Angelo would like to talk to you about this project.

I heartily recommend him and hope you will welcome him warmly. Please believe, my dear Julien, in my faithful friendship.

JACQUES MARITAIN

100

52 *bis* rue de Varenne
March 27, 1947

My dearest Jacques,

I should have written you long ago, and I do not even want to count up the months that have slipped away since I received your last letter, but I hope you will forgive me for this long silence. What you wrote me about the pamphlet deeply touched me, and I thank you with all my heart for the permission to print your Foreword. Still, the reissue of this book seems to me inopportune at the present moment. So I am going to wait a bit, and in any case I will do nothing without consulting you again. (The way things are going, I think I'll be waiting for some time.)

We are getting installed with difficulty in this apartment on the rue de Varenne which some friends found for us; for almost a month now we have been living in the middle of renovations, surrounded by old plaster, but little by little the work is getting done (we have so often been afraid of a general strike, which for us would be catastrophic!). The view of the garden is wonderful, and we are very near the Chapel on the rue du Bac.

We think often of the three of you. When will we see each other again, and where? If I could, I would go to Rome to visit you. I want you to know, in any case, that you are very near to us and that we love you very much.

This letter will be delivered to you by our dear Laurice who was kind enough to accept the task.

Good bye, my dear Jacques; I embrace you affectionately, wishing you a Happy Easter.

JULIEN

I have seen M. d'Angelo who wished that, dropping everything else, I write him a scenario of the life of St. Ignatius.[1] But he doesn't give me enough time, and I doubt whether the whole thing is possible, even though it does tempt me quite a bit.

P.S. March 29. I have accepted—with fear and trembling!

1. The movie company Universalia wanted first of all to make a film of *Minuit* (Letter 99), and then the life of St. Ignatius. Green worked during all of 1947 on the screenplay of the latter, but the film was never made. Because of a difference of opinion with the director, Robert Bresson, the project was abandoned. *Inigo*, Green's screenplay, is included in Pléiade III.

101

My dear Jacques,

An invitation from Eau Vive[1] informs me that you are in France, and I am writing to tell you of my joy. Unfortunately I can't leave Paris at the moment because of the publication of a new book[2] (which I sent to you in America), but I don't need to tell you how much we would like to see you, along with Raïssa and Vera with whom I beg you to share my deep affection.

JULIEN

When are you coming to Paris? Couldn't you send me a word? It would give Anne and me such great pleasure.

1. L'Eau Vive was a short-lived foundation loosely connected with Le Saulchoir, (a French Dominican House of Studies in a poor suburb of Paris, and center of Dominican intellectual ferment, particularly after the Second World War.) Maritain gave a number of courses there during the summers after his return to the United States from Rome. This letter, according to the postmark, is from July 25, 1950. It is addressed to Monsieur Jacques Maritain, L'Eau Vive, Soisy-sur-Seine, Seine-et-Oise. This address is crossed out and replaced with 4 Boulevard Raspail, Paris, 6e.

2. *Moïra* was published by Plon in 1950. (An English translation, by Denise Folliot under the same title, was published the following year (New York: Macmillan, 1951); see Letter 102.)

102

Princeton, New Jersey
26 Linden Lane
September 1, 1951

Dear Julien,

Raïssa and I have been wanting to write you for months now. Hindered at every turn by each day's obligations, we have ended up telling ourselves that we would be able to see you in Paris and that there we could better communicate with you than by letter, and now because of a stupid question of visas which has been dragging on for months and won't be settled for several weeks more, we have been forced to give up the idea of going to France this summer. So I am taking advantage of the sort of vacation we have now in the hot humidity of Princeton[1] to send you the letter so long overdue.

Before leaving Paris last year we had asked Father Couturier to tell you how much we think of *Moïra*. It's an admirable book. I do not know if it is the richest of your books or the one most laden with dreams, but I certainly believe it is the strongest and most perfect of your books. It has a rare power of truth; and the self-restraint of great classic art, and that active, dynamic role, so productive of terrible intensity, which is played by silences and by all that, just at the right moment, remains unsaid, all of which shows an extraordinary mastery. What you said in your *Journal* about the genesis of this novel was of enormous interest to us.[2] I see no reason for the scruples you seem to experience at certain moments. The book is terrifying—just like the human soul; it is constantly dominated by a rational vision that knows no connivance. It is an example of that art with "purified sources" whose possibility you seem sometimes to doubt.

As far as your *Journal*[3] is concerned, dear Julien, it has touched us to the quick. Its lucidity, its genuine sincerity, the depths of the spiritual experience with which it is nourished, the childlike spirit too which appears in it, as well as its gracefulness, make it very dear to us, and have moved us to the very depths of our affection for its author. I can't tell you of the many things that struck me; your conversations with dear Father Couturier and with poor Gide (who needs prayers more than the embarrassed panegyrics with which France is covering him since his death). I like that admirable notation on page 216: "What does that mean? What does all that mean?" and what follows, and your remarks on the metaphysical nobility of love and on its enemy, the sexual instinct, or on the day when man understands "that he never really knew very much about the little he thought he knew," and those remarks about the beauty of the human face, and the reminder of that famous Victorian phrase (about giving to the poor what is totally uneatable) which throws light on our present catastrophe. Must I tell you that a certain melancholy follows the reading of certain words which this or that priest said to you and which give witness of a most mediocre state of mind? Must I tell you that, though you are perfectly right to wrestle with those problems that are really decisive for the artist and for the human being, sometimes, in recalling St. Thomas' advice: "Do not dig any ditches that you fail to cover," I was disappointed that you did not push further on toward a solution? I am thinking of the problem of artistic creation and holiness, which is crucial for you. I am thinking of our conversations in New York during the war: it seems to me that such a problem cannot be tackled except in suffering and by suffering, but that this suffering should not obscure its real dimensions, which are already quite frightening. What I mean to say is that, on the one hand, the necessity for the novelist to be entirely identified with a character bears of itself, not on a lived or material identity, but on an immaterial-creative or "intentional" identity, as we ⟨philosophers⟩ are wont to say (God, in His totality, is also in each person He has created), and that, on the other hand, if tendencies toward a lived identity are inevitable in man and are part of his weakness, they remain or can remain accidental and involuntary, like movements to which we do not give our consent, however violent they may be, and to which we are all subject; and because of the fact that they are not sinful, they do not really stain the soul, and are not obstacles on the road to sanctity. Luther renounced sanctity because he thought that all the passions which wracked him were sins, whereas sin exists only in the consent of the free will. I wonder if Luther's temptation is not that of every great poet when he is on the brink of despair.

Excuse this little philosophical dissertation. You must realize that this is the way I speak as a philosopher. You must realize too that this problem is crucial for the philosopher as well as for the poet.

To Anne and to you, dear Julien, our deep affection. Until next summer, I hope! I embrace you.

JACQUES

Hélène Hersent is a friend of all three of us, but especially of Raïssa's, to whom she came in a very touching way in New York during the war, after having read *Les Grandes Amitiés.*[4]

1. In 1947, in the course of a meeting of UNESCO in Mexico, Maritain was offered the post of Professor of Philosophy at Princeton University. He accepted and resigned his ambassadorship in May 1948. He then embarked for America from Naples.

⟨2. In 1949, while Green was working on *Moïra*, he was recopying his *Journal* of five years before to prepare it for publication. He was copying out the entries concerning a novel he had tried to write at that time but had abandoned after several unsuccessful beginnings and then had completely forgotten, when he came across a page which contained an exact summary description of the novel he was

working on at the moment. Green was both disturbed and fascinated by this experience. (See October 7 and 8, 1948, *L'Oeil de l'ouragan*, Pléiade IV).⟩

3. Volume V of Green's *Journal* was published by Plon in 1951: *Le Revenant* (Pléiade IV).

4. This first volume of Raïssa's memoirs was published by La Maison Française in 1942. An English translation, by Julie Kernan, *We Have Been Friends Together*, was published by Longmans, Green and Co. (New York & Toronto) the following year. *Adventures in Grace*, its sequel, appeared from Longmans, Green and Co. in 1945.

103

Paris, November 22, 1951

My dearest Jacques,

Would you excuse me first of all for typing this letter? This is not habitual with me, but I hurt my left hand, and, although I don't write with that particular hand, it is hard to imagine how useful it really is, if only to hold the paper in place! Your letter arrived while I was still on vacation. It answered many questions I have been asking myself and which I still ask. How many times have I not noticed certain important letters arrive at a given moment and make us suppose some kind of foreknowledge on the part of him who wrote them. This is doubtless only an illusion, but I refuse to believe that certain coincidences are entirely the product of chance. Whatever the case may be, I want to tell you once again how much it means to me to know that you like those of my books in which I have tried to recount clearly certain things which will undoubtedly always remain obscure (and in that unequal struggle between what I want to do and what I can do, I always seem to lose the match—too bad!).

I was struck by what you said about the inadequacy of answers given me by priests. With time I have become used to this situation, but not without a deep sense of melancholy. What used to scandalize me in the early days of my conversion was the banality of what I heard from men I thought were supernatural. I was naïve then and still am. I have not lost all hope of some day hearing a man speak like an angel—but perhaps that will have to be a layman.

I don't know if you have read *Eve et Marie* by Father Dehau.[1] It seems to me that this book all by itself makes up for all that infamous pious literature which dishonors the Catholic world. From the very first pages where he speaks of prayer as a reconquered Eden, one is reminded of what Emerson says about the "accent of the Holy Spirit" which is recognizable in certain works. Has anyone ever thought of translating Father Dehau into English? Someone should do it, at least parts of his principal books. Who knows if in America he would not awaken an echo in many souls? When America pushes toward material success, it underestimates itself; it is really looking for something entirely different. It knows so little about itself.

You can't imagine what a disappointment it was for your friends not to see you this summer. You are nearer to us all than you can realize, and when I say you, I have the plural in mind. If next year doesn't find you in Paris, you will force us to make a trip to America in August, which would be absolutely dreadful. I have a very vivid memory of certain terrifying temperatures. But you will come to see us, I am sure.

I have reflected very much on what Raïssa told me about Hell. In truth, I hesitate somewhat to turn my eyes in that direction. I insist, however, that if the Church makes the existence of Hell an article of faith, it has never asked us to believe in the great number of the damned, whatever the opinion of the saints may be on this matter, and God knows they can be pessimistic when they put themselves to it! Perhaps it is because I need mercy more than anyone else that I believe more and more in the immensity of God's tender pity.

Goodbye, my dearest Jacques. Anne joins me in sending you, Raïssa, and Vera our most faithful and affectionate thoughts.

JULIEN

1. Green greatly admired the *Oeuvres spirituelles* of Pierre-Thomas Dehau, O.P., ten volumes of which were published in Paris by Les Editions du Cerf between 1940 and 1950, and frequently quotes from them in his *Journal*. See, for example, the entries for December 9, 1946 (*Le Revenant*, Pléiade IV), November 3, 1959 and February 4, 1966 (*Vers l'invisible*, Pléiade V), where he cites several of Dehau's thoughts as worthy of the great mystics.

104

Princeton, New Jersey
May 28, 1954

Dear Julien,

I have been very ill (heart attack[1])—am now convalescing, but I cannot write for a very long time. Thank you for sending me your book.[2] Raïssa and I like it very much. The character of Elizabeth is of rare beauty and has profound truth in it. There is a singular power in the double sense in which the words *Fire* and *Enemy* can be taken at the end.

From all three of us our great affection to you and Anne.

JACQUES

1. Maritain suffered a heart attack in March which immobilized him for more than two months.

2. *L'Ennemi*, a play in three acts, was published by Plon in 1954 (Pléiade III).

105

June 1954

My dearest Jacques,

I am writing you even though I have no news to send, but I have been thinking of you so much all these last few days that something pushes me to tell you so. Since the last time I saw you, I have not ceased to put to you mentally many questions you could have answered, I am sure, as you have always done, but for more than a year now I have found myself in such a state of incertitude that I need to hear a voice like yours. You can't imagine how much I miss you! I never seem to write you and it may be (I understand very well) that you mistake the meaning of this very long silence. And yet, it means nothing. It certainly does not mean that I do not love you! Ever since that far-away day when I first saw you at Meudon, I understood that God was sending you to me, as He later sent our good Father Couturier. There are moments when I feel alone and when I am seized by a great disquietude. Priests have little to say to us, apparently, and an enormous confusion reigns in Europe. One finds peace only when one is at prayer, for then one finds refuge in a fortress; but as soon as one leaves it the Demon is there. I don't want to complain. This is the lot of every Christian in this strange world about which I understand nothing.

I don't know why I am telling you these things. It is noon. I have finished my work. I was going to sit down and read by the fire, when a voice I could not resist said to me: "Write Jacques, write him now." So I am doing it to tell you that you must not hold it against me for not writing you. We must hasten to tell each other that we love one another while we still have the time. I don't see how the world can last very long in its present state. Perhaps I am all wrong; I understand nothing about politics, so perhaps it will go on for years and years. Whatever the case may be, my thoughts fly affectionately toward you, and I send a very tight hug to you, Raïssa, and Vera.

Your
JULIEN

106

Dear Jacques,

I should have written you long ago, and I hope you are not upset by my silence because I have thought of you very often and very affectionately. Your letter moved me and with all my heart I hope you are feeling better; knowing that you are ill caused us all great sorrow, and I wish I could say this better than I am saying it today. How much we feel the desire to see you, and to see you here! We miss you more than you can know. Your presence brought us all something no one else could bring in this time of general confusion. I was very appreciative of what you said about *l'Ennemi*.[1] I wanted to write a play for the glory of God, but that seems to have turned against me with the very first performance. I had never yet seen such an unleashing of savage rage! But I got to certain souls, I believe.

We felt very bad about the death of Father Couturier. He loved you and admired you deeply.

Anne joins me in expressing to you, Raïssa, and Vera all our affection. I feel myself very close to you and embrace you.

JULIEN

1. This play was produced at the Thé-   1954. The letter is postmarked July 9,
âtre des Bouffes-Parisiens on March 1,   1954.

107

26 Linden Lane
Princeton, New Jersey   May 22, 1955

Dear Julien,

Raïssa and I thank you with all our hearts for the sixth volume of your journal.[1] I'm the one who pounced upon it to read as soon as my work and my fatigue made it possible; Raïssa will read it on the boat, for we are leaving very soon for France.

I found this book extremely touching. It seems, more than the others, to give us a glimpse of that soul which is yours and where God is present. There are some admirable pages; there are others (those where you are at grips with the world—that world for which Christ did not pray) which caused me sorrow. Dear Julien, how can you write (p. 27): "Strange how that does not depend on the state of grace, since everything cries out to me that I am not in it"?[2] Can we ever know something like that? And can we ever give the impression of accepting such a situation, even for an instant? But what I feel pressed to tell you above all is the profound, immense joy which is given me by the affirmation, so pure and so lofty, that you give of your faith. There is in it a grandeur and a simplicity which, I think, will touch many hearts. Might I add that this desire to leave the world which haunts you is fulfilled in a very profound way by the simple fact of the Faith as you profess it? For what the world cannot tolerate in the Christian, what *separates* us from the world, is the Faith. (With Hope and Charity it is another matter entirely; the world would hate them too if it knew them, but Hope escapes its gaze and it is completely wrong about Charity, admiring it because it mistakes it for natural generosity. . . .)

I would like to say this too about the problems of the flesh and of religion which life itself and people who confide in you so often put in your path. Max Jacob died a saint.[3] Can we not believe that he showed us the only true solution to the problem when it takes its most painful forms? Max went to confession every day and to Communion every day. As you say with such force, we cannot escape St. Paul and the Gospels. And yet, in spite of everything, God wants our love and our union with Him in love. So then what? Max found the way, and was, more than anyone else, simply pushed to the extreme. To have recourse to these two sacraments each day, as he did, demands a kind of heroic, but not impossible, will; there is no problem stronger than God. This is how I would have answered, it seems to me, those visitors who questioned you.

About these things and about many others I hope we will soon be able to speak to one another. We should arrive in Paris in the early days of June; we will let you know as soon as we are a bit settled. To both you and Anne our profound affection.

JACQUES

1. This sixth volume of the *Journal*, entitled *Le Miroir intérieur*, was published by Plon in 1955 (Pléiade IV).

2. September 30, 1950 (*Le Miroir intérieur*).

⟨3. Max Jacob was a Breton French poet of Jewish descent who lived a bohemian life in Montmartre with Pablo Picasso and other friends until his conversion to Catholicism after an "apparition" of Christ in 1909. Picasso was his godfather. In 1921 he retired to the monastery of Saint-Benoît-sur-Loire where he lived in seclusion until he was arrested by the Nazis in 1944. He was sent to the French concentration camp at Drancy where he died in great serenity of spirit; he is buried at Saint-Benoît-sur-Loire.⟩

108

52 *bis* rue de Varenne, VII°
[November 19, 1955]

My dearest Jacques,

I always think of you very much, but particularly so these days because I can guess what sadness must be yours.[1] Mlle Garnier informed me of the tragedy that has befallen you, and I would like to be able to embrace you. What can one say after all? We can only pray for one another to lighten the burden of sorrow, and you know very well I am not forgetting you.

The few hours we spent with you, Raïssa, and Vera left with us a marvelous memory which Anne and I speak of very often. The world, which is so frightening, is always there. But you are there too, and the peace that you bring without knowing it. I have always felt, when I was near you, that nothing really evil could ever happen to me as long as you were there, and this is because, in a world which is rushing to perdition, you remain God's friend. Pray for me, Jacques, and you, too, dear Raïssa and dear Vera. I have an incessant desire to flee the world. And yet I feel that my place is here, but I must ask God to make me truly Christian.

I will not reread this letter, because I would be tempted not to send it to you since it does not really say what I want it to say. But it will tell you at least that I love all three of you very deeply and that my sister and I embrace you most affectionately.

JULIEN

1. Jeanne Maritain, Jacques' sister, died in October.

109

26 Linden Lane
Princeton, New Jersey   January 12, 1956

Dear Julien,

Your letter touched me very deeply, and I thank you for it with all my heart. Oh, you have done well to send it to us! It moved all of us, Raïssa and me, and Vera, in an extraordinary way because the message that it brought to us corresponded so perfectly to the affection which our souls have for you, an affection which is indeed absolutely unique—for you, Julien, and for Anne too. These things will be known in Heaven, for the mystery of God is involved in them. He alone knows what He has created between us. But we seemed to glimpse something of it in Paris in the marvelous sweetness of our conversations with the two of you. It was the obligation to leave behind the sensible presence of such a friendship that made our departure from France so painful this time in spite of the attachment we feel for your country.[1]

1. Raïssa added a few lines of affection   It was signed JACQUES and RAÏSSA.
at the bottom of this letter from Jacques.

110

[Postmarked March 1, 1956]

My dearest Jacques,

Your letter touched me deeply. It also moved me so much that I wrote you on the spot and, as I sometimes do, I slipped my answer into a drawer where it remains because I was not satisfied with it. If you were here, if I had the happiness of seeing you, I would tell you in five minutes what I could never explain to you in a letter. But I have to try. Excuse me if I seem indiscreet but it seems to me rather incomprehensible that a man like you could experience anxiety (what should I say of myself who have every reason in the world to live in a state close to anguish, but I'm not talking of myself here). I believe God hides from you all the good you have done. At any rate, I can tell you that he who writes these lines owes you more than you have ever realized. For me, as for so many others, you have been God's friend and witness. You have helped souls, whom perhaps you don't even know, to escape from the demon. How many times do I hear your name pronounced with respect, with affection! If good Father Couturier were here, he would tell you all this far better than I can. He loved you so much, and he was not easily mistaken about the quality of a soul; he saw you where you are, in the light.

I am not going to reread this letter. I am going to send it off with all its clumsiness. In spite of everything, it will express my gratitude for all that you give me. It is in great measure due to you that I have kept the Faith, because everything is of a piece in human life and your example has helped me preserve the essential.

I ask you to pray for me, and I embrace you with all my heart.

JULIEN

III

July 26, 1956[1]

My dearest Jacques,

I hope you haven't been upset by my long silence which has no other reason than the kind of agitation in which I am living, in spite of myself, because of a play I am to have produced in September.[2] You know that whatever has anything to do with the theater completely upsets one's daily life, and I think that after this new attempt I will never go near the stage again.[3]

I have no need to tell you that we have been thinking about all of you very much, and particularly about Vera since we learned that she has been ill.[4] I asked myself what I could do for her, and I went to Communion for her intention. If I tell you this, which I ask you not to mention to anyone, it is to let you know that I love all three of you with an affection which I hope you will never doubt. We were so happy when Fumet brought us marvelous news from you, but we know we won't see you this summer in Paris. We cannot pass in front of your house without looking at your windows and thinking about you.[5] If you could come back, what happiness it would be for us to have you as neighbors!

I would so much like to speak with you as in the old days. . . . How much I reproach myself today for not having gone to see you more often at Meudon! You have given me so much, you have been such a help to me, without ever realizing it, for, beyond words, there is a presence which is much more eloquent than anything that can be said.

Dear Jacques, tell Raïssa and Vera that we are praying for the three of you with all our hearts.

I embrace you.

JULIEN

1. On the envelope, which was saved, the postmark seems to date its sending as August 17th ("17–8"), and Maritain's answer (Letter 112), of September 26, 1956, also refers to "two letters of March and *August.*"

2. *L'Ombre* was produced at the Théâtre-Antoine on September 19, 1956.

⟨3. Green, in fact, wrote three other plays, two of which have been published by Le Seuil: *Demain n'existe pas*, in 1979, and *L'Automate*, in 1981. The third, "Le Grand Soir," remains unpublished.⟩

4. Vera too had a heart attack.

5. The Maritains' Parisian apartment, where Raïssa died on November 4, 1960, was at 36 rue de Varenne, very near Green's apartment.

112

26 Linden Lane
Princeton, New Jersey   September 26, 1956

Dear Julien,

Your two letters of March and August are incomparably precious for me. How I regret to be answering them so tardily. Tell Anne that it is also cruelly painful for Raïssa to be unable yet, because of the worry and anguish that have exhausted all her strength, to answer that precious letter which moved her so deeply; how many times has she spoken of it to me, in torment at not being able to write.

And how many times in turn have I written to you in my imagination. I would like to tell you so many things about an idea which impresses me more and more, that we all, in some way or other, fall short of what the precept demands of us—so it is by some insignificant little thing which comes in addition, a moment of pity, or of abnegation, an act springing from an evangelical counsel, or corresponding to a special intention that God has for us—for example, a certain obstinacy in carrying out for Him that so strange task He has given me (as He has to you and to Léon Bloy) to write books—

that we find our secret hope in the mercy of Christ our Savior. It is from this point of view that I read the story of the rich young man, who went away sad because he held fast to the precept, but refused to sell his goods. . . .

Vera continues to get better, and little by little is taking up her activities once again! You can imagine what these months of anguish have been for us. And how difficult things have now become, with the health of each one of us in so precarious a state. It is not very convenient to learn how to have confidence in God.

I cannot tell you how precious your friendship and Anne's is to us, and what a comfort it is for our hearts. The affection which unites us, Julien, is a part of the design of God's tenderness which we will see clearly only in the next world but of which all that you write gives me a kind of intuition. Your letters console me in so many sorrows.

I am also very late in thanking you for Le Malfaiteur.[1] All three of us have read it with very deep emotion, and I had intended to write you at length about it when Vera's sickness interrupted for a long period any correspondence whatever. The book is very beautiful, very pure. Our hearts have been touched by all that you have personally committed to it. I consider it as one of those very great testimonies where the heart is torn asunder in revealing the truth. It does not push a thesis, and here I think Mauriac has misunderstood it. You reveal the whole truth, and in that truth there is a boundless compassion, and a questioning so painful that it scarcely rises to the lips. What is not said, or is scarcely said at all, and whose invisible presence weighs so heavily, is more important than what is said in the book. Mauriac has not seen that it is not Gaston Dolange, but Jean, in the astounding chiaroscuro in which you have kept him, who is the center of the book. Only one question, which is almost a criticism—why have you given such importance to Blanchonnet? It seems to me that the reality of souls such as you show them is certainly sufficient to frighten us.

Would that we could see each other this summer in Paris! How we long to be able to take the boat this time, spend two or three months on the rue de Varenne, and experience the sweetness of having you and Anne as neighbors.

Pray for us. All three of us embrace both of you most affectionately.

JACQUES

1. Though Plon published a version of *Le Malfaiteur* in Volume IV of the *Oeuvres complètes* in 1955, followed by a separate printing several months later, the complete version was not available until the Pléiade (III) edition in 1974. (An English translation, by Anne Green, *The Transgressor*, was published by Pantheon Books in New York in 1957.)

113

August 7, 1958

My dear Jacques,

I would have written you sooner if I had felt better, but I have an intractable liver, which no longer allows me the most innocent of delicacies and which refuses to understand that when one is traveling one has the right to vary a bit one's ordinary diet! I am taking advantage of a respite to tell you how much I was touched by your letter as well as by the promptness with which you wrote it. Poor Rousseaux[1] must have thought he was doing good in writing that article in *Figaro*, and I even think he really intended to please me, but see what reason can come to without the help of intuition! I had to answer and tell him in the clearest fashion that he was mistaken. What a time this is when one has to take the trouble to explain that if one does not speak of God one is not necessarily an atheist! (In writing these words a phrase of Vivekânanda's comes to my mind: "We live like atheists. . . ."[2]

"*Dixit insipiens in corde suo: Non est Deus.*"[3] This sentence pretty well sums up what I have always thought, and I can say that doubt has never even crossed my mind. Faith is so deeply rooted in me that it is a part of my very existence, but it is hidden. And it is easy to be mistaken about me. But that has no great importance. We are all going toward God, my dear Jacques, the atheists like everybody else. Humanity will be saved in spite of itself. The spirit of rebellion seems inherent in man's very nature, which will always kick against the goad, but humanity will always continue to advance.

And what happens on a grand scale in the history of the world takes place on a small scale in each one of us.

I continue to read the Old Testament in Hebrew with the same sense of wonder. How is it possible not to require that Catholic priests know at least the rudiments of this language? What a renewal there would be in Biblical studies! Yesterday I was reading the Preface to the work of Father Moidrey's on the Book of Ruth.[4] It seems he wanted to translate all of Holy Scripture. "But what good does it do to write?" he said. "No one will read what I write."

I am ending this letter, my dear Jacques, but my thoughts are with you. I don't have to tell you what place you have been able to make for yourself in my heart.

Most affectionately,

JULIEN

1. A critic from *Le Figaro littéraire*.

2. ⟨Vivekânanda, a disciple of Râmakrishna, was an Indian philosopher who popularized the philosophy of Vedanta. During the late '30s Green read very widely in Hindu philosophy, especially concerning reincarnation and the transmigration of souls.⟩ This quotation is found twice in his *Journal*: March 16, 1942 (*Devant la porte sombre*; Pléiade IV) and January 17, 1959 (*Vers l'invisible*; Pléiade IV).

⟨3. Psalm 13:1.⟩

⟨4. Abbé Tardif de Moidrey was a famous nineteenth-century preacher known for his sermons at the great pilgrimage sites of Europe, such as Lourdes and La Salette, and at Jerusalem. A learned Biblical scholar, he wrote a famous *Introduction au Livre de Ruth*, which Gallimard republished in 1958 with a 100-page Preface by Paul Claudel on the figurative meaning of the Scriptures.⟩

114

26 Linden Lane
Princeton, New Jersey   Christmas 1958

Dear Julien,

I read *Le Bel Aujourd'hui*[1] with deep emotion.

First I want to tell you how much we were moved by what you wrote there about the three of us. You know how dear your friendship is to us; the witness you give of it is just as dear. As far as I am concerned, the expression that you report (of someone returning from Russia) about my "evangelical face" astonishes me and makes me want to hide (when I see my face in the barber's mirror, how foreign it seems to me!). But how precious are those few lines about our meeting in 1924.[2] I think of all this past. God alone knows what prayer has created between us.

But what I want to tell you most of all is that this book is very beautiful and that I love and admire it very much. There is an astonishing art in its grace and in the irresistible purity of its sincerity—and there is more than mere art in the way in which many very simple things that you speak of open the way to truths which strike the heart.

It is not without good reason that you cite Caussade[3] and that you like him so much. It seems to me that one finds here a kind of abandonment to Providence in the literary work itself of which I know hardly any examples outside of a few poets whom I love above all others.

It seems to me too that this book is witness to a spiritual experience which in a very singular way, by the grace of God, has become deeper and deeper, and because of it a lofty serenity envelops and shelters the difficult interior trials of which you speak with perfect sobriety, and in which you are not without great and holy companions.

My letter would never end if I entered into detail. What strikes me above all is that without any apologetic intention (you have been marvelously preserved from this) and by the simple statement of what there is and what happens within you, you bear witness to the Faith, and bring to many souls both the darkness of God and His light, in the very heart of this world, in which you expose the Demon so well, and which has made itself so strangely and so diabolically impenetrable to things from above. Father Crété, who is in Heaven, I hope, in spite of his imprudence, must be quite surprised to see by what paths and what extraordinary detours, and at what cost, God has traced out your destiny and leads you to accomplish, in fidelity to an interior light, a mission which in substance is the very one to which that impatient director felt you were called![4]

I said I could not enter into detail. There is, however, a point I would like to mention: the pleasure I got from what Father C

(Carré?)[5] told you about the phrase *Ne nos inducas in tentationem*. For a long time now I have felt the true translation would be: "Do not put us to the test." Didn't Jesus say to His Apostles: *vos autem estis, qui permanestis mecum in tentationibus meis* (Luke 22:28)? Here too *tentatio* seems to mean "test" or "trial."[6]

You make some remarks about old age that I do not find exact. First of all there is no old age. There is only a limitation of physical force and of the freedom of movement. But the soul does not grow old; it must grow stronger and more detached. It is not aging that is cruel, but rather sickness, and sickness comes at any age. All his life Bloy bore the trial of poverty; for us it has been sickness.

Julien, how well you speak of music! And how enlightening all you say about your work in writing your novels and your plays.

I'm the one who up till now has monopolized your book. Raïssa and Vera are going to read it now. Might I mention to Anne that Raïssa would like very much to receive a letter from her? She has been waiting for such a letter for a long time. All three of us express our deep affection for Anne and you. On this Christmas day we all send you both our warmest and heartfelt best wishes. I embrace you.

JACQUES

1. *Le Bel Aujourd'hui*, published by Plon in 1958, is Volume VII of Green's *Journal* (Pléiade V).

2. In his *Journal* entry for June 18, 1955, Green wrote: "One of the greatest favors God has bestowed on me was to put Jacques on my path in 1925. On this I insist" (*Le Bel Aujourd'hui*, Pléiade V).

3. Pierre de Caussade was an eighteenth-century mystic. His *L'Abandon à la Providence divine* is frequently quoted in Green's *Journal*.

4. Father Crété, who was in charge of the religious instruction of Julien Green at the age of sixteen, insisted that he had a monastic vocation. "When I announced to him my decision not to enter religion, he said he could not be sure of my salvation, a phrase which weighed heavily on me and angered Jacques Maritain" (Sep-

tember 14, 1956, *Le Bel Aujourd'hui*, Pléiade V).

5. In spite of Maritain's guess, "Father C" is, according to Green's *Journal* (April 20, 1956, *Le Bel Aujourd'hui*, Pléiade V), Rev. Louis Cognet, a good friend of Green's and the author of numerous books on the mystics. He was a professor at the Institut Catholique and a recognized authority on Jansenism and Port-Royal. It was he who furnished the French dramatist Montherlant with all the documents for his play *Port-Royal*. He died in 1970.

⟨6. Maritain was right about the meaning of the word *tentatio*. Newer translations such as *The New English Bible* and *The Jerusalem Bible* use "test" or "trial" for the passage from Luke and for The Lord's Prayer.⟩

115

January 8, 1959

Dear Jacques,

You will never know what joy your letter brought me. Like all those you have sent, it brought me so many things. . . . It replaced a bit, in the time I took to read it, your actual presence, which all those who love you need so much. If I myself do not write more frequently, it is because I can never say all I want to say in a letter. Doubtless too it would be easier for me if I could sit down at a table, as I used to be able to do, and spread all my papers about me, but, for almost two years now, I have had to write with a board on my knees, and make the best of it, as you see. An attack of rheumatism is the cause of this little change. This affects my work less than it does my correspondence, which suffers disastrous setbacks, inexplicable to those who don't know the situation.

I could speak of your letter in detail as you do of my book, and I think that if I listened to my heart, I would write you a letter *de senectute*, for what you said to me on this point struck me, and I want to be clear about what I meant to say, but said so badly. Dear Jacques, you are right, old age does not exist, or, rather, there is old age only where there is no love. We all know miserable beings in whose hearts sin in its ugliest forms has killed even the memory of God; but God takes care of His own, and it is for this reason that an octogenarian priest who, leaning on his cane, says his Mass at 7:00 in the chapel of the foreign missions, can lift his beautiful face to the altar and speak to the God Who gives joy to his youth, not in the past, but in the present. You, who are far from being so old, you like him will slip around old age. One of the greatest gifts of the Christmas Child is to give us the heart of a child. If we hold fast to such a gift, the deterioration of the body is of no account. When I was twenty-five years old, the idea of speaking to an old man (that is, someone past fifty!) filled me with sadness and ennui. Need I tell you that my point of view is completely different today? Nothing before forty years, Tauler used to say, but it seems to me that God reserves His greatest gifts for the end, as if He wanted to make the last season a springtime far more beautiful than the first. When we were younger we knew certain things without really understanding them. The light came only much later. In the love of God there is a tenderness which young people do not always understand. You remember William Cowper's song: "Oh, for a closer walk with God." This grace is rarely given at the beginning of our journey. I speak with you about these things because I think of them more and more myself. I look at what men do and listen to what they say, and it makes me sad to see them pass right by happiness without even knowing it is there.

Why aren't you here so that I could ask your advice! There are so many questions I ask myself which remain unanswered. God must wish this darkness and this great silence. Rest assured, in any case, that everything you have said and written to me is very important to me and that I have forgotten none of it. It is God Who has placed us on one another's path, so that you might speak to me, and speak to me in His place. Of that I am sure.

Your book on America[1] is very beautiful, because with you the way of the intellect always passes through the heart, something that is more and more rare. It touches me that you should love my country, which you nevertheless look at without any illusions, for your judgment is inflexible. I hope with all my heart that you will be able to give our friends in Europe a more exact knowledge of the United States. There are some absurd misunderstandings.

I must go now, my dear Jacques, but I think of you, Raïssa, and Vera with an affection that you must never doubt, in spite of my silence, which really means nothing. Morning and evening you are in my prayers, along with those whom I love the most and to whom I owe the most.

I embrace you with all my heart.

JULIEN

I have included a tiny picture for Raïssa. I always thought she resembled this portrait of the Blessed Virgin. Dear Raïssa, dear Vera, please pray for me.

⟨1. Maritain's *Reflections on America* (New York: Scribner's, 1958) was also available to Green in a French translation, *Réflexions sur l'Amérique*, trans. Philippe Lecomte de Noüy (Paris: Fayard, 1958).⟩

116

26 Linden Lane
Princeton, New Jersey

January 15, 1959

Very dear Julien,

Just a few lines—I will write more later—to tell you that your letter moved us to the bottom of our hearts and that for us it is a treasure. May God be blessed for the friendship between us. Raïssa thanks you for the picture which you sent her and which is very dear to her. Our affectionate wishes to Anne. I embrace you with great tenderness.

JACQUES

117

April 12, 1959

M. Jacques Maritain
26 Linden Lane
Princeton, New Jersey

Dearest Jacques,

A Dominican from Geneva just called to give me news about you and to pass on your affectionate message. It touched me deeply that you thought of me, and I need not tell you how near you are to all of us who love you.

The other day I had a visit from Stanislas Fumet and his wife. They spoke of you as of someone who is very dear to them, and yesterday afternoon Father Bars[1] of Perros-Guirec came to spend a moment with me, he too, principally to talk about you. I think you must have no more fervent admirer than this young Breton priest who has already written two excellent books. He asked me some questions about you that would have amused you as much as they would have touched you. "What kind of impression does he give? How does he speak?" etc.

All this to tell you how near you are to us, in our minds and in our hearts, from all the way across the ocean.

For my part, I don't have much news to give you; my life is so monotonous. I am working on a novel[2] and I am reading things you know much better than I do. There are many things you could explain, for to me they seem obscure—namely, in the books of Fathers Urs von Balthasar.[3] One would be grateful if he were a bit clearer, for what he says is often magnificent, but for me many pages are full of darkness (I am thinking especially of *Contemplative Prayer*). Wouldn't one be justified in asking a German to be profound and immediately intelligible as well?

Dear Jacques, I embrace you, Raïssa, and Vera, and think of you with most faithful affection.

JULIEN

P.S. In Balthasar's book I found some very beautiful pages on *Christian identity*, a theme so dear to Léon Bloy: Who are we?

⟨1. Rev. Henry Bars, whose essay on "The Friendship of Jacques Maritain and Julien Green" serves as an introduction to this volume, as a young man wrote an admirable book on Maritain—*Maritain en notre temps* (Paris: Grasset, 1959)—without ever having seen or spoken with the man. He became a close friend of Maritain's after the latter's definitive return to France in 1961. That same year he published a second book on Maritain, *La Politique selon Jacques Maritain* (Paris: Les Editions Ouvrières, 1961). In 1979, with the help of the Centre National des Lettres, Abbé Bars published a collection of Maritain's writings from 1940 to 1963: *Oeuvres*, 2 vols. (Paris: Desclée De Brouwer). He has also written a number of theological studies, particularly on the virtues of faith, hope, and charity.⟩

2. *Chaque homme dans sa nuit* (Pléiade III) was published by Plon in 1960; ⟨Anne Green's translation, *Each in His Darkness*, by Pantheon in 1961⟩.

3. Hans Urs von Balthasar, a German-speaking Catholic theologian, was the translator of Péguy, the author of a book on *Élisabeth de la Trinité* (Paris: Le Seuil, 1960) which is mentioned in *Ce qui reste de jour* (February 4, 1969). One of the major themes of his work is the Redemption considered from a philosophic point of view. The number of his publications is as astonishing as the variety of subjects he treats in them.

118

January 13, 1960
52 *bis* rue de Varenne, VIIe

My dear Jacques and Raïssa,

I am profoundly saddened by the news I just received because I know just how much you must be suffering, but our dear Vera is not far from you, and I am sure that in the great peace of God she is thinking of you and loves you even more than she could on this earth.[1] She is so good (I cannot bring myself to use the past tense, which seems to me to make no sense), and her love will be a treasure of which you will have a share each day. All those whom I love and who have preceded me are always so present that, once the first sorrow is past, I have never been able to think of them without a feeling of happiness. I ask God that it may be the same for you who are both so dear to me. One needs all of one's faith to bear up under such a painful trial, I know, but God is there and He loves you so much, dear Jacques and dear Raïssa.

I embrace you with all my heart.

JULIEN

1. Vera died of cancer on December 31st and was buried in Princeton.

119

26 Linden Lane
Princeton, New Jersey   February 6, 1960

Very dear Julien,

Your letter touched Raïssa and me to the depths of our hearts. I should have thanked you sooner but we are crushed with fatigue. Raïssa will write to Anne as soon as she can. May you both be blessed for your tenderness and affection which are a treasure for our souls.

It is true, Julien, and thank you for the way you say it: *Vera is so good.* We know that in the great peace of God her love watches over us more than ever. And we thank God for having delivered her and taken her to Himself. She has been very sick for the last three years. For more than a year she was bedridden, suffering ceaselessly, with great patience and with never a complaint. She prayed very much, for her friends, for the sick and the dying; she received Communion whenever she could—the last time was the day before Christmas Eve. On the day after Christmas her sufferings became intolerable, but the doctor did not consider her life in danger; he looked forward to long months of suffering. On December 31st she fell asleep at 10:30 in the morning under the influence of a sedative, but instead of waking up four hours later, her sleep or half-sleep continued all day long; the doctor whom we called refused to come, assuring us that this sleep was nothing to worry about and that we should awaken her gently. But she would not wake up. At 7:30 in the evening she let her head bow down a little, her face became white as snow, she was dead. It was as if someone had suddenly taken her off.

Yes, we thank God for having delivered her, but at the same time we are in a void and a solitude that is incomprehensible and insurmountable. The mental anguish we suffered for a year is flowing back on us, for we knew the name of that sickness which we kept hidden from her. Though we are completely at a loss as to what to do and seem surrounded on all sides by impossible situations, we are nevertheless at peace, hoping that Vera is helping us and will continue to do so. Here is something I will tell no one but you and Henry Bars (you may mention it to Anne, but to no one else). One day while I was reciting the rosary for her, in great dryness of spirit (it must have been in January or February a year ago), I heard these few words, as hard as stone: "She must not be deprived of her glory."

Julien, Anne, pray for us. We embrace you with all our hearts.

JACQUES

120

March 18, 1960

M. Jacques Maritain
26 Linden Lane
Princeton, N.J.

Dearest Jacques,

I would like to have been able to write you much sooner, but, scarcely back from Switzerland where your letter caught up with me, I received 400 pages of a new novel to correct,[1] and right away I had to give all my time to this task which I don't like at all.

All you told me about Vera moved me deeply, especially those words which you heard and which cast a great and beautiful light on the sufferings that chosen souls have to undergo. I thank you for having shown me this mark of confidence and friendship which touches me very much. It is useless to tell you what you are for me, what you represent in the eyes of so many persons who love you and whom you have helped in this life on their voyage toward the light. As I get older, I appreciate more and more God's graces, and it seems to me that they come to me on all sides from Christ to warn me that the time is short.

I read with great interest the book you were so kind to send me.[2] It is small only in its format and contains an abundance of riches. You and Raïssa bring us so much. This new work touches on many subjects in which I am deeply interested, but I wonder if the problem of literary creation will not always have a mysterious side to it. I have been reflecting on it for more than thirty years now without seeing much more clearly than when I was young. It seems almost certain to me today that for the novel the solution has not yet been found. Very recently, I was asked to read a book written by a religious whose life was surely exemplary. The book, which was written with a great deal of care, is nothing but white on white. The source has been purified. I am not saying, as you very well know, that one must live in sin to write novels! Yet I firmly believe that this kind of book is the fruit of sin and that where there is no sin there can be no novel. It follows from this that a novel is almost always a confession, often without the author's knowing it, for he exposes himself to the light of day, all the while believing that he has hidden himself behind his characters who are nothing else than himself. But I know we are of one mind on these points. There is, and this is of great importance for the novel, a kind of interior disposition to let oneself be led, pushed on by grace even when one writes novels which seem most frightening, and I hope God makes use of this. In the same way the temptation exists to let oneself be led by the hand by that enemy who is never disarmed and who has a marvelous knowledge of what must be done to tilt the work in his direction. He excels, sad to say, in what is called edifying literature. Dear Jacques, excuse me for carrying on like this on a subject about which you know much more than I, but it is my way of telling you how much your book has meant to me. We live in a world where literary confusion runs rampant (and the confusion is not only literary!). This can be said, probably, about every historical period, but for disorder I think we deserve the victor's palm.

Anne and I think of you and Raïssa with great affection and embrace you with all our hearts.

JULIEN

1. *Chaque homme dans sa nuit.*
2. *The Responsibility of the Artist* (New York: Scribner's, 1960) was published in French the following year (*La*

Responsabilité de l'artiste, trans. George and Christiane Brazzola [Paris: Fayard, 1961]).

121

26 Linden Lane
Princeton, New Jersey   May 12, 1960

Dearest Julien,

I just received your book. Its title is so beautiful. This word in haste to thank you and to tell you that I have been kept from reading it immediately by the proofs of an enormous book on moral philosophy which have literally submerged me.[1] It is only after finishing this fastidious work that I will be able to write you. Excuse the involuntary delay.

My heartfelt thanks for what you said about *The Res[ponsibility] of the A[rtist]*, which touched me deeply. I think we are indeed of one mind.

Would that we could go to Paris to see you and Anne! Will we ever realize this dream? Pray for us, my dear Julien.

Both of us embrace you and Anne with great tenderness.

JACQUES

1. Maritain is referring to his *La Philosophie morale. I. Examen historique et critique des grands systems,* which Gallimard published in 1960. (An English version, *Moral Philosophy: An Historical and Critical Survey of the Great Systems,* appeared four years later (New York: Scribner's, 1964).)

122

Wednesday morning [Summer 1960]

Dearest Julien,
    My heartfelt thanks for your letter to Raïssa. She is feeling better,
but what a trial![1] Pray for us. We will be in Paris on your return.
Our deepest tenderness to both you and Anne.
    I embrace you.

JACQUES

1. The Maritains had come to spend the summer in France. Raïssa fell sick in their room at the Hôtel de Bourgogne et Montana, at the corner of the Place du Palais-Bourbon. She never recovered from this cerebral thrombosis. Not being able to return to America, the Maritains went to live on the rue de Varenne, a few houses from Julien Green.

123

November 26, 1960[1]
Monday morning

My dearest Jacques,
    It will surprise you perhaps to receive a letter from me, even
though we have just parted, but when you gave me that beautiful
photograph of Raïssa, the thought came to me to write you over
there in her behalf. This may seem a bit absurd to you, I suppose,
but I could not put aside this kind of inspiration which came back
several times with singular force and insistence, so I am obeying it.
I firmly believe that Raïssa is with you incessantly and that she is
watching over you, that she is with you in your house at Princeton,
so that your sadness may not weigh too heavily upon you. *For Raïssa
is happy and she wants you to be happy too.*
    You are so dear to me, Jacques, and I feel so near to you every
day. I do not want you to answer this letter, which, I hope, will be
there in time to welcome you. You will have far too much to do to
find the time for writing me. When you return to Paris what a joy
it will be to see you again!
    I embrace you affectionately,

JULIEN

In rereading this letter I find it is very badly written, but I wanted to do it right away. Please excuse me.

1. This letter was addressed to Princeton, the envelope marked *to await arrival.* Jacques had just left on his first trip to the United States after the death of his wife and before settling permanently in France. The date 26/11/60 is inscribed in pencil, perhaps in the handwriting of the addressee.

Raïssa had died on November 4 at 36 rue de Varenne, and was buried in the cemetery at Kolbsheim. Jacques returned to the United States to settle his affairs and to put his house in Princeton at the disposal of the Louriés.

124

26 Linden Lane
Princeton, New Jersey

December 4, 1960

My dearest Julien,

It was certainly an inspiration from Heaven that you obeyed in sending me that letter and it touched me deeply. It didn't arrive until Friday (December 2nd) because my mail delivery was held up. But even that was providential, for what I felt even before receiving the letter shows me how true it is.

I had wept very much on the flight over (but not so much as in Paris), before passing my first night at Princeton in Sir Hugh Taylor's[1] house, and I felt a great fear at the idea of entering into our empty house the morning of December 1st. But no, it was not empty; *it was as if Raïssa were receiving me into her house.* Doubtless she had also guided those dear women, Jane the seamstress, Julia our cook, and Nini Borgerhoff,[2] who had arranged everything in the rooms with marvelous, delicate care so that all would be as it had been. (It is only into Raïssa's room that I find it so painful to enter.) At any rate, in the very midst of my sorrow I had the impression that Raïssa was waiting in the parlor filled with flowers. Her atmosphere, her spirit were there, with that grace, that sweetness, at once light-hearted and grave, that pure and elegant valiance that emanated from her. I firmly believe, as you do, that Raïssa is happy, and that she wants me to be brave. But happy, Julien, how could I be happy? I have lost the physical presence of her whom I have loved more than myself. I have witnessed the slow and implacable destruction of her poor body. (In one of her poems she said to God: "You want my destruction and my death.") But it is true that she is with me incessantly and that she is watching over me. And in my sadness I feel at the same time a kind of joy (the English word *elation* is more exact). May I never be found unworthy of this grace.

Thank you for your letter, my dear Julien, thank you for all that you and Anne have done for her and for me, and for saving me from despair.

Without waiting too long I would like to finish up the enormous material task which awaits me here and return to France about the 15th of January. I will be so glad to see you when I pass through Paris.

I embrace you with profound tenderness. Give all my affection to Anne.

JACQUES

⟨1. Sir Hugh Stott Taylor, a very close friend of the Maritains, was Professor of Chemistry and Dean of the Graduate School of Princeton University. He was also President of the Woodrow Wilson

National Fellowship Foundation.⟩
⟨2. Nini Borgerhoff, the wife of a Princeton professor, served for years as Maritain's secretary.⟩

125

26 Linden Lane
Princeton, New Jersey   January 24, 1961

Dearest Julien,

I have finished the dreadful work I had to do in this house that was hers and is now completely devastated. I intend to sail the day after tomorrow on the S.S. *United States*, with three small trunks containing my most precious souvenirs, and will go directly from Le Havre to Kolbsheim by car (I fear the disorder of the trains and I don't want to risk losing these trunks). At Kolbsheim I will await the arrival of my other belongings, which will probably take until the end of February. Then I hope to leave for Toulouse at the beginning of March, stopping at Paris a few days to see the two of you, my dearest Julien and Anne.

With what tenderness, with what gratitude, I think of you! I am sure that Raïssa is watching over you as she watches over me. You have known her and loved her so marvelously. If you only knew what you are for me, what a refuge! Wherever I am on the earth, I feel very acutely that *I don't belong*—with you I am not the kind of outsider and incongruity I am everywhere else. Pray for me. I embrace both of you with all my heart. May you be blessed for helping the way you have your poor

JACQUES

126

Kolbsheim
April 13, 1961

Dearest Julien,

I came to Kolbsheim during the Easter vacation to finish up my moving, but I have been put terribly behind by the lack of punctuality of some workers from Strasbourg from whom I had ordered a number of things. I should be in Toulouse the morning of the 20th (I will travel at night), and will be passing through Paris on the 18th and 19th. I'm afraid it may be difficult to see you. However, would you send me a note (marked "Please hold") to the Hôtel d'Angleterre, 44 rue Jacob, telling me if by good luck you and Anne have a few moments free for me on the 18th and 19th? I will try to telephone on the morning of the 18th.

How happy I will be to embrace you!

I'll see you soon then, perhaps. . . .

To you and to Anne the faithful tenderness of your poor

JACQUES

127

April 14, 1961

Dearest Jacques,

How happy we are to think that we will soon see you again! Can you take lunch with us on Wednesday, the 19th at 1:00? Come earlier, if possible, so we can have more time together. I have so many things to tell you. When I try to write them to you it just doesn't work any more! This explains my dreadful silence, which I hope you will forgive. You know very well that I think of you every day and with great affection.

I embrace you.

JULIEN

128

Toulouse[1]
April 26, 1961

Dearest Julien,

What joy and what sweetness it was for me to see you and Anne! I will never be able to express my gratitude.

I just received Gide's book *Ainsi soit-il* or *Les Jeux sont faits.* Thanks for sending it to me.

I have found the texts from Lautréamont I mentioned to you. They are in the Preface to the future poems (*Oeuvres complètes*, Paris, G. L. M., 1938), about which he wrote to the Belgian editor Verbroekhoven: "You know, I have renounced my past, I now sing only of Hope." He published them in 1870 in two separate bro-chures, under the title *Poésies* (the poems are not there).

In this extraordinary Preface we read for example: "If one recalls that truth from which all others flow, the absolute goodness of God, and His absolute ignorance of evil, all the sophisms fall to pieces on their own. And at the same time, all that literature, so lacking in

poetry, which is founded on them will also fall to pieces. All literature which calls into question the eternal axioms is condemned
to live only on itself. It is completely wrong. It devours its own
liver. . . . We have no right to question the Creator on anything
whatsoever."

And again: "All the water of the sea would not suffice to wash
away one intellectual blood stain." (If you have my bulky book
Creative Intuition,[2] these texts are cited on pages 206–208).

It seems to me it would be of great interest to study every aspect
of this Preface, which is generally passed over in silence. I don't
know what the Surrealists think about it. Perhaps they prefer not to
speak of it. I do not believe the idea that it may be a hoax has ever
been suggested, but it seems to me inadmissible.

We finally learned this morning that the military uprising in
Algiers has come to an end! We didn't know much about what was
going on (the Little Brothers have no radio), and we were very
worried. We must continue to pray for de Gaulle.

To you and Anne my profound tenderness.

I embrace you.

JACQUES

⟨1. After Raïssa's death in 1960, Maritain decided to pass his remaining years
in retirement and contemplation and accepted an invitation to live and write in
the community of the Little Brothers of
Jesus in Toulouse as lay adviser to those
Brothers who were studying philosophy.
Until his death in 1973, he spent the
academic months of the year in Toulouse.
The summer months he passed in Kolbsheim among his books and papers until
his failing health made the trip impossible. In 1970 this eighty-seven-year–old
"inveterate layman" asked permission to
make his religious profession as a Little
Brother (see Letter 237). In the autumn
of that year he took the habit of the Little
Brothers; after making his novitiate in
Toulouse, he pronounced his vows of religion one year later. In 1961, in his
Preface to Henry Bars's *La Politique selon
Jacques Maritain* (see 117.1), he wrote:
"I have retired from the world, thanks
to the very kind welcome of the Little
Brothers of Jesus, for whom Raïssa and I
have felt a very particular preferential
love since the time of their founding almost thirty years ago. I feel a deep thirst
for silence. I have returned to France, not
in an attempt to exert an active influence,
but to prepare myself to die here."⟩

2. Maritain's *Creative Intuition in Art
and Poetry* (Bollingen 35 [Princeton:
Princeton University Press, 1953]) was
published in French thirteen years later
(*L'Intuition créatrice dans l'art et poésie*
[Paris: Desclée De Brouwer, 1966]).

129

April 29, 1961

M. Jacques Maritain
Fraternité
École Théologique
Avenue Lacordaire
Toulouse
(Haute-Garonne)

Dearest Jacques,

As you do, I believe these texts of Lautréamont are irrefutable. We must never tire of quoting them when we speak of this great poet, and for my part, in the next volume of my journal,[1] I count on having reprinted those sentences where he speaks most clearly of his return to God. They are sometimes called ironic (which brings up again the idea of a hoax), but in their sound there is something that deceives only those who want to be deceived.

Eight days ago we passed through some very anxious moments.[2] The surprising thing is that it all began so suddenly and ended so quickly. I don't need to tell you that we thought of you. You are never far from our hearts, dear Jacques. God bestowed a great grace on me the day He put me in your path.

Very affectionately yours,

JULIEN

P.S. What I find sad, in the Preface you quote, is that the author seems to disavow so splendid a work. I cannot think God asked that of him. There is a lot to say on this point, on the respect one owes to texts which precede a conversion and which may perhaps be in contradiction with it.

1. Green, who considered Lautréamont one of the greatest authors in all of literature, often mentioned him in his *Journal* (cf. *Vers l'invisible* (Pléiade V, pp. 208, 278, etc.). (He did not reprint in his *Journal* the words Maritain quoted from Lautréamont in Letter 128. The entry for May 1, 1961, two days after his letter to Maritain, would seem to indicate that Green was less convinced that Maritain was right about Lautréamont's conversion.)

⟨2. Green is referring to the anxiety in Paris caused by the news from Algiers on April 22nd that Generals Challe, Salan, Jouhaud, and Zeller had staged a military Putsch in revolt against President de Gaulle's Algerian policy.⟩

130

May 17, 1961

Dearest Jacques,

I am sending you this little book which, I believe, is one you would want to read. It was given me by the editor, Richard Heyd, who later gave me another copy. So you can keep the one I am sending.[1]

Anne and I think of you *every day* with the affection that you know. You are so close to us, and we owe you so much.

I embrace you with all my heart.

JULIEN

P.S. I reread this morning, and not without sadness, the stories of Father Lebbe. I cannot believe that the blood of martyrs in those far-away lands does not produce new and magnificent harvests. All is not lost.

1. This was a copy of André Gide's *Et nunc manet in te*, published by the Swiss firm Ides et Calends.

131

Toulouse
May 28, [1961]

Dearest Julien,

Excuse me for not having answered such a sweet and good letter immediately. I am very tired and over my head in work.

I am deeply touched to receive Gide's little book inscribed by the publisher in your name. I reread it with strange emotion and a strange sense of pity. Raïssa used to defend him against those who accused him of egoism (because of the burned letters episode[1]). I will keep it since you have another copy. Thank you.

I have finished putting the final touches to Raïssa's notes on the *Pater noster*.[2] This work has done me good.

I will leave here on June 10th and will first visit Pierre Van der

Meer in Holland.[3] I intend to be in Paris on the 15th of June. What great joy it will be to see you and Anne! Could I have lunch with you on the 15th or one of the following days (except the 16th, when I have to be away)? I will be staying as usual at the Hôtel d'Angleterre, 44 rue Jacob. I should be in Strasbourg on the 23rd. Is the film finished? And will the new edition of your *Journal* be out soon?[4]

Pray for me, dear Julien and Anne. I have so many things to learn and there is so little time.

I embrace you both with all my heart.

JACQUES

⟨1. When André Gide deserted his wife, Madeleine, to live in London with a male companion, she reread, one by one, all the letters she had received from him and then burned them. Gide complained in his journal: "Did she realize that in doing so she destroyed the only archway where later my memory could hope to find refuge? All the best of myself I had confided to these letters: my heart, my joy, my changes of mood, my day-to-day activities.... I am suffering as if she had killed our child" (*Journal intime*, November 22, 1918). *Et nunc manet in te* is included in the Pléiade edition of Gide's *Journal (1939–1944): Souvenirs* (Paris: Galli-

mard, 1954).⟩

2. Raïssa's *Notes sur le Pater* was originally published by Desclée De Brouwer in 1962. ⟨An English translation, *Notes on the Lord's Prayer*, with a Foreword by Thomas Merton, was published in New York by P. J. Kenedy in 1964.⟩

3. Pierre Van der Meer, on the death of his wife, retired to the Benedictine monastery of Oosterhout and at the age of sixty-three was ordained a priest there.

4. The film was *Léviathan*, with Lili Palmer and Madeleine Robinson; the *Journal*, the one-volume edition covering the years 1928–1958, published by Plon in 1961.

132

Mougins, June 24, 1961

Just a word, dear Jacques, to tell you how happy I was at the news I just learned.[1] I am sure this gives pleasure to her who was always so near to you.

With all my heart I embrace you.

JULIEN

1. Maritain was awarded the Grand Prix de littérature de l'Académie Française.

133

Kolbsheim
June 28 [1961]

Thank you for having written, my dearest Julien. It does me good to know you are pleased with my prize, for to tell the truth my feelings about it are very mixed—this sort of prize bothers me no end. And also, with the exception of Gilson,[1] who, they say, took the initiative in this decision, the other members of the Académie surely haven't read a single one of my books; it's a longevity prize they have awarded me. But you are right; it would have given pleasure to Raïssa. I believe that she is pleased with the whole affair (this is all that counts for me) and that she is somewhat amused at my embarrassment.

On arriving here I found the complete edition of your *Journal*. What a beautiful volume! With what joy and what emotion will I read it. I'm sure that in the unity of the single edition, everything I already know will seem new.

I embrace you with profound tenderness.

JACQUES

1. Étienne Gilson was a Catholic philosopher who specialized in medieval philosophy. It was as professor at the University of Toronto that he arranged for several visits by Maritain beginning in 1932. As professor at the Collège de France he studied Thomistic thought in particular and published works on Duns Scotus, Dante, St. Augustine, and St. Bernard.

134

July 4, 1961

Dearest Jacques,

You will soon receive a book entitled *Sagesse de la folie* by Maxime Alexandre[1] whom I advised to send it to you. The work in question can be quickly read. It recounts the conversion of the author, an Alsatian Jew, who came to see me yesterday and who made the very best impression on me. He is about sixty years old, an ex-Surrealist, a devotee of German literature and culture, author of a book on Hölderlin[2]—and very poor. He is looking for a job. Perhaps you could give him some advice or a recommendation. He left Obernai for Paris, but would go back to Alsace willingly if he could make a living at teaching there.

His book seemed to me beautiful and very moving. I read it through at almost one sitting.

Excuse me for bothering you, but perhaps you have an idea.

I think of you and would like to see you. Will you perhaps be coming through Paris again this summer? I will be there till July 25th, then from August 15th till the end of summer vacation.

Remember me to Mme Grunelius.[3]

I embrace you with all my heart.

JULIEN

1. This spiritual itinerary, published in 1952 by La Revue des Jeunes, has a Foreword by Paul Claudel.

2. Hölderlin was one of Green's poets of predilection, as the number of quotations he uses from him attests. Maxime Alexandre's translation does not have the splendor of the original, but the difficulty of translating is also one of the subjects Green takes up frequently in his *Journal*.

(3. Mme Antoinette Grunelius and her husband, Alexandre, were godchildren and very close friends of Jacques Maritain's. At their chateau in Kolbsheim Maritain stored his books and documents after his definitive return to France from the United States. His archives are now permanently housed there at the Centre d'Études Jacques et Raïssa Maritain.)

135

Kolbsheim
September 26 [1961]

Dearest Julien,

I haven't been able to write sooner because I have been submerged with work.

Your *Journal* has been my dearly loved daily companion. I will read it a second time at Toulouse (and will try to note for you all the misprints which are rather numerous). It contains admirable human and spiritual riches and is an inexhaustible source of meditation.

At the very last moment the doctor forbade me to travel by airplane. I will sail on the *Flandre*.[1] I am leaving Kolbsheim tomorrow and will pass through Paris with lightning speed. I will try to telephone you but am not sure I can.

Pray for me. I embrace you and Anne with all my heart.

JACQUES

My frends, the Gruneliuses, informed me of some possibilities in Alsace for Maxime Alexandre. But nothing worked out. I wrote him. I had hoped to be able to meet him in Paris; but that won't be possible this time.

⟨1. Maritain returned to the United States for a brief visit to settle his financial affairs, dispose of his home in Princeton, and bring his books and manuscripts back to France. He put his home in the hands of his composer-friend Arthur Lourié and his wife, who were to live there until they died, after which time it would become the property of the University of Notre Dame where a Maritain Center had been established. The interior of this house, at 26 Linden Lane, was decorated by Maritain's artist friend André Girard with murals depicting, for the most part, scenes of Paris life. To the profound surprise and utter dismay of friends and scholars of Maritain throughout the world, the University, in 1986, sold off this irreplaceable relic of the Maritains to a private owner.⟩

136

52 *bis* rue de Varenne
November 26, 1961

Dearest Jacques,

This book of Raïssa's[1] is a work of light, and I thank you for having given it to me in her behalf. I refound her completely in these pages, with her piety, her sense of the divine, and her great insights. I would be at a loss to tell you what struck me most in her meditations, for I would have to copy out long and numerous passages. Probably more than any other, the place where she calls Heaven the human soul in the state of grace where God comes to dwell, or again the place where she speaks of God's pardon which goes out to those we also pardon. All this is of such great beauty and makes us love God.

I wonder where you are. I would so much like to see you and embrace you with all my heart.

JULIEN

I also received *Le Péché de l'ange* which I will read.[2] Thank you, my dear, dear Jacques.

1. *Notes sur le Pater.*

2. *Le Péché de l'ange, péccabilité, nature, et surnature* is a book written jointly by Charles Journet, Philippe de la Trinité, and Jacques Maritain (Paris: Beauchesne, 1961). ⟨William L. Rossner's

translation, *The Sin of the Angel: An Essay on a Reinterpretation of Some Thomistic Positions,* was published several years later (Westminster, Md.: Newman, 1969).⟩

137

Kolbsheim
December 5 [1961]

My dearest Julien,

How can I thank you for your letter about Raïssa's book? It caught up with me at Toulouse. Nothing could have done me more good. You know that I no longer live except for her and through her. You know too how important it is for me to know what you think of this little book.

I had a bad case of the flu, which became progressively worse for several days. I am getting better rapidly now. Out of prudence the doctor has confined me to my room until Sunday. This delay in my work bothers me very much. I hope I can make it to Toulouse a little before Christmas.

Excuse me for writing only a few words. All my tenderness to you and to Anne. I embrace you with all my heart.

JACQUES

My study on *Le Péché de l'ange* is terribly weighed down with Scholastic terminology, but it was necessary, alas, because I am taking a position opposed to a certain theological tradition. But I consider the point in question very fundamental.[1]

⟨1. Maritain is referring to the long-debated question of the essence of free will and of the relation of intelligent creatures to their final end as the two most profound aspects of the Mystery of Evil, a subject to which he would return in many of his writings, especially in *Dieu et la permission du mal* (Paris: Desclée De Brouwer, 1963; *God and the Permission of Evil,* trans. Joseph W. Evans [Milwaukee: Bruce, 1966]), in this correspondence and in his letters to Georges

1. Her letter is dated March 26, 1936. See *Journal de Raïssa*, 2nd ed. (Paris: Desclée De Brouwer, 1963), p. 239; (and *Raïssa's Journal* (Albany, N.Y.: Magi Books, 1974), p. 257).

141

Toulouse
June 6, 1962

Dearest Julien,

How happy I am at what you wrote about the *Journal de Raïssa*. I read your letter over and over with deep emotion. These notes bring many answers to me too, particularly on the points you mentioned. How I would like to speak of this with you and Anne! May I? At the last moment I have had to put off my departure from Toulouse. I have another case of the flu, and the doctor has forbidden me to travel. If this flu doesn't last too long, I hope to make at least a short stop in Paris, and to see you. I don't want to set any date in advance. I will telephone on arrival. I embrace you and Anne with all my heart.

JACQUES

142

Toulouse
June 13 [1962]

Dearest Julien,

Just a word (I have been obliged to rest) to tell you that my departure for Paris has been put off once more—because of a problem with my heart that had the doctor worried at first, but an electrocardiogram made yesterday evening shows it was due to nothing very serious. I have been authorized then to take up my normal activity once again but very gradually. As to my departure, it has been put off again for two weeks (hoping that no new snag appears). I will telephone from Paris to find out if you are still there. I embrace you and Anne with all my heart.

JACQUES

143

Toulouse
June 18 [1962]

Just a word, my dearest Julien (I am still obliged to rest), to thank you for your letter that was so sweet to my heart.

I still don't know when I will be able to leave for Paris. Toward the end of the month, I hope. I am almost at the end of my strength. . . .

I am very happy about the new edition of the *Pamphlet*. If it should appear with a Foreword by me, I would be singularly proud (but embarrassed too, to tell the truth, for the very idea that a book by you should need a Foreword is preposterous indeed). In any case, perhaps we could read it together in Paris to see if there is anything that doesn't ring true.

I hope to see you soon.

I embrace you and Anne with the deepest tenderness.

JACQUES

144

[After June 18, 1962]

Dearest Jacques,

Thank you for having accepted this text to which I attach great importance. The correction on page 3 is perfect, and you did well, I believe, to suppress the sentence on page 4,[1] which today would be obscure.

How happy we were to see you Sunday! I am so grateful that you thought to contact us. Need I tell you with what affection we think of you? You are always very close to us. I embrace you heartily.

JULIEN

1. Green is referring to the Foreword   Green's *Pamphlet contre les catholiques*
Maritain wrote for the revised edition of   *de France*, published by Plon in 1962.

145

Kolbsheim (Bas-Rhin)
July 13, 1962

Dearest Julien,

I am sending you the little work I spoke of to you concerning the last ends. Speak of it to no one; as I mentioned, this thing should remain absolutely confidential, between you and Anne.

Thank you for the letter you sent with Manu. How can I tell you how happy I was to see you and Anne. God's sweetness surrounds you.

I am glad you found the corrections in the foreword good ones. When is the book to come out?

I am feeling better. It seems to me that some of my strength is coming back, drop by drop.

I embrace both of you with great tenderness.

JACQUES

146

July 20, 1962

My dearest Jacques,

A first reading of your book convinces me that this is a very important work because it answers questions which many Christians have been asking for a long time, and because this response seems at least a reasonable one. It is certain that Hell is a scandal to souls. We are told too little or too much about this subject for it not to remain a danger to the faith of many, since (you know it as well as I do) a great number of Catholics go so far as to deny that it even exists—and this despite the affirmations of Christ and of His Church. What you say seems plausible and in accord with the ideas we have a right to form about God's mercy. You have evidently avoided speaking of a Hell that comes to an end, which would be the equivalent of Purgatory (I believe certain Protestants rally to this unacceptable solution). On the other hand, you have pushed to the limit an intuition which gives the clear impression of coming from God, because even if one calls up all the most terrifying texts, the love of God is stronger than all else, and His justice is only another aspect of His love. I am not a theologian and I speak out of ignorance, but what you believe, I believe too.

With all my affection

Your

JULIEN

147

Kolbsheim
July 28, 1962

Dearest Julien,

I was so touched by your letter and have thought so much about answering you in my mind that I no longer know if I answered you in fact. Probably not. So I am sending these few lines, in spite of my fatigue, to tell you how happy I am about the way you received my "daydreams," and about our agreement on this subject. This is *very* important for me.

With all this you are much too generous in your appreciation, but this generosity which comes from the depths of your heart bring me much sweetness and very much joy, as far as this word still has any meaning for me. For all you have written me in your so beautiful letter I am most deeply grateful.

You tell me that you wish this little book were published. Dear Julien, that is completely impossible, at least for a good number of years. For I have to think first of all about what I have had to say in philosophy. You know I have many enemies. If I gave the slightest reason, by such a book, for some blame or censure from the theologians, it would reflect on my whole philosophical work; in taking such a risk I would prove unfaithful to the task I believe I have been assigned. Later, if my philosophic work should be *accepted* intellectually (something that remains quite improbable), those who will have charge of my writings when I am no longer here can perhaps publish my reflections on the last ends, but only after much consultation. Now at least I have the consolation that a tiny number of friends who are dear to me, and you in particular, love these pages.

Little by little my strength is coming back; I have moments of invincible fatigue. Nevertheless I hope to work this summer and continue to go through Raïssa's notes.

Dear Julien, I embrace you and Anne with all my heart.

JACQUES

Monday the 30th. Before mailing this letter, I received the one Anne wrote me. It moved me deeply. Thank her for me. I will write her as soon as I can. She has a way of saying things that is marvelously fresh and touching.

148

September 30, 1962

Dearest Julien and Anne,

I was glad to embrace you at Patrick's[1] baptism but so disappointed not to have been able to contact you when I passed through Paris. There was so very little time. I had to settle certain affairs which took all my free moments. I had hoped at least to telephone you before leaving, but I was too worn out. They took me to Le Havre by car. The boat should arrive in New York the day after tomorrow, October 2nd.[2] Both of you are in my heart. You know with what tenderness I think about you. I embrace you both with all my heart.

JACQUES

1. Maritain was the godfather of Éveline Garnier's adopted son.

2. ⟨As he had intended to do every year, Maritain was returning to the United States to see his American friends.⟩ Since travel by plane was forbidden him, Maritain was going to New York by ship; this letter was written on board. ⟨During this visit, Maritain's friends flocked to see him both in Princeton and in the New York area where he remained for the most part (see Letter 150). He would make one more trip to the United States, in 1964. That time, besides going to Princeton, he made the long trek to Texas to visit his friend John Howard Griffin and then to Gethsemani, Kentucky, to spend some time with Thomas Merton (see 179.1).⟩

149

October 15, 1962

Dearest Jacques,

Just a word to tell you I have been thinking of you and have followed you in my mind through your whole trip![1] I hope it hasn't tired you excessively. Your charming letter touched Anne and me. You know we pray for you and love you more and more.

I wrote an Introduction to my *Pamphlet*. Need I say that I spoke of you and in a way that I hope will please you. This will be a way of acquitting myself, in a very feeble measure, of the immense debt of gratitude I owe you.

Take care of your health, my dear Jacques; it is so precious to all of us, but to no one more than to your

JULIEN
who embraces you.

1. This letter was addressed to Princeton.

150

Princeton, New Jersey
October 21, 1962

Thank you for your letter, my beloved Julien. Each letter from you brings such great sweetness to my heart.

I am very happy that the new edition of the *Pamphlet* is coming out soon and that you have written an Introduction for it. That you should speak in it of me and of our friendship touches me deeply. Be careful, however, Julien, to say nothing that would give the impression that I am anything more than a poor man, disappointed in himself, unworthy of the goodness his friends show him, and filled with regret and repentance.

The month of October here is incredibly beautiful. I am overwhelmed with visitors. I am floundering in the midst of the most difficult problems. Without the *guidance* and protection of Raïssa what will become of me? I have to pass alone through many banks of quicksand.

Will poor Lourié, like so many great musicians, never be recognized until two or three hundred years after his death?

A Little Brother will come to pick me up by car at Le Havre and drive me directly to Toulouse when I return in mid-November. It is only in June that I will be able to see you, my dear Julien and Anne.

Pray for me. I embrace both of you with all my heart.

JACQUES

151

December 8, 1962

Dearest Jacques,

I am writing this little note to excuse my long silence. I have been ill. It began about All Saints Day and on November 26th last they decided to operate. It was a rather banal operation (they removed my gall bladder) and told me this would be very good for me. I came home the day before yesterday and am gradually getting better. Please don't speak of this operation. It all seems to be going away, and I thank God for having taken pity on me.

I have not ceased to think of you and embrace you very affectionately.

JULIEN

152

Toulouse
December 12, 1962

My dearest Julien,
   It gives me great pain to know you have been sick and had to
undergo an operation (of which I certainly will not speak). As a
matter of fact, I think the removal of the gall bladder has very good
results. And I am happy that since your return home you are feeling better and better. But you have surely gone through some difficult days, and you must be very weak. Thank you for writing to me.
   I think of you with all my heart.
   My affectionate remembrance to Anne. I embrace you with deep
tenderness.

JACQUES

A little word of news shortly would give me great pleasure.

153

52 *bis* rue de Varenne
December 29, 1962

Dearest Jacques,
   Your letter moved me very much, and I am happy to be able to
tell you that my health has been completely restored. I only regret
that this operation couldn't have been done twenty years earlier.
   Plon has moved more rapidly than I had hoped, and the first
proofs of the *Pamphlet* have already arrived. If I send you the text
of your Foreword (with which I am delighted), it is because I think
you would prefer to correct it yourself. Might I point out a slight
detail that gives me pause? Do you think the reader of 1963 will understand the fourth line on page 1: "—twenty-two years ago ... "?
If he doesn't notice the date at the end of the Foreword (and one
must always make allowance for the inattentiveness of the reader),
he may well imagine that the book was written during the war, in

spite of my Introduction (which perhaps he won't even read!). On the other hand, if he sees the date 1946 under your signature, he will wonder what this means. Since you revised the text in 1962, would you be doing too much violence to the facts to give it that date? All obscurity would be dissipated at once, but it goes without saying that I will agree with whatever you decide (. . . "—thirty-eight years ago" would be even more striking than twenty-two!).

Then there is my Introduction and what I say about you. I prefer to warn you ahead of time that no protestation raised by your modesty against the terms I use will be given any consideration! I insist on this in spite of all the respect and affection I have for you. In rereading my text I feel I have said far too little and for too many years I have been awaiting an occasion to pay you this feeble homage.

Having mentioned these things, I think I have said all that has to be said, except that I think of you with all my heart and that, in embracing you most warmly, I wish you a very Happy New Year.

Your
JULIEN

154

Toulouse
January 4, 1963

Dearest Julien,

Thank you for your letter. I am so happy that your health is completely restored!

Yes, naturally, let's put *thirty-eight* years instead of twenty-two in the Foreword and let's date it 1962. (I indicated June 1962 on the proofs because it was last June that we were together in Paris. But if you prefer to indicate another month, do just as you wish. In a general way, I read through the galleys with care, but I am so tired that some mistakes may have escaped me.)

Yes, Julien, there is your Introduction which is very beautiful and explains so admirably the origin of the *Pamphlet*, but why say such things about me? You warn me that no protestation raised by my modesty will be given any consideration. It is not my modesty that raises the objections; it is my sense of truth. How can I tell you to what point these lines move my heart because of the incomparably sweet and generous affection they attest, and to what point at the same time they make me ashamed of what I am? Alas, Julien, I know myself. To see this printed makes me think I am an impostor. All that remains for me to do is to sink into my nothingness, as Mélanie[1] put it, and to tell myself that the reader will find it far too beautiful to be true.

You must love me very much to foster such illusions about me. This is why in spite of my grumbling, I thank you with all my heart, and I'm sure Raïssa thanks you too, and with what tenderness, not for your illusions, but for the gift of your friendship which is more precious than anything else.

Dear Julien, at present I am going through the notes of Raïssa's which I found at Kolbsheim this summer and which I want to add to the *Journal* for an eventual public edition. Among these notes there is one about you and Anne. I am enclosing a copy of it in this letter. If you prefer that this note not appear, or that I delete certain words, tell me in all frankness; I will do exactly as both of you wish.

I embrace you and Anne with all my heart.

JACQUES

1. Mélanie Calvat was the shepherdess of La Salette to whom the Virgin Mary appeared in 1846. In his Foreword to *La Vie de Mélanie par elle-même* (Paris: Mercure de France, 1912), Léon Bloy wrote: "above my perishable and dying pages, where nevertheless I have put all my heart, you will see the soul of this shepherdess of paradise, as sublime and naïve as the sky...."

155

January 8, 1963

Dearest Jacques,

You could say nothing that touches me more deeply than your letter in which I find your whole self, just as I have come to love you. Some day you will come to understand that of the two of us, the one who harbors the greater illusions about the other is not I, but I don't want to quibble over this point. I will say only that if on this earth there were more "impostors" of your type, the world would be a better place. Your sense of the truth doesn't do you much good in this case since you do not see yourself in the full light of love. The good opinion that we have of one another (when we finish doing what is stupid and forbidden, i.e., passing judgment) comes from God and is part of a truth whose totality escapes us. In the end you cannot prevent me from loving you such as you are.

There is not a comma I would change in Raïssa's note,[1] which I have read not without deep emotion. I remember perfectly.

Dear Jacques, I thank you and think of you with deep affection.

JULIEN

P.S. As if to prove what I said, a book has just arrived from the United States: *A Thomas Merton Reader.* In it you are not exactly dragged through the mud! If I wanted to tease you, I would copy a portion of page 265 where you are spoken of. At any rate, this Trappist and I are of the same opinion.

January 9.[2] Just this moment I received your letter and there is no need to tell you that I will do exactly as you wish, but notice that as far as the reader is concerned I have compared you to a statue of Christ and that strictly speaking the comparison goes no farther than this. If I have mentioned this medieval Christ (which is at Chartres), it is somewhat because of Raïssa to whom I had given a photograph of this beautiful statue, calling her attention to a resemblance which I found striking: "It's true," Raïssa said to me, "*and it's very moving.*" However, if you wish me to delete these two words (medieval Christ), it will take but a telephone call to Plon. But I will do it with regret—because of Raïssa.

Dear Jacques, I embrace you warmly.

JULIEN

1. Joined to this letter is a note, in Jacques Maritain's handwriting, from the *Journal de Raïssa,* which appeared in the edition made for the general public in 1963, but not in the private edition of

1962: "Thursday, February 13, 1936. — Saw Julien Green (and his sister Anne for a moment). He is studying the Bible enthusiastically. We spoke a great deal about the Bible. While taking me back, he said to me in a very serious manner which left me in a state of shock: 'Think of me from time to time, Raïssa'—by *think* he means pray—'I need it very much.' He and his sister must be resigned to not finding happiness, at least in this world." In *Raïssa's Journal*, this entry is found on p. 257.

2. This is the answer to Letter 156.

156

Toulouse
(January 8, 1963)

This is just a postscript to my last letter. I only want to point out to you that (in the passage where you speak of me) the words "medieval Christ" came to my mind, and upset me, somewhat more often than I had expected they would. Oh, if you could only change those two words. . . . But do what you prefer, or rather what you can do, for I know that an author cannot always do what he would like. I leave everything in your hands.

I embrace you with all my heart.

JACQUES

157

Toulouse
January 12, 1963

Dearest Julien,

Thank you for your so sweet and good letter. Whatever your illusions may be about this poor Jacques, one thing there is I welcome without the slightest reserve, and that is the affection you show me. It is very precious to my heart.

All right then, since Raïssa is a part of this plot, I no longer have anything against "the medieval Christ."

Excuse the brevity of this letter; at the moment I am suffering from lumbago and cannot write very conveniently.

Thank you for Raïssa's text. Thanks again for everything. With profound tenderness I embrace you.

JACQUES

158

January 21, 1963

Dearest Jacques,

Just a word to tell you that I am thinking of you and hope you are feeling better. I know what lumbago is; it is very painful.

In order not to cause you the slightest shadow of worry, I have somewhat modified the sentence in my Introduction that gave you pause. At present you have "the face of a medieval statue." If you are in agreement don't take the trouble to write.

I embrace you with all my heart.

JULIEN

159

Toulouse
February 8, 1963

Dearest Julien,

I was deeply touched by your letter and thank you for having modified your text and taken into account the phobias of your old Jacques. I find that medieval statue most reassuring.[1] I have not been able to write you sooner because of my fatigue (the lumbago is gone) and also because I am in the midst of an acute crisis in my work. I am so very afraid of being interrupted by some accident of health before I have finished what I am doing on Raïssa's notes (additions to the *Journal*) that I have stopped all correspondence.

I think of you and of Anne with profound tenderness. I embrace you with all my heart.

JACQUES

1. " . . . once again I see very distinctly   body" (Preface to the *Pamphlet*, Pléiade
that face of a medieval statue which was   I).
much more the face of a soul than of a

160

March 27, 1963

Dearest Jacques,

I am slowly getting over a sickness more painful than serious, which explains my silence, for I wanted to write you about my new book.[1] Grasset will send you a copy in a green jacket (unfortunately I was not able to inscribe it for you). I hope you will like it. It's more an examination of conscience than an autobiography.

I hope with all my heart that you are feeling better. I must cut this letter short because of the fatigue that writing causes me, but you know how much I love you. I embrace you very affectionately.

JULIEN

1. *Partir avant le jour* (Paris: Grasset,   Green four years later: *To Leave Before
1963) is the beginning of Green's auto-   Dawn* (New York: Harcourt, Brace, &
biography. (It was translated by Anne   World, 1967).)

161

Toulouse
March 20, 1963

Dearest Julien,

What sadness to learn that you have been sick and that you are still convalescing! I can scarcely write you. I am obliged to rest because of cardiac troubles and great weakness. Perhaps it is meant to be so for Lent. Maybe we will both get back our strength for Easter. Received your book this morning.[1] My heartfelt thanks, Julien; it will be my close companion. (And the *Pamphlet*—when is it coming out?) Pray for your poor Jacques. I embrace you and Anne with a profound tenderness. All my affection.

JACQUES

1. *Partir avant le jour* (Pléiade V).

162

[Postmarked April 9, 1963]

Dearest Jacques,

It gives me great pain to know that you have been ill and I hope with all my heart that you have recovered.

As for me, I am recovering very slowly from a sickness that was not serious but quite painful: a case of the shingles. I am sure Job had the shingles! Anne cares for me like an angel, but there were some difficult moments and I had to take some morphine. But it should all be over soon, say the doctors.

The *Pamphlet* is coming out at the end of the month. Excuse me for writing so badly, but I'm still not feeling very well.

I embrace you with all my heart .

JULIEN

163

Toulouse
April 29, 1963

Dear, dear Julien,

The day before yesterday I received the precious copy you sent me of the 1963 *Pamphlet*, with those lines in your dear handwriting on the first page. Thank you with all my heart. I am rereading the *Pamphlet* with the same joy and the same admiration as when I read it for the first time almost thirty years ago.[1] It is true that your whole work is there, like the ear of wheat in the seed. The fact is you began with a masterpiece—whose youthful naïvetés do not lessen, but rather underscore, its beauty.

And what emotion for me that this new edition contains the testimony of our friendship (this is more important than my modesty). All this is most mysterious. We'll figure it out in Heaven.

Julien, I haven't been able to write you as I would have liked about *Partir avant le jour*. Really just too tired. I love this book deeply. It required all your extraordinary talent. But it required much more—the spirit of childhood, and that love and reverence for souls, which brings light to all you say. In reading you I seem to get a glimpse of the light in which the angels see the miseries of the flesh in our poor humanity. It is in no way a question of vocabulary and language (a perfectly pure language can be used to wound and soil the soul). It is a question of interior light—of grace and charity.

Tell Anne again how grateful I am that she has consented to become the godmother of little Raïssa-Marie. It will be a joy for me to be at her side. I am still very weak (I was sicker than I thought all during Lent), but my strength is returning little by little and I hope to be able to leave Toulouse on the 7th or 8th of June. How happy I will be to see you in Paris.

I embrace you both with deep tenderness.

JACQUES

I would expect that the shingles are completely over and almost forgotten. Yes, Job must have had a case of the shingles, or several. . . .

⟨1. Maritain miscalculated. He should have written "almost forty years ago."⟩

164

July 5, 1963

Dearest Jacques,

I was so happy to see you last month and need not tell you with what joy I look forward to your next visit. The moments Anne and I spend with you always bring us so much happiness. . . .

If I am writing today it is because I have been charged with a certain commission by a Mr. Abrami, an Italian journalist and collaborator on the *Osservatore Romano*. He is by birth a Jew, who has converted. I have had several rather long meetings with him, and my impression is excellent. Recently he telephoned me several times to tell me that a letter from you to the Holy Father would be very warmly welcomed. "I think I know," he said to me with an insistence that finally struck me very forcefully, "that such a letter would certainly not remain unanswered." But he added that the reply would perhaps have to wait a bit, because the Pope receives

5,000 letters a day. At any rate, they seem to count very much on a letter from you, which is all quite natural. I myself who, thank heaven, am no Pope, have been keeping all your letters since 1926! Dear Jacques, I embrace you very affectionately.

JULIEN

165

Kolbsheim
July 7, 1963

Dearest Julien,
Thanks for your sweet letter.
I knew Msgr. Montini very well when I was in Rome, and I had for him a very deep affection and admiration (we were friends, if a word so simple, true, and human can be used in the rarefied world of protocol).[1] Likewise I immediately sent him a telegram of congratulations when I learned of his election, which he answered with another telegram whose kindness touched me deeply and in which he sent me his apostolic benediction. I replied naturally with a little letter of thanks.

You see, then, *I have written* to His Holiness Paul VI. But I must say, I can't understand Mr. Abrami's insistence that such a letter from me be sent to the Pope. What importance could that have? And I must say too that this insistence disturbs me a bit. I fear even the shadow of eminent personages, and I fear some Italians full of friendly pressures which get one involved in their projects and private intrigues. But these fears are rather minimal, because I can't see for the life of me what they could expect. I embrace you with great tenderness.

JACQUES

All my love to Anne.

1. After the death of John XXIII, Paul VI was elected pope on June 23rd. Maritain had been linked to Msgr. Montini while the latter was Secretary of State to Pius XII during Maritain's tenure as French Ambassador to the Vatican. (As a young priest, Msgr. Montini had translated Maritain's *Trois Réformateurs: Lu-*

ther, Descartes, Rousseau into Italian. While he was archbishop of Milan, Msgr. Montini, at Maritain's suggestion, invited Maritain's close friend Saul Alinsky, the famous organizer of the Back of the Yards Movement in Chicago and author of the bestseller *Reveille for Radicals,* to come to Milan to help the Catholic Trade Unionists organize in opposition to the powerful Communist unions. Paul VI often referred to Maritain as his "teacher," and in his encyclical *Progressio populorum,* cited Maritain directly several times. It was to Maritain that he delivered the message to the intellectuals of the world at the close of the Second Vatican Council.)

166

July 9, 1963

My dearest Jacques,

I thank you for having written me so quickly and regret a bit having bothered you, but that journalist was so insistent that after some hesitation I thought it better to do as he asked. As is the case with you, zeal makes me very uneasy. You certainly would not have to be pulled by the sleeve to get you to write to the Pope, but behind it all doubtless was the desire to obtain the testimony of a great French writer. So forget my letter and retain from this one only my tender and faithful affection.

JULIEN

167

Kolbsheim
September 23, 1963

Dearest Julien,

I hope to be in Paris October 1st. (Don't mention it to our friends. I will have very little free time.) Do you think that tentatively you and Anne could have lunch with me (at noon on *Thursday, October 3rd*) at the *Lutetia*? I say "tentatively" because nothing is certain when there is question of my state of health. Would you perhaps have the time to send me word before the 30th, here—or a note that would be waiting for me at the hotel?

In any case I will see you soon. I embrace you and Anne with all my heart.

JACQUES

Do you know if Cocteau is still at Milly, or has he already left to spend the winter in the Midi?

168

November 15, 1963

Dearest Jacques,

I am getting over a slight sickness, more painful than serious, which kept me from writing you earlier to tell you what joy you brought me in sending that marvelous journal of Raïssa's. It is like a long trail of light in the world where we are and where we need so much for someone to speak to us of God. I cannot help believing, today, that the decision to have these papers printed was inspired by her who is always so present to you and whose secret but powerful action will continue to make itself felt.

One follows Raïssa's journey with great emotion. One's only regret is that interruption of several years, but the thread is never lost, and it is a grace to be permitted to see God at work in a predestined soul. Suffering, alas, is necessary, and Raïssa had her share of it, but who would not now envy her her place in God's Kingdom?

I was touched by the memory she had of me, who am so conscious of still being terribly *in via*.

The morning paper brought news that filled Anne and me with great joy. The esteem of men does after all make some sense when it is a question of someone like you.[1]

Dearest Jacques, my eyes hurt me a bit too much to continue this letter, and I wonder if you are going to be able to read my handwriting. Know, in any case, that I love you with all my heart and that Anne joins me in embracing you.

Your

JULIEN

I like very much Stanislas'[2] column in *Le Figaro*.

1. The Grand Prix national des lettres   the man and the philosopher in the high-
had just been bestowed on Maritain,   est esteem.
thanks to General de Gaulle, who held   2. Fumet.

169

Toulouse
November 28, 1963

I am ashamed, my dearest Julien, of not having replied sooner to
your sweet letter. I could not because of a whole pile of extrav-
agantly annoying situations. (*This nonsensical prize.*) It pains me
very much that you have been ill again and that your eyes were
giving you trouble. I hope everything is going well now. You must
rest, Julien.

All you write me about the *Journal de Raïssa* is infinitely precious to my heart—you, my beloved Julien, who were so near to
her till the end, in those months of agony. I believe as you do that
the decision to publish these notes was inspired by her—if you only
knew how she helped me in this work. I think she wants her witness
to be made public among men. For she has many things to teach us.

And I must learn to let myself be led like a blind man. My God,
I had planned everything so that this publication would be as discreet as possible, convinced that all by itself the book would make
its way among souls. I had persuaded the editors to use no press
releases.... And then, just as the book appeared, all that exasperat-
ing fanfare about me! Even then Raïssa protected me by sending
me a slight case of the flu which made it possible for me not to see
any of the journalists and photographers who invaded the property
of the Little Brothers. Now I am submerged under a pile of aber-
rant letters from people who have never read a word I have written.
Now too indirectly because of me and this prize there is all the pub-
licity I feared so much. The first printing of the *Journal* is already
sold out. At first I took all of this with the greatest of ill temper. But
now I say to myself that Providence works out its plans in ironical
ways and that of all those people who have bought the *Journal*,
most of whom did not know what they were getting, it is enough

that there be only a half dozen who needed that meeting with Raïssa to turn them toward God.

I found Father Pézeril's[1] article in *La Croix* wonderful. I have written to thank him. I bless you for having brought this holy priest to her. I was also very touched by all that Mauriac said about the *Journal* and about Raïssa in his Bloc-Notes. But when it comes to me, Zut! Dear Stanislas' fidelity and affection are deeply moving, but his article in *Le Figaro* gives me the impression of having been written about someone else, as if I were being told over and over again that I was nothing but an impostor. Julien, I thought immediately of you on learning about the atrocious tragedy in Dallas. The assassination of the President plunged me into a state of horror, and I realized then to what a point your country has become my second homeland. But how can one put up with the general silence on the true meaning of this crime? I am very much aware, through Thomas Merton and John Griffin, of the expressions of sordid hatred and violence which the fear of "integration" arouses among whites (in Texas especially, and in Mississippi). There is no doubt in my mind that this crime (which, in order to save their skins, they are trying to camouflage as a Communist plot) was plotted (with what complicity on the part of the police) by some fanatics resolved to take vengeance on Kennedy for the march on Washington and in him to punish all "niggerlovers." Alas, why did they let several days go by before calling in the F.B.I.! During this time the criminals were able to cover up their tracks. It seems to me now that, by delicate hints, the officials let it be understood that they know the truth. But they will say nothing as long as they have not gathered legal "evidence." And when will this evidence be gathered? The terrible thing is that Americans don't believe in the Devil; and they do not believe either that "nice people," good fathers of families, good church-goers could become possessed by demons and *monsters*, so possessed by hatred that the crime would inevitably happen some day. If only the blacks could know that the President died *for them* and for their rights!

Julien, pardon me for letting my anxiety overflow like this.

I embrace you and Anne with all my heart.

JACQUES

1. Msgr. Daniel Pézeril was auxiliary bishop of Paris and author of *Pauvre et saint curé d'Ars* (Paris: Le Seuil, 1959), about which Green wrote: "A book which forces one to a general examination of conscience, one of the rarest lives of the saints that I have been able to read" (June 13, 1959, *Vers l'invisible*, Pléiade V).

170

December 4, 1963

My dearest Jacques,

It would be up to me instead to make excuses for being so late in writing, but this liver attack has thrown my correspondence into chaos.

Your letter touched and moved me deeply. What a commentary on the tragedy in Dallas your book is (I will return to your book[1] later)! How can one avoid asking "Why?" And in view of what good, which perhaps we will never see? It is certain that all this has a meaning which escapes us and that all the investigations in the world will never reveal the essential aspect of this diabolical act. My mother never really got over the assassination of Lincoln, and I believe I felt something like this on hearing of the death of Kennedy.

I read your book with passionate interest. It illuminates certain aspects of a mystery that has always preoccupied me. In other times I tried not to think about it. In a bookstore window I once saw a book entitled *L'Irréprochable Providence*, and that was enough for me. I followed the advice of the *Imitation* which tells us not to ask questions about these enormous problems, but what you say is important and will be an immense help to troubled souls. I would be lying if I told you I understood *everything* in your book. For that I would need a theological formation I do not have, but what was accessible to me I found admirable. What good fortune to believe and how I pity those who do not have the Faith! As I grow older I become more and more conscious of the obscurity in which we live and I know perfectly well what Father Dehau meant when he spoke of the "burden of darkness" with which God weighs us down in proportion as our faith increases.

You are so dear to us, Jacques. It is a joy for Anne and me to know that we have a place in your heart. Would that we could see you again soon!

While awaiting that day, I embrace you with all my heart.

Your
JULIEN

1. *Dieu et la permission du mal*; see 137.1.

171

December 27, 1963

My dearest Jacques,

I am reading *Amour et Amitié*[1] with an interest that is difficult for me to explain to you in a few words, because I find in this new book the answer to many questions I have asked myself. The definitions you give of *l'amour fou*[2] are very moving, and I don't remember ever having read pages of this importance on a subject so close to our hearts. From all I can see, you have written an inspired book, but I think the passage that moved me most is the one about the moment of death. That fourfold and magisterial affirmation on the salvation of each one of us is made with a kind of angelic authority. Really, one has the impression that you open the gates of Paradise to souls who had lost hope of ever entering there, because it was too difficult. That it is difficult, I have never ceased to believe, but if I were a theologian I would prefer to take my place on the side of the merciful, like you, rather than on the side of the rigorists who have cast such a somber shadow over religion. Those pages were given to you. I do not say this to lessen your merit. In many cases, for a Catholic writer, merit comes with obedience to inspiration, don't you think?

I would need so much time to speak in detail about all the rest, which is so beautiful and where Raïssa's memory is always present. I do not know your work very well, my dearest Jacques, because I do not have the philosophic formation necessary to understand it, as I have told you so often, but I wonder if you have ever written anything superior to this, where you seem to have surpassed yourself.

I have a request to make of you on behalf of the Carmelite seminarians on the rue d'Assas. If, on some future trip to Paris, you could visit them and speak to them, even for only a few minutes, they would welcome it as a gift of grace. It was my good friend Jacques Robinet[3] (he will be ordained a priest this year) who charged me with this commission. Your presence alone would have an unforgettable effect on these young men who need to be encouraged. They will not assassinate you with questions, as is done in America, but you could say just a few words from which their hearts would draw such strength.

I love you so much, my dearest Jacques, and it gives me great pleasure to tell you so once again today in sending you all my best wishes for a very good year in 1964.
I embrace you heartily.

> Your
> JULIEN

P.S. You will have noticed the inadvertence I corrected above![4] It probably betrays my fundamental outlook, that invincible optimism which forms the basis of my true nature and which I have fought against all my life, because I feared it as a temptation! Today I cannot believe that the Church would impose on us the obligation to hope and that one day we should be disappointed in that hope.

⟨1. "Amour et amitié" is Chapter 7 (pp. 301–74) of the *Carnet de notes*— "Love and Friendship" (pp. 219–57) in the translation, *Notebooks*—not a separate publication.⟩

⟨2. Maritain distinguishes numerous levels in human love. There is, first of all, the love of concupiscence, a purely sensual love or carnal desire that humans share with the animal world. This love is purely selfish.

Love that is truly and properly human begins when, to the attraction of the senses, is joined, even in its most primitive form, the gift of the self as a person. Thereby the lover gives himself or herself wholly to the beloved who alone exists fully and absolutely for the lover. Maritain distinguishes three levels of this properly human love.

First of all, there is passionate or romantic love, in which the lover gives himself or herself to the beloved, but in imagination and dreams rather than in reality, for here sensual or carnal desire, often without the lover's realizing it, plays an essential and preponderant role. It is the means the human species uses to ensure its preservation. It is good, Maritain says, for human beings to pass through this kind of exultation, on condition that they do not remain there.

There is a second form of authentic love which humans ordinarily attain after a certain maturation that comes with the experience of life and of suffering. Here there is a very real donation of the self, not only in what one has, but in what one is. There are many degrees of giving, and at this stage the gift is not entire and absolute.

Finally, when the gift is absolute and unreserved, the lover reaches the level of authentic human love in its extreme and absolute form, the summit of love between Man and Woman. Then the lover gives himself truly and really to his beloved, and she to him, as to his or her Whole, "and, though remaining ontologically a person, makes himself or herself a part that no longer exists except through and in that Whole which is his or her Whole. This extreme form of love is *amour fou* [literally, "mad love"; there is a similar expression in English, "to fall madly in love," but it does not translate

Maritain's thought], and such a name befits it, because it accomplishes precisely . . . that which is in itself impossible and senseless in the order of simple existence or of being as such, where each person continues to be a whole and cannot become a part of another whole." This is the paradox of love, Maritain says, "which, on the one hand, demands the indestructible ontological duality of persons, and, on the other, demands, and *in its own way* brings about, the faultless unity, of these same persons" (*Carnet de notes*, pp. 306–308; the translations are my own). In his English version of the *Carnet*, Joseph W. Evans translates *amour fou* as "mad, boundless love" (p. 224).)

3. Jacques Robinet, then a Carmelite seminarian, later became a psychoanalyst.

4. Earlier in the letter Green had first written "I have never ceased to *doubt*" which he crossed out and replaced with "*believe*."

172

Toulouse
January 6, 1964

You are the one person in the world, my dearest Julien, whose judgment carries the greatest weight with me in those things I can still write about, now that God has dismissed me from my old job as a philosopher, and now that I am attracted solely to what Raïssa lived for. This is to tell you in what a marvelous manner your letter reassured and strengthened me. Oh most surely, I believe like you that those pages on *Amour et amitié* were given to me. It was Father Voillaume[1] who had asked me to write them, and I did so against my inclination, for fear of plodding ahead into something I could not get out of. I prayed constantly to Raïssa to help me, and I'm sure she did so. For I wrote it all without preparation, as quickly as I could, just as it came to me on the blank page, the terrible blank page. And I had the constant impression of being guided. Then too it was a few lines from the *Journal* which set it all in motion. I can answer you in no other way than with these confidences.

I am especially happy with what you told me about the passage on the moment of death—the moment which, insofar as I am concerned personally, I think about almost ceaselessly, and which still remains inconceivable.

I was so worn out that I was unable to answer your previous letter. It is likewise of great importance to me that you liked my book on evil (where on the subject of Judas I have tried to answer a question which, if I rightly recall from a page in *Partir avant le jour*, was often asked in your family . . .).

The tragedy of Dallas continues to haunt me. Am I wrong to believe that there is a kind of American *understatement* which concerns, not the words, but the very idea itself, by virtue of which they scrupulously circle around the pot, sometimes very intelligently, without ever daring to look inside at the essential? Articles that friends send me from America about Kennedy's death leave me with this impression in such a way that I begin to ask myself with fright what it is that the collective subconscious is so afraid to look at.

You know very well, Julien, that I could not bring myself to disregard a request coming from you. I will include in my plans then (not without some apprehension) a visit to the Carmelite seminarians on my next trip to Paris (if only I don't fall ill suddenly), but tell your friend Jacques Robinet that I insist on two indispensable conditions: namely, (1) that there be nothing official about the affair; (2) that I have to do with seminarians only, not their professors, whose presence would paralyze me.

I hope you are feeling very well. May the holy angels who dwell in your house make you sensitive to the gentleness of their love. I embrace you with profound tenderness.

JACQUES

1. René Voillaume was the first prior of the Little Brothers of Jesus. Maritain first met him at Meudon in 1933, at the time of the founding of the order in the Sahara.

173

January 14, 1964

My dearest Jacques,

I have waited several days before answering you because I wanted to speak first with Jacques Robinet, whom I saw yesterday. He is most grateful to you for agreeing, if it is at all possible for you, to pay a short visit to the young men at the seminary. The professors are never present at such gatherings, he told me (and he will assure you of this himself). Naturally it will have no official character whatsoever. In fact, it seems to me that all the conditions are present to make you very satisfied with the situation at the rue d'Assas!

I do not have to tell you how much I was touched by the way you answered me. Jacques, it is such a grace for me to know you. I cannot resist telling you. The Lord will call me to account for the light He brought into my life when He let me meet you. Thoughts like these terrify me sometimes because I have *responded* so poorly, but there is no limit to God's mercy.

I will write you again in a few days. This is no more than a short note to tell you that at the seminary they are in perfect agreement. They will be so happy!

I embrace you with all my heart.

Your

JULIEN

P.S. A car will be put at your disposal to take you from your hotel to the rue d'Assas and later to bring you back to the *Lutetia*.

I told Jacques Robinet to write you a note of thanks. He would have done it himself, but I had to give him your address asking him not to confide that letter to anyone. You can count on him as you can on me.

174

January 28, 1964
M. Jacques Maritain
Fraternité
École Théologique
Avenue Lacordaire
Toulouse
(Haute-Garonne)

My dearest Jacques,

I would like to have been able to write you sooner but most of my time has been taken up, for several days now, by an affair that might have been invented for the movies. But this did not keep me from thinking of you, you can be sure. It's too bad we can't arrange some kind of mental correspondence.

Jacques Robinet must have written you. I have made all kinds of recommendations to him about your visit, if you judge that it should take place (as I hope it will).

It is very curious, this young Church, the Church of the seminaries. One has the impression of its will to break with the past, with all that is static and paralyzing in the past, and up to a certain point I understand, and agree, but I'm afraid it may be going too far. Fortunately we have great Popes who are docile to the Holy Spirit. The pictures of Paul VI in Palestine moved me deeply. He does what must be done; he goes out as Paul went out. I would have liked so much to speak of all this with you, for there have been moments, especially before John XXIII, when I was very worried, seeing the turn things were taking in ecclesiastical circles as well as among laymen, that enormous confusion of ideas, to say nothing of the beliefs we used to consider beyond question. Without being integralist in the slightest way, I wonder if the very essence of the Faith is not in danger. I have heard priests say some really stupifying things. It is very probable that about 1900 some very strange opinions were also expressed, but the ground swell of Modernism did not carry off the Church. Such trials showed that it was built upon a rock.

To turn to a different subject, I saw Jean Cocteau[1] on television the other evening. It was as if he wanted to pay us all a last visit, and he almost made me cry. His look was slower, more attentive, and seemed to be asking a question, but what question? Poor Jean! The last time I saw him, in his room at the Palais-Royal, he had over his head a picture of the Blessed Virgin, and on the table near him a crucifix. Shortly before that he had said to Jean Denoël:[2] "When I'm dead, who will pray for me?"

These last days I have been re-reading St. Catherine of Genoa's *Treatise on Purgatory*. This is the book that brought me back to the Church. Why this one more than another? But I have always loved the souls in Purgatory. They are holy and they are saved, and without a doubt, if they can pray, they pray for us.

Dearest Jacques, I don't know what makes me run on this morning. It's doubtless the longing to be with you, for I love you with all my heart.

I embrace you.

JULIEN

1. Jean Cocteau died at Milly-la-Forêt on October 11, 1963. He had said to his cook: "This is my last day in this world," and almost immediately after going to his room to rest fell ill.

2. Jean Denoël, an adviser and friend of Gaston Gallimard's, was the executor of the wills of Gide, Cocteau, and Max Jacob.

175

February 7, 1964

Dearest Jacques,

A short time ago I had a visit from Robert Marcy and Denise Bosc, who proposed a new production of *L'Ennemi*. On the one hand, I have no way of judging their merit as actors, and, on the other, I think it is too early to give another run to a play which was not very well received in 1954. I'm afraid Robert Marcy and Denise Bosc were disappointed, and I regret it deeply because they came to me from you. This letter will tell you how sad I was to hurt two of your friends. Believe me, it was completely unintended. I took great care to tell Robert Marcy all the reasons which forced me to refuse his offer (omitting, of course, one of the principal reasons, which is that I know nothing about him as an actor) and I thought I did it in the most courteous manner, but Denise Bosc was very upset.

I am writing these things to you so that you learn about them from me and to tell you once again this evening of my faithful and profound affection.

Your

JULIEN

176

Toulouse
February 13, 1964

Julien, my beloved Julien,

I am abominably behind with you and I ask your pardon. This is due to the conditions under which I have to work. People just can't imagine what it is for a man of my age to have certain *necessary* things to finish (if God is willing) at a time when the number of hours available each day has become too small, and when on the other hand the approach of that great *Deadline* is constantly on his mind. So there are periods when I work like a madman (last January, for example); and as soon as such a period is over, I feel completely annihilated for some time—which is the case at the moment—after which I must begin again.

I understand perfectly, Julien, your reaction to the request of Robert Marcy and Denise Bosc. Strictly speaking, you could not have responded otherwise, given the fact that you have no way of knowing the quality of their acting. I love them dearly, which is another matter entirely; but I would in no way want to interfere on a professional level. I *believe*, according to the indications I have had, and a scene from Péguy's *Jeanne d'Arc* which they were kind enough to play for us at Kolbsheim, that they are very good from a professional point of view, but how can one know this to the point of entrusting a play to them as long as one has not seen them act?

(As for me, the theater, concerts, the cinema, all that is over for me.) I am sure, moreover, that they understand very well, in spite of Denise's first reactions, which were probably somewhat desperate. Forgive her, Julien, and keep your friendship for them. They need it for they are very lonely. I myself cannot help them as I should. For more than a month now I have been unable to write them (I will try to do it tomorrow, despite my fatigue).

Everything has been arranged with Jacques Robinet. I have written him. He answered with a very good and very touching letter (to which I fear I haven't yet replied. I can't remember). But I forgot to mention something in writing to him. Perhaps you could do it for me. Given my troubles with my heart and my stomach, the only time when the meeting could take place without too much inconvenience for me is at 5:00 *p.m.* I hope this is possible for them.

Dearest Julien, how could I not accept what these young people ask of me at your behest? The depths of my tenderness for you has no measure; nor can you know the depths of my gratitude. Oh yes, all is grace. And God's tender mercy envelops us all.

How touched I was by what you told me about Jean Cocteau's kind of "visit" to television. Poor Jean! He was far more *true* than people think. And he never gave up his Faith. I remember how he prayed (like a child) next to Raïssa on the rue de Varenne. And the last letter he wrote me was perfectly clear in spite of everything (just as was his choice, it seems to me, of Jean Denoël as literary executor). I have very great confidence in God's mercy toward him.

Like you I believe that the souls in Purgatory can do a good deal for us. I believe also that we should pray to the *uncanonized* saints, the unnoticed saints who are in Heaven, much more than we are accustomed to.

I agree with you completely, Julien, on the situation of the young Church, the Church of the seminaries (and to tell the truth, on the entire situation of the Church at present). We are at the heart of an extraordinary mystery. That kind of throwing of the reins on the horse's back by John XXIII was absolutely necessary, but what a risk at the same time. Poor Paul VI. All that is *professionally* intellectual (professors, universities, seminaries) seems to me either spoiled or in a very dangerous position. A certain exegesis has gone mad and become stupid. There is a new modernism full of pride and obstreperousness that seems to me more dangerous than that of Pius X's time. (It was after all a rather strange spectacle to see all the bishops of the Council—the Teaching Church—each one flanked by his *experts*, professors, scholars, and pedants of the Taught Church, of whom a good number were off their intellectual rails, and of whom almost none had any *wisdom*.) So, it is in the middle of all this hubbub that the work of the Holy Spirit is carried out.

In my opinion the attitude of the young clergy is very understandable, because we are face to face with a *general mentality* which has been taking form since the Middle Ages and the Baroque period, but which is for all that formless and untamed, as violently uncontrolled as a tidal wave, and which, instead of having found its normal forms of intellectual expression, hurls itself against a sea wall raised up by a *theology* that is faithful, but has not known how to renew itself (the intelligence is always too late). For many years now I have been shouting that we have to ask St. Thomas to open doors, not to close them. But the theologians continue to close them (unless they are modernist, although to tell the truth there are no longer any modernist theologians, but only historians, exegetes, and other rabid specialists who want nothing more to do with theology), and the general mentality that I speak of wants nothing more to do with St. Thomas (who alone could save the situation, if they understood him as he should be understood). . . .

Like you I was both moved and deeply upset by Paul VI's pilgrimage to the Holy Land. As you know I was very well acquainted with Msgr. Montini in Rome, and we are true friends. But he reflects with prudence and scrupulosity, always looking for the most perfect exactitude, whereas John XXIII followed the impulses of an Italian peasant instinct, full of intuitions at once poetic, cynical, and holy. I admit that I was deeply disappointed that Paul VI himself did not place the six candles which were placed instead by Cardinal Tisserant in memory of the six million massacred Jews. . . .

Julien, excuse my running on.

I embrace you and Anne with all my heart.

JACQUES

177

February 20, 1964

Dear, dear Jacques,

Your letter was more than a letter for me. It was a visit in which we spoke heart to heart about the only things that count, for there was something within me that responded to everything you said to me. In this so disquieting world of 1964, so uplifting too from a certain point of view, you are for all those who love you a great and good presence. I know very well that you don't like to be told these kinds of things but they are true nonetheless, and it is quite possible that we see you better than you see yourself.

All that you tell me about the Church and the action of the Holy Spirit fascinates me. There will certainly be great changes which will bring moans from many people, but the essentials will remain. It seems that some Brazilian bishop declared that one day the Pope would no longer be in Rome but in Jerusalem. Why object, if it turns out to be true? I see no reason to be disturbed about this. Certainly, if the Holy Father established himself in Palestine, the consequences would be infinite from the temporal point of view, but real religion is quite another matter.

I regret as you do that the present Pope himself did not place the six candles in memory of the massacred Jews. The gesture would have been magnificent (and the Italians ordinarily have such a sense of gesture); it would have struck the thousands of souls—both Jewish and Christian—who were waiting for something of this kind. In spite of everything, one loves this man who does not back away from great risks, however prudent he may be.

I have been thinking very much about Robert Marcy and Denise Bosc. My sympathy went out to them immediately and I would have liked so much to tell them yes, but this play is perhaps the only one of my works of which I can say that it was given to me from one end to the other. I wrote it without crossing out a single line and almost without knowing what I was writing.[1] Nothing in the world could lead me to expose it to another failure. All my secrets are in those three acts. The whole story of my return to God shines through it. I understood this when I saw it on the stage.

I hesitate to tell you now that I have a new favor to ask of you. Here it is: I saw a photograph of you that I would like very much. It is a recent one. You gave it to Desclée De Brouwer. Doubtless you must get many requests for it. Of that I'm sure. It is so beautiful, and then too it is so unbelievably you. When I saw it just a moment ago I thought: "Jacques is more himself today than he was in 1925 when I saw him for the first time." Something has happened. Ordinarily, according to the words of St. Paul, one sees the outer man gradually fall to pieces and one would hope that the inner man take more and more solid form at the same time, but in your case, it is the inner man that appears visibly in the traits of the outer man. There simply are no ruins; there is nothing but light. But once again I am beginning to say things that may very well upset you. You must see in this nothing more than the mark of my affection, dearest Jacques, and pardon your old

JULIEN
who embraces you.

1. The play in question is *L'Ennemi*. In *Le Bel Aujourd'hui*, Green has this to say: "They do not realize that the key to my conversion is found in *L'Ennemi*. Yet the key is there. It is the story of Poe's purloined letter; it is on the table, in full view, and no one sees it" (October 5, 1970, Pléiade V).

178

Tuesday of Holy Week, 1964

Dearest Jacques,

I had written you a letter on February 20th which I hesitated to send you because of the request at the end of it, and also, I have to say, because the whole letter seemed to me insufficient and because I proposed to write a better one! But too bad. You will receive two letters instead of one. I don't have the gift you do of writing effortlessly and without revision things at once so weighty and so clear. Then too there is always your heart which speaks, such a generous heart which has given us all so much.

The house where I am writing this is in Eure-et-Loir, not far from Dreux.[1] This is a kind of refuge for us in the countryside, where the tumult of the world ceases. Until 1906, this house, which is quite old, was the presbytery of a beautiful and very old church whose vault is being restored at the present moment. (I can hear the noise made by the carpenters with their hammers; the barrel vault was made of chestnut, and on it they found the name of one of the artisans and a date, 1560; now the chestnut, which has become so expensive, is being replaced by fir, which won't last as long, but at least the holes will be closed up—why am I telling you all this?)

I am thinking of you very much during this Holy Week. I would like to see you, dear Jacques. You are so near me, so near to all of us who love you. May Jesus keep you and bless you.

With all my heart I embrace you.

JULIEN

1. Green is describing the old presbytery at Faverolles, which belonged to him. Victor Hugo hid in this house on his way to exile in 1851, and later described it in *Les Misérables*, but situated it in Digne; it was here that Jean Valjean stole the candlesticks of Msgr. Myriel.

179

Easter Wednesday, 1964

My dearest, my beloved Julien,

It is a great joy to receive two letters from you at once. All you write me is so precious. How I would like to see you! I hope this will be possible at the beginning of June.

What you tell me about your play explains why both Raïssa and I loved it so profoundly, I could even say so marvelously. You certainly are right to refuse to expose it to a new failure (although the word failure really makes no sense for a work of such grandeur).

I don't know exactly which photograph you are referring to. You say it is recent. Then it must be the one taken at Princeton, two years ago, by John Griffin (the author of *Black Like Me*).[1] So I am sending it to you, dear Julien. If this isn't the one you are thinking of, you must tell me. It is of nothing but a broken piece of wood, a branch which the lightning has shattered and whose bark it has somewhat destroyed. Pray for me. I live in a kind of mental aberration. Raïssa runs everything. I have been thrown into a new work which is beyond me. I will tell you about it. I embrace you and Anne with all my heart. Tell Anne I hope to write her soon.

JACQUES

I suppose that you are still at your place in the country but that the post office will forward this letter.

⟨1. John Howard Griffin, Thomas Merton, and Jacques Maritain were very close friends. It was Griffin who chronicled in words and in photographs Maritain's final visit to the United States, including his final visit with Merton at Gethsemani, Kentucky, and his last years in Kolbsheim and Toulouse. Griffin's best photographs of the aged Maritain, along with notes from his own diary, and a text by Yves Simon, were edited by An-thony Simon in *Jacques Maritain: Hom-age in Words and in Pictures* (Albany, N.Y.: Magi Books, 1974). Griffin is best known for *Black Like Me*, the powerful chronicle of his travels through the South as a black after he had artificially and temporarily altered the pigmentation of his skin. It not only was a bestseller in the United States but was widely known in Europe, and was eventually made into a successful motion picture.⟩

180

April 3, 1964

Dearest Jacques,

This is exactly the photograph I saw at Desclée, and you have caused me immense pleasure in giving it to me. Thank you with all my heart. Of all the portraits I know of you, it is this one which best captures those traits of the inner man which have had such an influence on all of us. Then too, it is the faithful reflection of your physical presence, which is so dear to us. What happiness it will be to see you again in June!

I am going to have the second volume of my autobiography brought out in May and I have no idea what kind of a welcome it will receive. Father Pézeril has read it and told me to change nothing, but I have nevertheless made a few cuts here and there. I wonder what you will think of this book.

You are very close to us here on the rue de Varenne. We speak of you often and with the greatest affection, and also of Raïssa who is still so present in our life.

Pray for your friends, dearest Jacques. You can have none who loves you more tenderly than your

JULIEN

181

Toulouse
June 3, 1964

Dear, dearest Julien,
I love and admire your book.[1] Like the first, it moved me to the depths of my soul. There is a grace hovering over you, a grace in these books. That sincerity Gide spoke of so often and could never achieve is there, extraordinarily authentic, and purifying, indeed purity itself—because it proceeds from the Holy Spirit and from His gifts (I mean the gifts of Knowledge, of Counsel, and of Fear . . .). Thank you for having given us these treasures.

I cannot write you more than this. For two months now my health has been declining at an alarming rate, and I know what it is to feel fatigue *usque ad mortem* (even unto death). In spite of it all I intend to leave soon for Kolbsheim (in a station wagon, on a mattress) and pass through Paris. Alas, my doctor will permit only a very short passage and I have to attend some indispensable "business" meetings (in particular, I would like to consult a homeopathic doctor). I would like so much to see you and Anne, even if only for a few moments. Will I be able to? I can be sure of nothing. In any case I will try to get the Little Brother (Brother Joël), who will be driving me, to telephone you.

I embrace you with all my heart.

JACQUES

1. *Mille chemins ouverts*, the second volume of Green's autobiography, was published by Grasset in Paris (Pléiade V).

182

Kolbsheim (Bas-Rhin)
August 2, 1964

Dearest Julien,
Rouault's eldest daughter (Mme Geneviève Nouaille) writes me that she has loved your work for thirty years and that she wants

very much to make your acquaintance. But she feels intimidated and dares not write you to ask for a short interview. I gladly pass on to you her wish because I like her *very much*—she has an admirably generous heart. (And very humble.) Let me know if she can write or telephone you. She will return to Paris on September 10th.

In her letter she adds that her mother (who is in her nineties) and her sister Isabelle (who was Rouault's guardian angel, and is in charge of his paintings) would be happy if you and Anne would agree to dine with them. This would give you the chance to see some of Rouault's great paintings.[1] Be good enough to tell me too what you think of this.

I regained some of my strength in Alsace and no longer have the lamentable appearance that you saw in Paris. But my heart has just lately been causing me some problems. That is why I can scratch out only these few words in haste.

Julien, Anne, if you only knew how precious your friendship is to me and how I bless God for it! I embrace you both with all my heart.

JACQUES

I suppose you are no longer in Paris and that this letter will be forwarded. . . .

1. Georges Rouault was a French ex-pressionist painter who out of scrupulosity burned a part of his work. Like Maritain, Green admired his canvases, especially the *King* and the *Veil of Veronica* for their suggestive power and their religious intensity. They are now in the Musée d'Art Moderne.

183

Kolbsheim
August 11, 1964

Dearest Julien,
    Just a word to thank you for your letter.
    I transmitted your message to Geneviève Nouaille. I am happy that you are writing a Foreword to the letters of our Father Surin

(his spiritual Catechism has played an important role in our lives).[1]
The Gruneliuses send their faithful and friendly greetings.
I embrace you with great tenderness.

JACQUES

1. The *Correspondance du père Joseph Surin*, edited by Michel de Certeau, S.J., was published by Desclée De Brouwer. Green's Foreword to this volume, together with his *Pamphlet*, was reprinted by Gallimard, in its Idées series, under the title *La Folie de Dieu*.

184

52 *bis* rue de Varenne, VIIe
[February 24, 1965]

Dearest Jacques,

Excuse my long silence. My life and Anne's have been darkened and somewhat disorganized by a recent bereavement. My eldest sister, Éléonore, whom, I believe, you met once, died a month ago.[1] She very literally fell asleep without ever having suffered. Her faith was very deep. We think of her with affection and sorrow. She took with her a part of our lives, our youth especially. Please pray for her, won't you?

Dear Jacques, we love you so much. May we see you again soon! I embrace you with all my heart.

JULIEN

1. Julien Green's eldest sister—whom he described as "beautiful, amiable, always kind, and of such a steady disposition that she ended up appearing mysterious" (October 6, 1966, *Vers l'invisible*, Pléiade V)—died in London where she had been living (on Brompton Road) since the war.

185

Toulouse
March 1, 1965

Julien, Anne, my very dear friends,

I am united to you with all my heart in this great sadness on the death of your sister Éléonore. Yes, I saw her one day, and in my memory her faith and goodness still shine bright. It seems to me that by letting her gently fall asleep in Him God wanted to manifest to her, and to you too, His own gentleness. But I find hard to bear the thought that you are suffering and that you feel deprived of a part of yourself, which has suddenly been torn away. To be sure, I am praying for her along with you.

All that death swallows up continues to live elsewhere.

Dear Julien, I would like to have answered each of your letters in turn, but I could not; I was so worn out. (Sick in January. Then too much work.)

I embrace both of you with all my heart.

JACQUES

186

March 27, 1965

My dearest Jacques,

I have just spent some marvelous hours with you, for you have never given me a book which has touched me more profoundly than this *Carnet de Notes*,[1] where once again I find you, Raïssa, and Vera just as I have always known and loved you, as we know those whom we love, by intuition. In fact, you have taught me many precious things about the three of you which I did not know and which bring you still closer to me, in my heart. My only regret is to have found all this out too late, but it could not be otherwise. This book is full of treasures, yes, and, I am not afraid to say it, treasures of grace. From the very first pages, I was seized by the tone of your words, for God already made use of you long before your conversion, to reach us who owe you so much. I know you well enough to realize that you give no importance whatsoever to admiration. Let me say, at least, that I admire God in you. After all you have opened to us the grand avenues of your soul and there I see nothing but light.

If I had to tell you all that struck me in your book, I would have to write you much too long a letter. What you said of Raïssa went straight to my heart, and in the same way the pages about Vera are incomparably beautiful and moving. This *Carnet de notes* will touch many souls, I am sure, and do an enormous good. This is a book filled with love, and you have done well to publish it now. I could never tell you enough how precious you are to me, my dear Jacques, and it is with all my heart that I embrace you.

JULIEN

⟨1. See 2.1 for bibliographical information.⟩

187

Toulouse
April 1, 1965

May you be blessed, my dearest Julien, for your affection, which warms my heart, and for that letter, so full of a marvelous charity. It touches me all the more deeply as I find myself now in a kind of very thick night, and as I cannot see what you liked in that book (except for the chapter on Vera for which I feel a kind of satisfaction). But I believe you, Julien, and for me that is infinitely sweet. You would never believe how much I need that encouragement, which seems to come to me from Heaven, like many things that come to me through you.

In fact, during the whole time I was working on this book, it was only of our friends that I was thinking and to whom I was speaking. The idea of the general public never crossed my mind. And then, when I saw the book printed, I felt a shock that disconcerted me enormously. To surrender all those things to the public, to readers who had never known and loved Raïssa and Vera, are you mad, I asked myself. You reassure me as only you can, and I had a terrible need of that. Thank you for telling me I did well "to publish this book now." This has dissipated my doubts, and puts me back in my place before God.

At my age you feel bizarre sensations. You are a stranger everywhere. You are not in eternity, and everything seems to chase you out of time, to deny you your poor little place, your poor little instant in which you existed in the past, and all the while the present instant means nothing at all. (There was still an oasis of peace for me in daily Mass. Now even that is finished, with this invasion of ugliness and vulgarity.) If you only knew how I long to be with you and Anne! I think that in June, if I am not feeling worse than I do now, I will risk climbing the five flights of stairs to see you *in your home*, to be with you in your home.

Pray for me, Julien. You are dearer to me than any words can say. Thank you with all my heart. I embrace you with all my heart.

JACQUES

188

Paris
June 9, [1965]

Dearest Julien,

I forgot to give you the name and address of the homeopathic doctor in whom I have great confidence: Dr. Jacques Lehman, 12 rue Margueritte, Paris, 17ᵉ (Wagram 93–31). I should return to see him on July 14th. If you want me to ask for an appointment for you either at the end of September, or in October (or later!), I can take care of it at that time. (But you must tell me whether you will be in Paris at that time. I seem to recall that you will be going to Marseilles at the beginning of October. . . .[1])

Seeing you and Anne fills my heart each time with an inexpressible sweetness for which I give thanks to God. Blessed be your dear friendship.

The letters from Raïssa that Anne entrusted to me moved me deeply. I will return them to her from Kolbsheim.

Pray for me. And thank you once again for those marvelous hours spent with the two of you.

I embrace you and Anne with all my heart.

JACQUES

1. *Sud*, an opera based on Green's play, and written by K. Coe, with sets by Jacques Dupont, was to have its opening performance in Marseilles. Stravinski had wanted to turn the play into an opera to be produced in Marseilles, but he felt too

old not to leave this subject to a younger   go to Marseilles, but *Sud* played later at
American composer. Julien Green did not   the Opéra de Paris with another set.

189

June 13, 1965

My dearest Jacques,

I would like to have thanked you sooner for your letter, but neither Anne nor I can remember the address of Mme Manuel, and she is not in the telephone directory. So you will receive this note only in Alsace. It will tell you how grateful I am for the address of the homeopathic doctor whom I will visit on my return.

What a joy it was for both of us to see you again in our home just like the old days! Your presence gives us more than you could believe in this period when the Catholic world is passing through such a difficult trial. It is a comfort to listen to you and to see you still the same as you were on that far-off day when we met for the first time. I consider the visits you pay us as so many graces.

Thank you, dearest Jacques, thank you for everything.

I embrace you.

JULIEN

190

December 28, 1965

Dearest Jacques,

Excuse me for typing this letter, but I am a prey to a tenacious attack of rheumatism which keeps me from writing by hand. Nevertheless I must tell you how much I am thinking of you. I have had some echoes about your trip to Rome.[1] What you had the chance to say there must certainly have been taken seriously into account, because you speak for all of us. I hope you were not too worn out on your return. Will you be coming to Paris this winter? We would like so much to see you.

Our dear Jacques Robinet gave me your message about my next book.[2] A year ago I still hesitated to bring it out, but I have made my decision and the day before yesterday I got an idea of the good that may come of it. You will receive this third volume some time in February. I hope it doesn't disappoint you. I wanted to tell the whole truth in the simplest fashion possible and, I hope, the most readily acceptable. At any rate, there will be no more misunderstanding on my account. One might ask why I wrote this book. I can reply only that I felt myself pushed irresistibly to do so. It cost me very much to write it, but I hope some good will come of it.

I am writing from an old house I don't think I have ever mentioned to you. We go there from time to time to spend a few days. It is not far from Nogent-le-Roi. It is a former presbytery which is separated from an old and very beautiful church only by the breadth of a garden which I stubbornly insist is spacious, even though they tell me it covers no more than an acre. What charms me is that the apse of the church is in this garden. Unfortunately, the church is not heated, and this poses some problems—especially for rheumatics! The countryside seems as beautiful to me in winter as in summer, and Anne and I take long walks there together. It seems to me at these times that we are people on a road in the most marvelous paintings of the Impressionists.

The other day I received a letter from a lady at the *Osservatore Romano*.[3] She wanted to ask me questions about the Council, and I did not want to conceal what I felt, because I believe one does not have the right to do so in times like these, but I did not have at hand the text of my oral responses and I must admit that this bothered me a bit. I'm afraid I said poorly what I felt so deeply.

Couldn't I somehow see you and speak to you, dear Jacques. I would have so many things to say to you as well as so many questions to ask. One's view of life changes rapidly with age (I am speaking for myself), and in many cases it is better this way. When one glances back, one is stupified at what one found so passionately moving as a young man. In spite of all this, the heart remains the same, thank God, with the same impulses and sometimes the same enthusiasm. This makes me think of Psalm 42, which, unfortunately, is no longer recited at the foot of the altar (I would have complained to the Pope about that!): ". . . *ad Deum qui laetificat*

juventutem meam..." ⟨"...to God Who gives joy to my youth..."⟩.
At present I am thinking of your youthfulness, your youthfulness
today, which is a youngness of the soul and the mind.
Dear Jacques, I must stop. Anne joins me in telling you of our
very deep affection. With all my heart I embrace you.

JULIEN

I received your last book[4] a little before my departure for the
country and I count on reading it as soon as I get back, in three or
four days. I was happy to see that you included some very beautiful
texts which I already knew, in particular the conference you gave at
the *Ambassadeurs* in '38.[5] I was there. I remember, I was very moved.

1. Paul VI gave Maritain the original
text of the message destined for the intellectuals at the closing of the Council.
It was bruited about at the time that
Jacques Maritain had been named Cardinal *in petto* by the Pope, but this new
secret was never confirmed.

2. *Terre lointaine*, the third volume of
Green's autobiography, recounts in par-
ticular his university years in Virginia
(Paris: Grasset, 1966; Pléiade V).

3. Ada Carella.

⟨4. *Le Mystère d'Israël et autres essais*

(Paris: Desclée De Brouwer, 1965).⟩

5. In 1938 at the Théâtre des Ambassadeurs Maritain gave a conference entitled "Les Juifs parmi les Nations" ⟨in
which he attacked the virulent anti-
Semitism rampant in France and in the
rest of Europe at the time. Maritain was
almost alone among Catholics, lay or
cleric, to come out publicly in defense of
the Jews. This conference inspired a rash
of abusive attacks on Maritain from the
Far Right, particularly from Catholics⟩.

191

January 11, 1966

My dearest Jacques,

If I wait till I am completely well to write you, I don't know
when you will hear from me. Today I am taking advantage of a
slight rheumatic respite, but you will have to excuse my poor handwriting.

I read your book with great emotion, for it stirred up in me all
manner of memories. I was already familiar with a great number of
these pages, and I am happy to see them collected at last in one
volume. I can see you again, dear Jacques, at the *Ambassadeurs*,

shortly before the war. What anguish was felt there by all your friends who heard you! We all knew only too well that the worst was no longer avoidable, but it was a comfort to know you were there, so generous and so firm. I hope that what you have done for Israel will never be forgotten.

You say so many things that are so beautiful and so striking that one would wish to quote them all. I found quite remarkable what you wrote about the hatred that a Christian arouses in the world today, a hatred that should make of him a brother to the Jew. This has perhaps changed a bit since the Council, but I'm not so sure.

The pages on the persecution of the Jews are terrifying. It is good to read them again. What love there is in your heart, what true charity for all those who suffer! I have the impression that with each book you outshine yourself once again—and yet the preceding books have great beauty of form and tone.

In the past days I had a visit from a lady sent by *Osservatore Romano*, who wanted to know what I thought of the Council. My answer, very general and unfortunately oral, was that I was certainly *for* it, but there is so much to say, not in a restrictive sense, but in entering a bit into detail. I tremble to think of what my visitor may do with an answer I had to give on the spot.

My book will be out in February. For a long time I hesitated to make it public. We will see what kind of welcome it receives and if it will be understood that I wanted to speak the truth without cheating. I wonder too—and you realize that such a book poses serious problems—if the readers will recognize the shadow of God's hand on my unhappy youth.

How I want to see you! I have so many things to tell you. But will you be coming to Paris soon? Anne and I speak of you very often. No one, I am sure, thinks of you with more affection than we, and it is with all my heart that I embrace you.

JULIEN

192

Toulouse
January 19, 1966

How can I tell you, my dearest Julien, how much your letter moved me? I cannot find the words. I can only say that I thank you with all my heart.

All that you write me is infinitely precious—even though I know clearly I do not merit it—and perhaps precisely because of that fact. There is that marvel of friendship that God has put in your soul for the poor man that I am, and to think of such a mystery is overwhelming.

Thank you for remembering as you do that conference at the *Ambassadeurs*.

Has the hatred against the Christian diminished a bit in the world since the Council? It's possible, but, at the cost, I believe, of a misunderstanding (which runs the grave risk of spoiling the Christian).

I would like very much to know what that lady at the *Osservatore Romano* will say of your conversation with her. For my part, as a result of circumstances that I shall tell you about later, I have imprudently undertaken something way beyond my strength—a little book that I will probably never finish but in which I would like to try to say certain things that only a *very* old man can say (if he has the strength). We are in a very serious modernist crisis. (This has not prevented the Council from accomplishing admirable things.) I do not find much consolation in the ugliness and stupidity introduced (along with French) into the sacred liturgy. Alas, my pen is not that of the author of the *Pamphlet contre les catholiques de France*.

I have learned from dear Jacques Robinet that your book will come out very soon. This gives me great joy. God's angels have surely guided your hand. This I know for a fact.

I hope I'll be able to go to Paris at the beginning of March—and see you and Anne. I have an appointment with my doctor. Did I give you his address?—Dr. Jacques Lehman, 12 rue Margueritte, Paris 17ᵉ (Wagram 93–31). I would like very much for you to consult him. I am heartsick that you are suffering from rheumatism. I know from experience that Dr. Lehman uses exceptional therapeutic methods (homeopathy–radiesthesia). He put me back in shape when I was very, very sick. The same thing with Msgr. André Baron[1] (who brought him to my attention) and very recently Antoinette Grunelius was literally "transformed" after a treatment of only a few days. We are beginning to discover only now the power of the infinitely small. Lehman has a very direct mind and conducts his research with great scientific rigor.

I'll see you soon, dear Julien. With what tenderness I think of you and Anne! I embrace you with all my heart. Pray for your poor

JACQUES

1. Msgr. Baron (1893–1981) made Maritain's acquaintance through Léon Bloy. He was rector of Saint-Louis-des-Français and worked for a rapprochement with the Eastern churches.

193

Toulouse
February 10, 1966

My dear, my very dear Julien,

I have just finished *Terre lointaine*. I read it with profound and sustained emotion and with an inexpressible feeling of presence— yes, it is the student of 1922 who wrote this book. It is an admirable book whose extraordinary sincerity has its source in the divine. At the same time it breathes an inviolable purity and self-restraint; and the reader senses in an almost painful way with what charity—both for God and for your neighbor—you have given, surrendered, your- self. Your guardian angel wrote this book along with you. I do not know what people will tell you—but for me, what emerges above all else from these recollections is the force of the religious witness you bear and the grandeur of God's love for you and of the protec- tion with which He has covered your life, according to His infinitely mysterious ways. One might say that all those things from which you have suffered so cruelly are a light veil that He has placed be- fore your eyes, with a kind of slightly ironic tenderness, in order to carry out His work, without your realizing it, in the depths of your soul, a marvelous work, and to lead you to where He has always wanted you to be. May He be blessed.

Pardon me, Julien, if I express myself badly. I am so worn out; my head is spinning because of the ungrateful work to which I have condemned myself.

I hope to see Anne and you at the beginning of March. I have asked Paule Manuel to telephone you to find out on what day I might have lunch with you on the rue de Varenne.

I embrace you with all my heart.

JACQUES

There is an overwhelming melancholy in your book. The faces of all humanity pass before us—especially those of your family—each face so attractive, so irreplaceable, so charged with mystery, and now they are, all of them, in the grave. How can we understand this? I believe that the slightest gesture in time, *everything*, is preserved in God's mansion. . . .

How you make us love the South![1]

1. The South is one of the privileged places in Green's works. Many of his books, in whole or in part, take place in one of the southern states, especially Virginia and Georgia: *Le Voyageur sur la terre, Sud, Terre lointaine, Moïra, Les* *Pays lointains, Chaque homme dans sa nuit*—to say nothing of the many passages in his *Journal*. Love for America supplied an additional bond in the friendship between Green and Maritain.

194

February 17, 1966

Dearest Jacques,

You cannot know what good your letter did me. I read it over and over again with as much joy as gratitude for it came just at the right time, when I was very worried, and it seemed to me that in the pages I was reading I saw God watching over me. Everything you say to me is so important—always. You see what is in the depths of my heart, and you speak of it with a marvelous simplicity. In you the soul speaks more and more clearly. What a grace for me to know you!

I am pleased you spoke of *irony*, a divine irony, the smile of charity, or, if I dare put it this way, a supernatural *sense of humor* which we too should answer with a smile. It is sad—and a bit stupid—to take oneself perpetually too seriously.

I thank you for having sent me the Pope's message for the closing of the Council. I was particularly sensitive to the words he addressed to artists and writers. Our dear Father Couturier used to say to me at times: "We must increase the sum of beauty in the world." This is what you do, Jacques, with your books, each of which seems to me more beautiful than the last.

What a joy it will be for us to see you! The day you are to come to the house, a car will pick you up at Passy. We are looking forward to this very much, and you certainly won't refuse us this great pleasure. It is enough that you let me know at what time you want the car to be there.

I spent a marvelous evening with Father Bars. He came to dinner with Anne and me. Doubtless he does not realize how important these hours were for me.

Dearest Jacques, there is just enough space left for me to embrace you with all my heart.

JULIEN

P.S. I am rereading your letter. Ironic tenderness, that's what it is. God's smile. They never speak of it; they dare not. They want us to look on Him with the eyes of slaves, whereas we are really His well-beloved children.

195

Toulouse
February 26, [1966]

How sweet your letter was for me, my beloved Julien. Thank you with all my heart for having written me like this.

Completely overworked, I can scribble only a few lines today. Yes, I agree about that car since you insist (but Paule Manuel could very well drive me . . .). I will telephone about the time. What joy to see you soon.

Pray for me for I am involved in some rather difficult things.
I embrace you and Anne with all my heart.

JACQUES

We will speak of Henry Bars. I'm so glad you like him.

196

June 15, 1966

Dearest Jacques,

Excuse my too long silence. I should have thanked you long ago
for the very beautiful pages which you sent me and which recalled
to mind the conversation we had about time and the contempo-
raneity of events, but I must admit that I understood better what
you said to me than what you explain in your book, and this comes
from my ignorance of philosophic discourse, an ignorance that has
deprived me of the joy of following you in a whole segment of your
work. However, what I was able to grasp in these pages on Christ
seemed to me of great beauty and great importance, and stirred up
in me a whole world of ideas. I hope I will be able to speak to you a
bit about them and ask you to help me see clearly.[1]

I'm glad I'll be seeing you at the end of the month. Each of your
visits is a *grace* for me.

With all my heart I embrace you.

JULIEN

⟨1. Maritain had obviously shared with Green a few pages of the manuscript which he was then working on and which would be published as *De la grâce et de l'humanité de Jesus*; see 203.1.⟩

197

Toulouse
June 18, 1966

My dearest Julien,

My heartfelt thanks for your letter. This word in haste (excuse
my poor handwriting, I am half dead with fatigue—I was able to

finish my manuscript on time, and deliver it to the editor, after an insane amount of work) to tell you that I expect to spend a few days (a very few) in Paris beginning on June 27th (I have an appointment with my doctor on the 28th. Then I leave for Kolbsheim). Could I dine with Anne and you on Wednesday the 29th (or on Thursday the 30th)? I have such a great desire to see you. It would be best if you had time to send me back word before I leave. Otherwise you can write to *Lutetia* (Boulevard Raspail), where I will be staying (the Manuels are leaving on vacation)—writing "hold" on the envelope. I will arrive in Paris on the evening of the 27th.

I'll see you soon. I embrace both of you with profound tenderness.

JACQUES

198

Kolbsheim
July 11, 1966

Dearest Julien,

Just a word to tell you with what joy I read your *admirable* Foreword to the *Correspondence* of Father Surin. I am delighted that Father de Certeau asked you to write the Foreword for this volume.

Father Surin, whom we knew through Léon Bloy, played a great role in the lives of all three of us, and I still love him tenderly. Sick he was, for sure, but what a blessed sickness. Don't you think that literary form is a precious indication of the interior state of the soul? A single sentence of Father Surin is enough to convince me of his sanctity. (I admit it is just the opposite with Teilhard.) (I mean that a single sentence of his is enough to show that he was a dangerous and ambitious dreamer.[1])

I cannot express the sweetness of the peace I feel when I am with Anne and you like the other day. I love both of you with all my heart.

JACQUES

⟨1. Like Étienne Gilson, Maritain was very critical of the famous palaeontologist. In *Le Paysan de la Garonne: Un vieux laïc s'interroge à propos du temps présent* (Paris: Desclée De Brouwer, 1966), he devoted fourteen pages to a criticism of "Teilhard de Chardin et le 'teilhardisme'" (pp. 173–87). He treats Teilhard more as a poet than as a scientist, philosopher, or theologian. "One does not expect a poem," wrote Maritain, "to bring us any rational knowledge whatever, whether scientific, philosophical, or theological. One can expect only that it reveal to us a little of what the poet, through a kind of obscure contact, has grasped at one and the same time about himself and the world about him" (p. 186). In the translation, *The Peasant of the Garonne: An Old Layman Questions Himself about the Present Time* (trans. Michael Cuddihy and Elizabeth Hughes [New York: Holt, Rinehart and Winston, 1968]), "Teilhard de Chardin and Teilhardism" is found on pp. 116–26, and the passage I translated above, on pp. 125–26.⟩

199

July 13, 1966

Dearest Jacques,

Your letter gave me such intense pleasure that I will not wait a single moment to thank you for it. What you say about the pages of Father Surin is reassuring, for, I admit, I was a bit worried. It is so difficult to write about such a man! For years, and still now, he has been and is still for me the essence of *religion*. I don't mean that no one speaks better than he on the relation between God and the soul, and you are right to say that each of his sentences has the tone of sanctity—a tone that cannot be imitated (even though the counterfeits are as numerous as they are dismaying). How far from his words are those "pious" books that I always suspected of being written by the Devil! They lead one away from God, in fact. I am thinking of the whole abject literature of the nineteenth century which speaks so basely of divine things. It must be admitted in justice to the seventeenth century that it often had—Surin more than any other—what Emerson called the accent of the Holy Spirit.

Dear Jacques, I cannot be happy with what is going on in the Church. This is a singular trial that the Lord is imposing on us. It takes joy from the heart, but I am confident it will all pass.

What happiness it is to know that you are there, in Alsace, in that beautiful region I love so much—surrounded by people who love you.

Anne and I embrace you heartily.

JULIEN

200

July 18, 1966

Dearest Jacques,

This is not a postscript to my last letter. I forgot to tell you in fact, and I very much wanted you to know, that there is no press service for the letters of Father Surin and that consequently I haven't been able to send it to anyone. I only half regret this, after all, not being sure of having said what should have been said in that Foreword. If they had given me more time, I think I could have done a better job.

I think of you very much and of the marvelous friendship you offer me. How I would like to have seen you more often in the old days! But you have helped me so much, and there are so many of us who can say that. . . .

With all my heart I embrace you.

JULIEN

201

Kolbsheim
September 6, 1966

My beloved Julien,

Will you be in Paris at the end of September, and could I have lunch at your house on Tuesday the 27th? (And could I arrive a little before lunch; I will be coming from my editor, with whom I have an appointment that morning?) Send word quickly if you can.

I am half dead with fatigue. Too much work. And I leave for New York at the end of the month.[1]

I hope to see you soon.

I embrace Anne and you with all my heart.

JACQUES

1. Maritain made his last trip to America to visit his friends there, and arrived in Princeton in time for the burial of Arthur Lourié. See 135.1.

202

September 8, 1966

Dearest Jacques,

Agreed for Tuesday, September 27th. As you know, it will be a *joy* for us to see you. Come as early as you can. You can have the whole morning and all the time you can give us after lunch.

Anne and I embrace you heartily.

JULIEN

203

October 28, 1966

Dearest Jacques,

I was about to write you about your pages on Christ[1] when your *Paysan de la Garonne*[2] arrived. Let's begin first with the brochure of which I read one part with passionate interest, whereas the other part, because of my ignorance, remains obscure for me. But what I understood moved me—and informed me. Doubtless, there is question of no more than hypotheses in what concerns the moment when Christ became fully conscious of His divinity, but they give the impression of passing too close to the truth not to touch it. This is the first time I have read such beautiful and profound things on this subject which will come into its full light only in the next world.

As to the *Paysan*, this is the book I have been waiting for from you for years without knowing what form it might take. I was certain it would be something important, but you have gone beyond my hopes. But I can't keep on telling you, each time I receive one of your books, that the last is more beautiful than all the others. I would end up doing an injustice to the books that came before. But this one is something different. I think this comes from the fact that you have attained so great an inner freedom that it permits you to say everything with a simplicity that disregards the obstacles, and you say what has to be said at the moment it appears indispensable that someone raise his voice. If anyone has defended the Faith at a moment when, in spite of certain appearances, it is so bitterly attacked, it is you, my dear Jacques, and it is just as we know you and just as we love you that you show yourself in this book. Those who know you well, as Anne and I do, will not be astonished at that smile which appears from time to time to light up pages that would otherwise risk appearing too severe, but I think you will only be loved the more for it. Your irony has about it something both surprising and enchanting—and it is not without its usefulness in a country where a good sense of humor still counts. I will have many things to say to you, when I will have the pleasure of seeing you again, about this book which in my eyes has capital importance and whose reverberations will be great in the Catholic world.

Can you give us soon a sign that you are coming, my dear Jacques? You know with what affection you will be received at the rue de Varenne.

In anticipation I embrace you heartily.

JULIEN

1. *De la grâce et de l'humanité de Jesus* (Paris: Desclée De Brouwer, 1967) was first published in two parts in *Nova et vetera* (41, Nos. 1 and 3 [January–March and July–September 1966], 1–23, 161–218). (The volume has been translated by Joseph W. Evans: *On the Grace and Humanity of Jesus* (New York: Herder & Herder, 1969).)

2. The printing of Maritain's biography at Desclée De Brouwer was completed on September 29, 1966.

204

December 4, 1966

Dearest Jacques,

I found you whole and entire in the telegram you sent. I was profoundly touched. I can tell you now that one of the reasons why

I accepted this prize is the fact that you received it before I did.[1] Today I cannot write you as long a letter as I would wish; you know what the day after receiving a prize is like—and tomorrow there will be a reception which I cannot think about without worrying, for I don't know how to shine in the social world!

I think of you very often, and always with great affection, dear Jacques.

I embrace you.

JULIEN

Your *Paysan* is selling marvelously, I hear from every direction. I'm certainly happy about this.

1. The Grand Prix national des lettres, which Maritain received in 1963 (see   Letter 168), had just been conferred on Green.

205

December 31, 1966

My dearest Jacques,

I am recopying my journal with a view to its publication which should take place in September '67 and, as you will see in the enclosed pages, I have come to the story of the Greek Bible, which I told you. I am a year behind because I hesitated somewhat to do this.[1] Would you please read it and tell me if I should include it in my journal? The form will be slightly modified, and, I hope, improved, but I will say no more or no less than what you are going to read, if you would be kind enough to do so. Excuse me for inflicting this little task on you, but whatever concerns you and Raïssa has very great importance for me as you know.

I hear you spoken of on all sides with as much admiration as affection. It could be said that your *Paysan* has brought you closer to all of us. For my part, is it necessary to say it, I didn't need this to love you. You are in my heart forever. Anne joins me in wishing you most affectionately a very happy New Year in 1967.

I embrace you.

JULIEN

P.S. In a few pages which will arrive later, I recount the conversation I had with you about this mysterious Greek Bible. You told me then that the Germans confiscated your books, particularly those you considered most precious and which you had placed in a cupboard. Among these was the Septuagint in question. Is that the way it was?

1. In *Vers l'invisible*, the story of the Greek Bible is recounted at length, with all its developments, as in a short story of Edgar Allan Poe's (June 8, 1965, etc.).

(See above, "The Friendship of Jacques Maritain and Julien Green," note 4, for a summary of it.)

206

Toulouse
January 5, 1967

Dear Sir,

I am writing you on behalf of Jacques Maritain for right now he is overwhelmed with such a mountain of work that he must beg you to excuse him for not replying immediately as he would like to have done, but only within four or five days. Jacques asked me to write you because, as a member of a Dominican community which is attached to him by the bonds of a very old friendship, I have the privilege of serving as his secretary. Until he can do so himself, he asks me to tell you without delay of his full agreement concerning the pages you sent him. I send you also the most affectionate expression of his deep friendship and faithful remembrance.

Please accept, dear Sir, the expression of my very religious respect.

SR. MARIE PASCALE

207

Toulouse
January 9, 1967

My beloved Julien,

Finally I can write you. I am completely worn out because of a work I have undertaken (foolishly, but I think it was necessary, and

Raïssa helps me along as I go stumbling over the stones in my path). It is for a seminar that I will have in a few days with the Little Brothers on the origin of man (and there will have to be two more in the coming months, if I can handle it all).

I was profoundly moved, Julien, by such beautiful pages of yours on the Greek Bible, which in such an extraordinary way fell into your hands, and I'm very happy that you speak of this in your *Journal*. I find perfect all that you have written in this admirably just and sober account (except for the words "great writer" in which I do not recognize myself at all). Thank you for having sent it to me. My *nihil obstat* is enthusiastic.

The last lines touched my heart. Yes, I believe as you do that this was Raïssa's way of accepting your challenge. This is just like her. And she wanted to teach you, with a smile, something very important.

Julien, how would souls who are in Heaven and who see God need a brain to remember a world which they knew through their senses and to recall all those whom they loved and whom they wish to help? They see all of that—both the past and the present—in the vision of the divine essence (on the other hand, St. Thomas explains that, even in the natural order, separated souls know things as the angels do, by *species infusae*—an expression that defies translation, I would say by infused intuitions), wherein, according to His good pleasure and to the degree that their love is involved, God shows them things as He sees them Himself. There is nothing more certain than this communication between the dead who have eternal life and those who are still living here below. Otherwise, how could we pray to the saints, or how could they come to our assistance? I live much more (I do not want to say in my thought alone, but in the reality of mutual communication) with Raïssa and Vera than I do with the people living around me.

To get back to your *Journal*: it is true that all the books which we held most dear and which were in a cupboard in the salon at Meudon (they were all tied together) were stolen while we were in America. And the Bible you gave me was with them. I mentioned the Germans because several friends told us that the Gestapo had visited the house, but this fact has not been established with certainty, so perhaps it would be better not to mention the Germans?

I will most likely go to Paris in the course of this month to consult lawyers, alas (up till now I have been—for purely sentimental reasons—an "alien-resident of the U. S.," but this has created so many difficulties with my bank that I have just re-established my legal residence in France, and now this has caused other problems . . .). Naturally I have the deepest desire to go see you. I will give you a sign if this is possible, but I am not sure of being able to prolong my visit enough for that. (And do not speak of this trip, which I want to remain incognito.)

I hope to see you soon then. I embrace Anne and you with all my heart.

JACQUES

208

January 15, 1967

My dearest Jacques,

Thank you for the very beautiful letter you wrote me. It is very important to me, as it would be, I believe, for many readers who are trying to see clearly into the difficult problems you are grappling with. Would you permit me to quote a few lines from that letter in my journal? It goes without saying that I will show them to you first and that I will do nothing without your consent.

Need I tell you that I believe, as you do, in the Communion of Saints? It is indeed one of the truths of religion to which I hold most strongly. It has never crossed my mind to doubt that the separated souls intercede for us. They love us and remember us, that is sure, but from this to the belief that they can communicate with us directly, there is an enormous step to take. I wish with all my heart that it might be so, but, unless I am mistaken, this is one of the points about which the Church proposes no truths that must be believed. Your opinion has a value for me I'm not sure you realize, and what you tell me about the relations we are able to have with our dead (I do not like this word very much . . .) is of a nature to make me reflect, all the more so as I would want to believe what you believe. Perhaps some day I will be convinced. For the moment I feel the presence of all those who have gone before me and who watch over all those who are dear to me. The "millions of spiritual beings" Blake speaks of protect us all. This is part of my faith and my hope. Morning and night, for many, many years I have been praying for all those dear to me who have disappeared and for all those whom I do not know. Likewise I hope they will help me go to God. You spoke of the saints. I venerate them and pray to them, but I'm afraid they are being abandoned more and more.

The story of the Greek Bible is very strange and in it what strikes me is the fact that each of the incidents which make it up has nothing extraordinary about it in itself. Everything can be explained in the account. The mystery is in the juxtaposition of the facts which in themselves are perfectly natural. One might compare them to the words of a messenger whose meaning is obscure even though each single word is clear. In truth, I don't know what to think about it. It may be, as I first believed, that Raïssa was trying to communicate to me some truth that is still poorly defined, but I am not sure, because I am not persuaded that this type of communication is really necessary at the point where we are right now. Yet a little while and we will be, yes we too, and this I look forward to with all my heart, in what Henry James called "the great good place." (I wouldn't want to try putting that in French!) St. Teresa of Avila used to say that life lasts no more than a quarter of an hour!

I will have much more to tell you in a letter if you cannot see me in Paris. My poor Anne was bitten by our cat and suffered cruelly, but she is much better now. She joins me in sending you our faithful and deepest affection.

> Your
> JULIEN
> T.S.V.P.[1]

P.S. Concerning our departed (who are not *absent*) I find myself in the situation of a man who receives no news from those he loves, but who says to himself: "Even if they never write, I know they love me and are thinking of me."

Let me add this, not without a shadow of hesitation, but you will understand because you know how dear you are to me: perhaps this message from Raïssa—if there is a message—was destined more for you than for me. Indeed, more than once the idea crossed my mind that I was serving as an intermediary. . . .

⟨1. Téléphonez, s'il vous plaît (Please telephone).⟩

209

Toulouse
April 8, 1967

My beloved Julien,

Henry Bars wrote me that today a taping will be made for Italian television in which you have agreed to take part.[1] I want to thank you with all my heart, but to tell you also that I am angry that such a heavy task should be demanded of you; I do not like at all the idea that I am imposing, even without having wished it, sacrifices of this kind on my friends (I know you find this sort of thing hateful, as I do). Forgive me, and may your precious friendship be blessed.

I embrace Anne and you with profound tenderness.

Your poor
JACQUES

1. "There was a question of a tribute to Maritain organized by Italian television. I had accepted, but very much against my will because I speak poorly on television. What I did say came from my heart . . . " (April 10, 1967, *Ce qui reste de jour*, Pléiade V).

210

April 29, 1967

Dearest Jacques,

I would have written you much sooner to thank you for your letter if I had not been ill. I had a liver attack and am getting over it very slowly.

I was so happy to be able to speak of you and to say publicly how much I owe you, but you know that words don't come easily to me on television, and I am afraid I did not take very good advantage of the opportunity offered to me. Luckily dear Father Bars was there too! His presence was an immense help.

I must leave you, dearest Jacques, but I will be thinking of you as always with profound affection.

JULIEN

211

June 6, 1967

Dearest Jacques,

What joy to think that we are going to see you again soon! There is only one problem which, I hope, can be resolved. As a matter of fact, we won't be in Paris on June 24th, so we propose the following Wednesday, June 28th.

I am recovering very slowly and with some difficulty from an attack of infectious hepatitis which has worn me down considerably, and I must go to the country to rest as much as possible.

I am thinking of you and hope with all my heart that you have completely recovered by the time this letter arrives.

The news these days must move you as it moves us all. Little David's sling seems quite formidable![1]

Anne and I embrace you very affectionately.

JULIEN

1. The reference is to the lightning-like Six-Day War between Israel and Egypt.

212

Toulouse
June 8, [1967]

Dearest Julien,

Thanks for your letter. I feel very bad that you have been sick; I wish you were able to take a real rest in the country and then come back to Paris totally recovered.

I already have some engagements on June 28th. Could I come to lunch with you on Thursday the 29th or on Friday the 30th? Be good enough to send me word quickly so I can arrange my schedule.

Forgive me for writing you only these few lines in haste. I am at the end of my strength, and with a philosophic work on my hands which is tormenting me very much and which has completely *emptied* my memory of everything else.

Pray for poor Jacques. I'll see you soon!

I embrace Anne and you with all my heart.

JACQUES

213

Toulouse
October 30, [1967]

Dear, dear Julien,

I just read your interview in *Le Figaro littéraire*, with the quotations from the *Journal* which follow it.

I cannot resist the desire to tell you what joy and what admiration was brought to me by all you gave us there.

More exhausted than ever (I just can't seem to go on). I have to be satisfied with these few lines.

The blessing of the *Truth* is upon you.

I embrace Anne and you with profound tenderness.

JACQUES

214

52 *bis* rue de Varenne VIIe
November 5, 1967

Dearest Jacques,

It is always a joy for me to see your beautiful handwriting on an envelope, and the last letter you wrote has given me a pleasure you cannot imagine, for I am always worried when one of my books comes out. What you tell me about the extracts you read in *Le*

Figaro littéraire is rather reassuring—I say rather because there is all the rest that you still do not know. I hope, however, that you will soon receive the volume in question. To my great regret, I had to suppress many passages concerning you, but, I believe, you would have found them indiscreet. Those that remain will tell you, as I do again this evening, of my faithful and profound affection.

I embrace you with all my heart.

JULIEN

215

Toulouse
November 11, 1967

My dearest Julien,

Your *Journal* moved me to the depths of my heart and enchanted me completely from beginning to end.[1] This is a book of exceptional grandeur. I want to write you more at length but I just *cannot* do so now because of the abyss of fatigue into which I have been plunged. (For the same reason I will not be able to write until much later to Robert, whose book I liked so much.[2] Tell him how sorry I am.)

I embrace Anne and you with profound tenderness.

Your poor
JACQUES

1. The eighth volume of Green's *Journal, Vers l'invisible,* was published by Plon (Pléiade V).

2. Their mutual friend Robert de Saint Jean had just published *Julien Green par lui-même.* See 68.1.

216

Toulouse
February 23, 1968

Dearest Julien,

I am so ashamed for not having been able to write the long letter I promised to send you. I have been kept from it by my work and a fatigue that leaves me half dead.

At the beginning of March I must go to Paris to see my doctor. If it doesn't inconvenience you and Anne in any way, could I have lunch with you on Friday the 8th?

Be kind enough to send me word before the end of the month.

I embrace both of you with profound tenderness.

JACQUES

217

February 24, 1968

Dearest Jacques,

Just a word to tell you that we will expect you on Friday, March 8th. What a joy it will be to see you!

Anne and I embrace you with all our hearts.

JULIEN

P.S. Don't wait till 1 o'clock! Come as early as you can.

218

August 5, 1968

My dearest Jacques,

My long silence must have puzzled you, but it was difficult to write you without mentioning something about which I wanted to say nothing for the moment. My dear Anne has been ill, and very ill. An operation was necessary in June, and she has been very long in recovering. Today, thank God, she is getting stronger, and I really believe the danger has passed, even though she has a tendency to consider herself completely cured, whereas I see very clearly that there is still a long way to go before she is back to normal. Because of this, I have been through some difficult hours. Anne had asked me not to tell any of our friends about the operation, but I am sure she herself will speak with you about it as soon as she feels well enough to write. It is a joy for me to see her coming and going in the house once again, but I have to fight with her to keep her from doing too much.

I thought of you time and again during the sad days of May. I hope we never have to go through the like again.

Need I tell you that you are always near us, dear Jacques? You know how much we love you.

I embrace you with all my heart.

JULIEN

Give our friendly best wishes to the Gruneliuses.

219

Kolbsheim
August 10, 1968

My dearest Julien,

What a pity to think that Anne, our sweet, our incomparably good and blessed Anne, has been sick and in danger. The suffering of the innocent is unbearable for the heart. I thank God that everything turned out well and that she is regaining her strength and moving toward a complete cure, but I think with sorrow of the hard days the two of you have lived through.

I embrace you and her with all my heart.

JACQUES

I can write only a few lines, worn out as I am with fatigue. I hope I can stop in Paris in October to see you then.

220

Kolbsheim
September 24, 1968

Dearest Julien,

It is a sick man who is writing you these few lines. My heart condition has only gotten worse in the course of the summer, and the cardiologist whom I saw in Colmar will permit me to spend only a few days in Paris on my way back to Toulouse at the beginning of October, but he has absolutely forbidden me to go up any stairs.

So, Julien, would it be possible for you and Anne to come to lunch with me at the *Port-Royal Hotel*, 5 rue de Montalembert, on Sunday, October 6th, at about 12:30? I have such need to see you and to have news about dear Anne.

I embrace both her and you with all my heart.

JACQUES

Send me an answer in Kolbsheim if I can get it before October 3. If not, be good enough to send it to the *Port-Royal Hotel* with the notation "Please hold."

221

52 *bis* rue de Varenne, VIIe
October 21, 1968

My dearest Jacques,

I read with emotion those beautiful pages on Bloy, so filled with understanding and with love as is everything you write when you speak of your friends.[1] How they would have touched that great writer and what a consolation it would have been for him too if, in 1917, he had been able to foresee that a half century later you would be there, you whom he loved, to tell the story of his life!

Your considerations on the problem of God's suffering fascinated me for several reasons. I think I told you that in 1945, upon my return from America, I had put some questions on this subject to a Dominican, who was visibly scandalized. I wanted to know, as a matter of fact, if the Passion of Christ had not troubled the heart of His Father. You approach the mystery of divine suffering in a different way and from a much deeper point of view. I can only read, wonder—and question myself, but not too much, I must admit, because it seems to me that here there are abysses over which it is better not to lean, if one is as ignorant as I am. It is not that I *believe* that faith is endangered by the study of this problem. But how can one avoid seeing that a shadow is cast upon our hope? Will our Paradise be spent in contemplating a God Who suffers? On the other hand, I realize that there exist, if I may put it this way, certain thoughts that the human brain cannot succeed in *thinking.* They seem even intolerable. You understand that I am oversimplifying in order to see clearly, but this is a terrifying mystery, one more mystery which is proposed in your pages with admirable profundity. Nevertheless, when one thinks of the mystical experience of many saints, one could ask if joy and suffering are not aspects of the same phenomenon, on a certain very elevated plane. An analogy, doubtless absurd, comes to mind: extreme cold burns. It appears almost certain—no, it is certain—that we cannot go to God except through suffering, and that this suffering is transformed into joy, because it is, after all, the same thing. I express myself very imperfectly, my dear Jacques, but you must see in all my gibberish no more than the desire to understand you. To put it simply, I believe that all true joy comes to us from God alone, but it is of a nature that remains mysterious, as does He Who gives it to us. Didn't St. Paul say that it surpasses all our understanding?

How I would like to see you and hear you speak of all these things, which are the most important things in the world! You know how much we love you, Anne and I. Each one of your visits is a marvelous gift that Providence offers us *in sign of friendship.* This is what you are for us.

With all my heart I embrace you.

JULIEN

There comes to mind all that Saint Catherine of Genoa said about the joy–suffering of Purgatory.

1. "Léon Bloy" was published in *Nova et vetera,* 43, No. 2 (May–June 1968), 81–103.

222

Toulouse
October 27, 1968

My dearest Julien,

Your letter touched me to the depths of my heart, and I thank
you for it from the bottom of my heart. Yes, you did speak to me
of the question you had put to a Dominican in 1945, and that is
what I had in mind as I wrote. It is a very great comfort to me that
you liked these pages and all that you write me on this subject is
precious. I like very much the analogy you pointed out in the intense cold that burns. . . .

The lines "it seems to me that here there are abysses over which it
is better not to lean" and "there exist, if I may put it this way, certain
thoughts that the human brain cannot succeed in thinking" struck
me especially because they correspond to a profound feeling which
made me tremble during the whole time I was writing. I had the
impression I was advancing into a forbidden terrain.

But it seemed to me it had to be done. *Revue thomiste* has asked
me to publish this study (I am in the process of fixing it up to send
them) and this encourages me very much, but does not take away
that dark anxiety!

Thank you too for what you said about my conference on Léon
Bloy. What strange paths Providence makes use of! He was so surprised to have a philosopher for a godson.

Since my return to Toulouse I have been feeling better, at least as
far as my heart is concerned. But my fatigue is still the same—
crushing—and makes me speak in a kind of fog, having the sense
that I am uttering nothing but stupidities. I need your charity and
Anne's to repeat what you tell me about my visits. Because seeing
you and hearing you each time is a sign for me of the friendship of
Providence, a mark of God's tender-loving kindness. I love both of
you tenderly. I embrace you with all my heart.

JACQUES

We will not spend our Paradise contemplating a God Who suffers, because the idea and the words of suffering cannot be applied

properly to God, and correspond in Him to a mystery of His beatitude for which we have no name. But we will see for all eternity what Christ has suffered for us, that *beata passio* of which the Liturgy speaks in the Canon of the Mass (they have translated this expression by inverting the words, *passion bienheureuse,*[1] which doesn't mean the same thing at all).

⟨1. When placed before the noun, the French adjective *bienheureuse* means "blessed"; when placed behind the noun, it means "happy," "fortunate," or "lucky."⟩

223

52 *bis* rue de Varenne, VIIe
February 18, 1969

Dearest Jacques,

You did very well to re-edit those pages of Raïssa's and to add to them the unpublished texts which are a real enrichment for the book.[1] I have always thought that, in her poems, Raïssa surrendered a part of herself which remained almost inaccessible in her other writings where it had to be guessed at. For her, poetry was the language which permitted her to say what she would have been kept from saying otherwise. In her verses she surrendered to us a part of her secret. Certainly there was the spiritual journal which you gave to the public, and there she hid nothing of her deep inner life, but it seems to me that her journal and her poetry cast on each other a light that helps us understand each more deeply.

What joy it must be for you, my dearest Jacques, to find again in this beautiful book a soul so tenderly loved by God and by you.

With all my heart I embrace you.

JULIEN

1. *Poèmes et essais de Raïssa Maritain* was published by Desclée De Brouwer in 1968.

224

52 *bis* rue de Varenne, VIIe

October 28, 1969

My dearest Jacques,

I hope you are not upset by my long silence which can be explained only by a great deal of extra work that has caused my correspondence to suffer. But I don't want to put off any longer telling you with what joy and interest I read your two studies on the angels and especially on the mystery which touches on the vulnerability of Our Lord.[1] These are pages of capital importance from which I drew nourishment this summer, as glosses to the Scriptures, which they illuminate sometimes with a new light. Everything you say about the angels and about their role is most beautiful and can offer no difficulty; on the contrary, you give courage to the reader while instructing him. In regard to what we have to call the suffering of God, many questions arise to which we will get no answers in this world, but the very fact that you approach this problem as you do seems to me of utmost importance. I read and reread these pages with great emotion—especially when I had the feeling that I finally understood them. It is indeed a rather frightening truth that you propose for our consideration and it is not always easy to follow you. We who are not theologians find ourselves somewhat in the situation of Peter before the divine obscurities of Brother Paul and it will always be like this. But you have this in common with Paul, something that has always touched me deeply, that is, a profound knowledge of those things that count the most, joined to true humility. And if you find this compliment excessive, I ask you to remember that Saint Paul recommended that we be his *imitators*, and the wisdom which you have received, you communicate to us with that modesty filled with authority which was his. How agreeable it is to notice that the most recent works you give us are just as beautiful as the best of your youth! Your presence among us is a pledge of God's friendship in an endangered world. I am happy to be able to tell you these things which come from my heart and I embrace you affectionately.

JULIEN

1. These articles are "Quelques réflexions sur le savoir théologique," *Revue
thomiste*, 69, No. 1 (January–March
1969), 5–27, and "Le tenant-lieu de
théologie chez les simples," *Nova et
vetera*, 44, No. 2 (April–June 1969),
81–121.

225

Toulouse
October 31, 1969

My dearest Julien,

I was reading your *Journal* this morning when your marvelously
sweet letter was delivered to me. I am so happy, more so than I can
say, that you liked those two essays: what you say about them
touches my heart and I thank you for it with *all my heart.*

But I am completely disconcerted by what the generosity of your
heart leads you to say about me. You seem to be mistaking a dusty
old puppet for a poet. If you only knew how I struggle in the midst
of the misery and impotence that overwhelms me. . . .

Forgive me for writing you only a few lines today. I am laboring
under a crushing fatigue against which I have to struggle each day
to continue my work—I will tell you about this.

I hope, if I am given the words I need, to write you at greater
length when I have finished reading your *Journal.*[1] I began with the
second volume which is less familiar to me, and I'm reading it very
slowly, line by line, and at each moment I am deeply moved and
filled with admiration. I have gotten only as far as page 1032. It is
like a long conversation with you which continues within me all
day long. How I would love to see you! Perhaps this spring, if at
that time I am able to go to Paris to bring my editor the manuscript
I had the imprudence to begin.

Dear Julien, I embrace you with a profound tenderness.

Your poor

JACQUES

1. The *Journal en deux volumes*
(Paris: Plon, 1969), which appeared after
the single-volume edition, included the
final two portions of his journal. (Volume
I covers the years 1928–1949; Volume
II, 1949–1966.)

226

52 *bis* rue de Varenne, VIIe

November 9, 1969

Dearest Jacques,

Your letter has touched me so deeply that I cannot keep myself from telling you so and thanking you for it. You don't have to answer this letter; you have too much work, but I want to cite you a passage, which you know very well, from *Le Pèlerin de l'absolu.* You tell me that you really are not a poet. Here is what Bloy thought (there is question of your article about "Les Deux Bergsonismes"): "I knew he was superior, my beloved godson, and in how many ways! But I never expected to see so strong an arm emerge from the tattered rags of a philosopher. The arm of an athlete, the strong cry of a mourner. At the same time I recognized *a wave of dolorous poetry, a powerful ground swell that came from very far away.*" How he loved you then and how he would love you today, now that you are even more yourself than in those days. You push your gifts to their limits; you make truth lovable. We all love you tenderly, my dearest Jacques, but no one more than he whom you have helped so much in this life.

Your

JULIEN

who embraces you with all his heart.

You see, I was right. And this athlete's arm resembles very much the arm of St. Paul that I spoke to you about in my letter, always apropos of you, dear Jacques.

227

Toulouse
June 22, 1970

My beloved Julien,

I thank you with all my heart for having sent me *Les Années faciles*,[1] which I am going to read at Kolbsheim where I will be before the end of the month. I am filled with remorse toward you. I would like to have written you at length on the two volumes of your *Journal*! To tell the truth there was absolutely no way I could do so because of this book on the Church which for more than a year now has devoured all my time and all my strength, and has thrown me into a veritable agony of fatigue. I have just now finished the manuscript.[2] My doctor does not want me to stop in Paris on the way to Kolbsheim; so I won't be able to see you now as I had hoped. It will have to wait till October when I return to Toulouse. Julien, I think of you with an immense tenderness, and each day I thank God for you. Pray for your poor old friend. I embrace you and Anne with all my heart.

JACQUES

I had great joy from the prize you were awarded.[3] Finally some justice has been done! It is marvelous to think that an American is the greatest French writer of our time.

1. Maritain is referring to a reissue of Volume I of Green's *Journal*, with numerous unpublished additions. This version of *Les Années faciles*, published by Plon in 1970, and now the definitive edition, is included in Pléiade IV.

2. In *De l'Église du Christ: La personne de l'Église et son personnel* (Paris: Desclée De Brouwer, 1970), Maritain tries to explain the Church in the light of the Second Vatican Council. (An English translation by Joseph W. Evans, *On the Church of Christ: The Person of the Church and Her Personnel*, was published by the University of Notre Dame Press in 1973.)

(3. Green was awarded the Grand Prix du roman de l'Académie Française.)

228

52 bis rue de Varenne, VIIe

June 26, 1970

My dearest Jacques,

Your letter touched me more than I can tell you, but you must feel no remorse. You are giving your time to an important work, and I understand perfectly well that you no longer write as often as those who love you, because your book, which we are all waiting for, must come before letter-writing.

Les Années faciles, which you have received, is a sort of confession and shows how God set about leading me back to the Church. I had to make an open avowal of certain things I had always kept more or less secret and naturally it cost me dearly. Three hundred pages of supplementary indiscretion!

On the other hand, I have written for *Le Monde* a kind of introduction in which you and all that I owe you figure very prominently. This is a testimony I had always wanted to make, and this occasion seemed a good one. I will send you these pages, but you must not thank me for them before October, and then you can do it *viva voce!* Your work comes first.

Your congratulations gave me great pleasure. They want me to become a member of the Académie (this is the meaning of the prize, I am told), but for that I would have to renounce my American citizenship. And you know very well there can be no question of that. Besides I just can't see myself wearing that cocked hat!

Dear, dear Jacques, I am happy to know that you are at Kolbsheim, on that beautiful estate, among people who love you. Anne and I are thinking of leaving for Eure-et-Loir in a week. I feel we both need a change of air. Anne is worn out, and I intend to arrange matters so that she has nothing to do. I will do my work, but, alas, I have never been able to write more than three hours a day, and that only with great difficulty.

I will say nothing of what is going on in the Church today, but there are some things that break my heart. Certain priests have simply lost the Faith. That you are here is a grace and a comfort for many.

May I ask you to remember me to M. and Mme Grunelius. And as for you, my dear Jacques, I embrace you with all my heart.

JULIEN

229

52 *bis* rue de Varenne, VII[e]
July 5, 1970

Dearest Jacques,

Excuse me for sending you only a photocopy of my article, but it appeared in *Le Monde* so shabbily illustrated that I could not bring myself to send it you so disfigured in this way.[1]

The last page, which concerns you, will tell but poorly what I think of you, but you can add what is lacking in it.

I embrace you with all my heart.

JULIEN

1. In "Tout dire sur soi-même," which appeared in the June 6, 1970, issue of *Le Monde*, Green wrote: "Maritain only seemed more and more distant in my life, like a sort of luminous shadow. I had an affection for him that was troubled only by what he never reproached me for: namely, my gradual separation from the Church. He never preached to me, for which I was very grateful. Others did not hesitate to sermonize me, and in their case it was not so much the message that I refused in the depths of my heart as the messengers themselves, whose indiscreet zeal, though very touching, got my back up, which no doubt was profoundly unjust on my part. Maritain had nothing of the proselytizer about him. His very presence was enough to say what was essential, for in his 'blue gaze' which never lied dwelt that faith whose language I recognized. What he believed, that he was from head to foot. I could not see him without there coming to my mind such words as transparency and purity which are very difficult to use, but I could find no others. More so than long speeches, his reserve made me reflect. This came from his faultless courtesy as well as from his infinite respect for the freedom of a human soul. Only once he risked saying to me, apropos of *Le Visionnaire*: 'You were made for the mystical life.' And that was all, but what a stone he had thrown into the abyss. . . .''

230

Kolbsheim
July 15, 1970

My beloved Julien,

It was not until today that I have been able to answer your precious letter of the 5th. I have been in an agony of fatigue for the last two weeks here, and still now my eyes can scarcely see the words I write.

Thank you for the photocopy of your article. All you say about this new edition is admirable and infinitely precious. Regarding the page (so perfectly beautiful) which concerns old Jacques, I have no words to tell you how very much it moved me and with what tenderness I thank you for it—and with what confusion too, for I know my misery. (The same goes for the passages about me in the two bound volumes which appeared before the new edition of *Les Années faciles*.) But precisely because it is so undeserved, this marvelous generosity of your friendship is even dearer to my heart. It is a grace for which I bless God.

You will find in this envelope a copy of the text I sent to Jean Denoël for the volume of *Renaissance de Fleury* which is dedicated to you. I am sending you these poor pages so that you may be able to tell me if there is anything in them that displeases you and that I could correct.

Give Anne all my affection. I hope she is feeling well. What are your plans for this summer? My friends the Gruneliuses have asked me to tell you that they would be most happy if both of you could spend a few days at Kolbsheim. Preferably in September (before that the house is invaded by their children and grandchildren). And what a joy it would be for me!

Dear Julien, I embrace you with all my heart.

JACQUES

[Text included with the letter]

I am grieved that the state of my physical strength hinders me from contributing to this tribute to Julien Green in a manner I would consider worthy of him. I insist, nevertheless, on being among the contributors, however brief my offering may be and in which I am afraid I may not find the words I need.

For Julien Green I have an admiration without compare. I find it marvelous that an American should be the greatest French writer of our time. In this I see an eminently remarkable sign of the universality of the human spirit, and also of the excellence of that instrument which is the language of my country.

This fact is due not only to the exceptionally profound poetry which dwells in Julien Green, and to his perfect discipline in all that concerns the demands of his art. I believe that the secret of his grandeur is his absolute *fidelity to the truth* which possesses his entire soul and reigns over every level of his interior life. Centered entirely in what can be called the truth of the imagination, this fidelity is manifest primarily in his novels and forces him to write only if he *sees* his characters; but it animates as well, from beginning to end, and in every respect, his life as it does his work as a writer.

This is why for him the *Journal* is the completely natural and indispensable complement to the Novel. Both the one and the other introduce us into the very heart of the mystery of human existence.

As is the case with every great poet, his characters are an aspect of himself, and with such truth that they make us feel the ineffable communion of all men in the measureless depths of their nature and its miserable and sacred night: a darkness sown with stars.

And in his life he has had the astounding and wrenching privilege of knowing in their implacable force all the attractions to which we are given over, and which all beauty, whatever its source, exercises on the sons of Adam redeemed by the blood of Christ. The spirit, in us, is at once enchanted and incurably wounded by the impermanence of time; being itself immortal, it would like to eternalize the fleeting moment. There is nothing more moving than the passion with which Julien Green sets himself to fix the matchless glow or shadow of that which passes away, and which is all the dearer to us because it will never come back again.

But what I would like to say above all, and it is here I feel my words betray me, is that in Julien Green, who carries within himself those immense—and torturing—human riches of which I have just spoken, one finds absolutely no mixture, no confusion, of the values of contrasting orders of which this richness is so full, no adulteration of the one by the other. Entirely different in this respect from Baudelaire, with whom, nevertheless, the cruelties of royal poetry create certain affinities in Green—but in Baudelaire there was a measure of that element of mystification and of complicity in the lie and in those artificial paradises, all of which was responsible for the weaknesses and inequalities of his admirable work—the indomitable primacy of Julien Green's will to truth keeps strictly in its place and in its rank each of those attractions whose empire extends over man, with never the slightest illusionary mixture or the slightest deceitful encroachment. He has known all the attraction of carnal joy and of "pleasure." He has known all the attractions of the spirit. And never has either of these attractions been contaminated by the other— with the result that his invincible fidelity to the truth has always left intact in his case an invincible fidelity to the spirit. To express as best I can what my mind is trying to grasp here, might I say that in the high circles of our culture the story and the sufferings of Green have redeemed those of Baudelaire?

In no one more so than in him do I find the feeling and the respect for the essential spirituality of the delights of painting, of music, and of poetry, which are in the order of nature a secret pathway toward the divine. From this comes the singular purity of the trajectory of his personal experience and his personal life. Even during the period when he almost abandoned the faith of his childhood, God never abandoned him. The angel of Truth remained ever close to him.

This is why his witness has a unique value for our times and for those who for their part consider the experience of pleasure and the freedom of desire a necessary ingredient of human life. It is enough to read the new edition of *Les Années faciles* to understand that in reality human life aspires to be delivered from this by an infinitely greater love, and to glimpse how the God of love can turn even that experience itself to the Good, when the heart is pure and seeks above all else the *truth*.

I hope I will be excused for having mumbled so miserably what I so wanted to say well. And may Julien Green himself permit me to add that his friendship has been and is for me one of the most precious gifts bestowed on me in this world here below.[1]

1. *Renaissance de Fleury* (October 1970).

231

July 21, 1970

My dearest Jacques,

Those pages you sent me are very beautiful and moved me very deeply, because I found in them, along with the writer I admire, that heart filled with marvelous charity which makes you so dear to us all.

I have no reservation to make except that you see me in too good a light! I feel that I in no way merit such praise, and all I can do is protest affectionately, for I know only too well what is missing in me to make me correspond to the idea you have of me. I leave with you the responsibility for this far too favorable judgment, which nevertheless touches me more than I can say. If only I could think that one day the Lord might say to me: "Jacques was right," then as of today I would feel assured of my salvation. I believe, however, that our neighbor, if he has any charity at all, sees us in a better light than we see ourselves, but you go too far in your optimism! Happily you have pointed out my faults with all necessary clarity. What would I have become if I had not met you? Would there have been someone to guide me, or at least show me the way? Between 1918 and 1940 I had not a single opportunity to speak to a religious. It is to you and Raïssa that I owe my meeting that Polish Dominican who brought me back to the Church. You have a claim on my gratitude, and I am always happy to remind you of it.

With what joy would I come to see you at the Gruneliuses' if that were possible! Actually I don't know what I'm going to do. Our vacation has been thrown into confusion by the fact that our cook has left to go back home to Spain, and we seem unable to find someone to replace her. I think we are going to return to Paris at the end of the month. Robert de Saint Jean has fallen ill, and Anne is very tired, too tired to travel. I am thinking of spending a little time with her in Versailles, but she prefers to return to Paris and not budge from there. There are times when her health worries me. She has always been so brave, but now I believe she is almost completely exhausted. You can imagine how this worries me, for I love her deeply.

Thank you again, my dearest Jacques, thank you for everything, from the bottom of my heart.

I embrace you.

JULIEN

P.S. In spite of all, may I be so bold as to say that, in the admirable text you sent me, there is a sentence that gave me pause. It gave pause likewise to Anne who just mentioned it to me. Here is the sentence (page 2 at the end of the second paragraph): ". . . might I say that in the high circles of our culture the story and the sufferings of Green have redeemed those of Baudelaire?" This thought will surely be completely misunderstood, not because it isn't true—it is perhaps in a way we cannot understand—but because I am, in the eyes of almost all those who have written of me, someone who must be ranked among the more fortunate of this world. The reasoning is simple: when one has suffered neither hunger nor cold, it is forbidden to speak of suffering. Interior trials just don't count.

Excuse me for telling you this, my dear Jacques. You know the respect I have for your thought, but I know very well the mentality of today's critics and I would prefer that there be no misunderstanding. That I should suffer from it all has no importance, but not you whom I love.

It goes without saying that if you judge best to keep the sentence as it is, I will be in complete agreement, but I feel bound to state my point of view in all frankness—and in all affection.

232

Kolbsheim
July 23, 1970

My beloved Julien,

Thank you with all my heart for your dear letter which moved me so deeply.

This word in haste to tell you that naturally I will change the inopportune sentence you pointed out; I am writing immediately to Father Gregory, at the abbey of Fleury, asking him to delete that sentence and replace it with the following lines: "I am thinking here, at the same time, of the realm of that spirit which is the human soul, and which finds its expression in the splendid diversity of the works of beauty, and of that other infinitely transcendent realm to which we are called by the Spirit who created and loved us first. In no one more so than in Green do I find . . ."

To tell the truth I never supposed that there was anyone stupid enough to believe, after having read your books, that you are among the fortunate of this world. But it is true that such people exist and that it is better to avoid their miserable commentaries. Then too my sentence was obscure and clumsy.

I am absolutely convinced, Julien, that what I said about you in those all too brief pages is the truth, pure and simple. And I have no doubt that Anne and Robert (and Our Lord too) have the same opinion of you as old Jacques.

I am heartsick that Anne is so worn out, and that at the same time she is without the domestic help she needs so much. Tell her of all my tenderness for her.

I would like to write you more at length, but I just cannot. I am still sunk in that abyss of fatigue. I count on seeing you in Paris at the beginning of October.

Antoinette and Lexi[1] send both of you their faithful affection.

Pray for me. I embrace you and Anne with all my heart.

Your poor
JACQUES

1. Antoinette and Alexandre Grune-lius. Raïssa and Jacques Maritain are buried in the cemetery at Kolbsheim near their estate in Alsace.

233

July 24, 1970

Thank you, my dearest Jacques. You are like the man in Scripture who gave "like a king." The new sentence you wrote to replace the other is extremely beautiful and rich in meaning. The first was too and seemed quite clear, but one must always make generous allowance for the stupidity of certain readers. From the publication of my very first books, I was berated for this absence of any material cares, which is a favor that the Lord has been pleased to show me (with certain intervals which they seem to know nothing about, for along with Anne I have known some difficult moments), but let's forget about that. I am angry with myself for having taken up your time by suggesting a change, but your answer goes beyond all my expectations. This is what strikes me about you: in addition to the magnificent intellectual gifts you have received, there is that unfailing spontaneity of the heart. May you remain long with us, my dearest Jacques, you who are for us an older brother filled with the tenderness of God.

My dear Anne read your letter with great emotion. She loves you as do I, who can never tell you so enough. If I had been able to meet you earlier, for example, just after my conversion, in 1917, my life would have been completely different, but I thank Providence for those visits to Meudon which counted so much for me because of you and because of dear Raïssa whose name I write with tenderness.

With all my heart I embrace you.

JULIEN

How moved I am by what you tell me about the Gruneliuses! Anne and I love them very much.

234

Kolbsheim
September 23, 1970

My beloved Julien,

I have just finished correcting the proofs of my book[1] and I am dead with fatigue. This is a word in haste to tell you that I will pass through Paris on my return to Toulouse at the beginning of October and that I have an immense desire to see you and Anne. Could you receive me for lunch on Saturday, October 3rd (I will arrive about

12:30)? Be good enough to send me a line telling me if this is convenient for you.

I embrace both of you with all my heart.

JACQUES

I just read with unspeakable emotion your masterpiece *Les Clefs de la mort.*

1. *De L'Eglise du Christ* (see 227.2).

235

52 *bis* rue de Varenne, VIIe
September 24, 1970

My dearest Jacques,

Agreed, with joy: Saturday, October 3rd, you will take lunch with us, and I don't need to tell you how happy we are. Come as early as possible; don't wait till 12:30, unless you cannot do otherwise.

Thank you for what you said about *Les Clefs de la mort.* You repay me for all the effort this book cost me.

With what impatience we await your book on the Church! From all sides I hear it said: "It is time that someone say something." Those who like to gossip do their gossiping, certainly, but they really say nothing because they have no authority. Happily, dearest Jacques, you are here.

Anne and I embrace you with all our hearts.

Your
JULIEN

236

October 6, 1970

Dearest Jacques,

I wrote you last summer to thank you for these very beautiful pages which appear today in Father Gregory's review,[1] but I am taking advantage of this occasion to tell you of the joy I had in reading "Fidelité à l'esprit" once again, which will remain for me a very precious testimonial. May I never show myself unworthy of it.

We were so happy to see you the other day. Believe me, we love you *more and more* tenderly.

I embrace you with all my heart.

JULIEN

1. See Letters 230 and 231.

237

October 14, 1970

My dearest Jacques,

These few lines will get to you tomorrow morning, I hope, to tell you that I feel nearer to you now than I ever have since the day the Lord accorded me the grace of meeting you. For some years now you have separated yourself from the world, and I have seen that you were completely given over to God, but today this is so in a very particular, visible, way since you have taken the habit of the Little Brothers of Jesus.[1] Now you must not forget those who love you tenderly, my dear Anne and me, who have such need of your prayers.

Dear, dear Jacques, my beloved brother in Jesus Christ, I embrace you with all my heart.

JULIEN

1. Jacques Maritain received the habit of the Little Brothers of Jesus the following day at Toulouse where he lived a part of the year. ⟨He was granted a special dispensation to enter the religious life at his very advanced age.⟩

238

Toulouse
October 23, 1970

My beloved Julien,

I would like to have answered immediately your marvelous letter of October 14th which arrived on the morning I took the habit; I have been kept from doing so by the atrocious labor of the top-speed correction of the second set of proofs of my book. It all swooped down on me immediately afterward and drained me completely of my strength.

Dear Julien, all that you wrote moved me to the depths of my soul. I have the very strong feeling that I am nothing but a grain of dust which begs for mercy, and at the same time I see more clearly than ever what grace and what sweetness from Heaven your blessed friendship is for me. Anne and you are constantly in my heart and in my prayers; I would gladly give my life for you two if it were worth anything.

O my beloved brother, I embrace you with a boundless tenderness.

JACQUES

I was happy to read in *Renaissance de Fleury* the excellent article by Robert de Saint Jean and your admirable pages.[1]

1. *Une voix secrète* (Pléiade III).

239

Toulouse
December 14, 1970

My beloved Julien,
How can I thank you for your marvelous letter?

Since my return from Kolbsheim, I experience more than ever the impotence of my miserable head; and a few days ago at Mass, Jesus Himself seemed to show this to me with a force and a severity that struck me heavily. He knows infinitely better than I do that it was Raïssa who did all the work on my last book (I prayed to her during the whole time)—a book which has become for me like a strange object that astonishes me but is so dear to me. I have the trembling desire to see it loved by those I love. This is to say that your letter is very important for me and consoles me more than all others I could receive since I love you most of all. It gave me back my courage to go on living, even though I have so little desire to do so.

Your old Jacques does not deserve what your blessed friendship leads you to say. But what does that matter, once such things *are* in your heart.

May you be filled with grace for loving that "person"[1] of the Church about which the theologians in general speak so badly and so little. I am in profound agreement with you in all that you write me about the cheerful and complete disregard for truth which reigns today: this is what has caused all desire for conversion on the part of Protestants and non-believers to disappear and all religions to be considered equal. We were too hard on non-Catholics in the past— but at least the Faith was there, with a love for the truth, however unenlightened. At present, by going to the opposite extreme, and by losing both the Faith and the love of truth together, stupidity becomes the object of adoration.

Dear Julien, the last lines of your letter touched me to the bottom of my heart. In my turn let me tell you that I love you in a way that is unique and has no limit. I embrace you.

JACQUES

Tell Anne of my profound tenderness.

Excuse the disorder of this letter. Fatigue is crushing me; I had to write out, because of an emergency, an article for the issue of the *Revue thomiste* prepared in honor of Cardinal Journet.[2] I finished it yesterday, but at what cost. I have no strength left.

⟨1. Maritain is referring to the subject of his *De l'Eglise du Christ*. See 227.2 for the subtitle of the volume.⟩

2. Charles Journet (1891–1975), professor of theology at the University of Fribourg, was the founder of *Nova et vetera* and the author of many important theological works. Profoundly ecumenical, he took a position clearly opposed to what he considered the ideological waverings of Taizé, the ecumenical Protestant monastery founded in 1940 in Burgundy. ⟨The community there contained a number of Catholic monks, particularly Franciscan, and became a center of pilgrimage for French youth. A *Concile des Jeunes* was held there in 1974.⟩

Cardinal Journet was a close friend of Maritain's and in correspondence with Green. ⟨He and Maritain spoke frequently about the theological problems of the day, and each produced books that treated those problems from very similar points of view. For example, at the same time as Cardinal Journet published *Destinées d'Israël, Le Mal, Exigences chrétiennes en politique*, and *L'Église du Verbe incarné*, Maritain published *Le Mystère d'Israël*,

Dieu et la permission du mal, Man and the State, and *L'Église du Christ.*) Cardinal Journet died two years after Maritain and was buried at the Chartreuse de Valsainte, where Maritain had frequently urged Green to make a retreat.

240

Toulouse
May 11, 1971

My dearest Julien,

I am filled with remorse toward you. As soon as I received *L'Autre*,[1] I read it with overwhelming emotion and admiration; I wanted to write you immediately, and a long letter too, but I was just getting over a case of bronchitis and was worn out by antibiotics. All words escaped me. I put it off from day to day, hoping that my strength would come back. And instead of this—and it's not the fault of antibiotics this time—I have been engulfed in an abyss of fatigue; each day I sink a little deeper. I have been reduced to silence, and my silence makes me ashamed. *Forgive me*, Julien.

I have just found out that now you are French without having asked it (they found an elegant solution, but I find this ruling of the Académie odious) and that you will succeed to Mauriac's chair. I want to tell you of my intense joy.[2]

Let me add that *L'Autre* is an extraordinary masterpiece in which you have succeeded in bearing witness to your personal faith in a book which in no way smacks of being a "Christian novel," but streams with love and with humanity.

I am at the end of my strength. Pray for your poor friend who is moving steadily toward death, more and more clearly conscious of his impotence, his imbecility, and his measureless misery. But Raïssa sustains him.

JACQUES

The doctor claims that in a few weeks my heart will not be as weak as it is (this would certainly astound me). If I can go to Kolbsheim and on the way stop for a few days in Paris at the end of June, what joy it will be to see you.

1. *L'Autre* (Pléiade III) was originally published by Plon in 1971; ⟨*The Other One*, Bernard Wall's translation, by Harcourt Brace Jovanovich in 1973.⟩

2. To be elected to the Académie Française the candidate has to be a French citizen. Julien Green refused to give up his American citizenship, and the rule was bent in his favor. He was declared an honorary French citizen and thus succeeded François Mauriac to the chair of Saint-Amant, the lyric poet of the seventeenth century.

241

Toulouse
June 9, 1971

Dearest Julien,

Thank you for your letter which was so sweet to me.

Jean Denoël wrote me that you and he intend to go to Meudon on the 12th, and this greatly embarrasses me, as I wrote to him yesterday. To tell the truth I accepted the idea of a plaque on the house[1] thinking of Raïssa and Vera, but against my will as far as I was concerned, and I am angry with myself that this should be the occasion of a trip and of fatigue for friends like you. Your intention to be there moves me deeply, but I would be more at peace with myself if you gave up this little trip.

To my great regret, the cardiologist whom I had to consult after some very difficult weeks, and whose prognostication (medical style) is "very reserved" has forbidden me to pass through Paris on my way to Kolbsheim, and he wants me to go there directly by car. It will not be at the end of the month, then, but on my return, at the beginning of October, that I hope to dine with Anne and you, according to my precious custom. Could our beloved Anne send a few lines giving me news about the state of her health?

Julien, I am far from holding the Académie in any reverence, but your election has a value and significance unique in the history of French letters. You are the only one who has forced the Académie to bend its rules in order to receive you among its members. Now that's true grandeur and fills me with intense joy.

I embrace you and Anne with all my heart.

JACQUES

⟨1. A commemorative plaque was to be placed on Maritain's house in Meudon where the meetings of the Cercles Thomistes had taken place during the 1930s.⟩

242

[no date]

Thank you, my dearest Jacques. Your congratulations have touched me to the depths of my heart. Excuse my long silence, due only to an enormous weariness. Will we see one another soon in Paris? Anne and I ardently hope so. Need I tell you this?

I embrace you very affectionately.

JULIEN

243

July 25, 1971

My dearest Jacques,

I hope you will pardon me for my long silence which is due to nothing but a weariness such as I have never before experienced and which was caused no doubt by the laborious days that followed my election to the Académie. Here, at Faverolles, I am recovering little by little, but I am beginning to feel the weight of days. It has to be admitted that almost all the members of my family have suffered, with all the external signs of good health, from a sort of congenital asthenia from the earliest years of their youth, and all the touted tonics have been of no avail. Excuse these tedious details which I would not bring up at all except that I did not want you to think that I was suffering from laziness of the heart, for I think of you with profound affection.

I would like to have been able to go to Meudon with your friends. I had to content myself with being there in spirit, calling up from the past the marvelous hours I spent there with you, Raïssa, and Vera. You should know how much these visits meant to me. Meudon was a refuge in a world weighed down by so many dangers. At your house we found the peace of the Gospels. I have forgotten none of these things, so very precious to me.

If you could stop in Paris on your way back from Kolbsheim, it would be a great joy for Anne and me. You need only let us know two or three days before you arrive.

I have been rereading some pages from Raïssa's journal. Among the many sentences which struck me, this one in particular awakened wonderful echoes: ". . . let him then whom God has drawn to the repose of contemplation not become involved in the darkness of worldly affairs . . ." (pp. 74f.). To attain this repose how many renunciations are necessary! I who know contemplation only by definition, I have my part in that darkness referred to in the last part of the sentence with such Pascalian beauty. In spite of it all, I have great hope. Pray for me, my dearest Jacques, as I pray that your health be restored. It is important that you be here. We all love you, but no one more tenderly than your

JULIEN

244

Kolbsheim
August 3, 1971

My dearest Julien,

Thank you with all my heart for your blessed letter. I am very upset that you are suffering from that fatigue I know only too well. I hope your stay at Faverolles can give you back your strength!

Oh, don't excuse yourself for not having been able to come to Meudon for the placing of the plaque! When some nameless individual in charge of "town-planning" asked me for authorization to do this, my first reaction was to answer no. Then I accepted because of Raïssa and Vera, but the whole affair has not ceased to displease me, and the idea that my friends should be invited to assist at this little ceremony made me feel bad. What I would like is to be forgotten. At eighty-eight one knows only too well one's misery, and only too well also the illusions that people entertain—when it happens that they think something good of me, I feel like a liar. What warms my old heart, Julien, is the memory that *you*, Julien, you have kept of that house, and the marvelous way your incomparable friendship leads you to tell me of it.

I'm the one who feels filled with remorse toward you, for not having written you in so long a time, as I would like to have done, and for not having been able to tell you at length of my admiration for your masterpiece *L'Autre*. I was hindered by an insurmountable weariness.

As far as my cardiac condition is concerned, I am beginning to feel better, but the fatigue is still there (this is why I couldn't answer sooner)—and along with that, my work; for after my book on the Church I have decided not to publish any more, but I still have the proofs of a few small things to correct (an article on Bérulle for the next issue of *Revue thomiste*, and a brochure, which will not be for sale, on the Canticle of Canticles, which I hope to send you in October).[1]

Thank you for having reminded me of that admirable passage from the *Journal de Raïssa*. But don't tell me that you know contemplation only by the definitions given of it! You might as well tell me that I have no eyes to see with, and that the stars I observe in the firmament are products of my imagination. For I am persuaded you are a born contemplative.

The doctors forbade me to pass through Paris on my way to Kolbsheim where I went in a station wagon stretched out on a mattress. But I count on spending a few days in Paris on my return, and to have the joy of seeing you and Anne. Brother Heinz, my dear novice-master, came here with me. How astonishingly good Providence is! This Little Brother has a superior mind, and the most beautiful philosophic gifts I have ever encountered, and which give me hope for the future. I hope some day he is able to see you.

Dear Julien, dear Anne, I never cease thanking God for you. Pray for me. I embrace both of you with boundless tenderness.

JACQUES

⟨1. Cardinal Pierre de Bérulle (1575–1629) introduced the Carmelite order into France and founded there the secular congregation of the Oratory. He left a profound mark on the French school of spirituality, certain aspects of which Maritain criticized rather severely in the article "A propos de l'École Française," *Revue thomiste*, 71, Nos. 2–3 (April–September 1971), 463–79.⟩

245

April 14, 1972

My dearest Jacques,

I read and reread your very beautiful pages on *L'Ecole française*[1] with the same pleasure I get from whatever you write, i.e., when I succeed in understanding you! All that you say so clearly of the priesthood is fascinating, and I don't need to tell you how opportune it is to speak of these matters. Bérulle, along with his magnificent intelligence, had a certain naïveté and even a strange ignorance about the most current psychology. Perhaps this is an utterly stupid remark, but I believe that in certain great souls like his the simplicity I admire so much may very well do prejudice to rigorous good judgment.

As to the indelible character of the priesthood, I have always believed in it and I see the tragic difficulties it brings about in the lives of those clerics who are leaving the priesthood today. We are living through painful times. You will find an echo of our anxieties in a new volume of my journal which will be sent to you in May.[2] You are often mentioned in it and always with very affectionate admiration. Once or twice I have let myself allude to certain lapses of memory that you complain about, and which I sometimes *envy* you, because they would make things so much simpler and easier for me. I believe there is question of a painful renunciation willed by God. What strikes me about you, and what I never cease to point out, is that marvelous quality of intelligence which you have received and which remains intact, as lively and as luminous as in those far-off years at Meudon where I had the good fortune to make your acquaintance.

I hope with all my heart that you are well and that you are not working too much. How happy I find you to be where you are, among believing and prayerful souls! For my part I feel a very profound anxiety when I see the world such as it is in Paris, but God is here. This is what keeps one from losing one's mind and slipping into despair.

Anne is very tired, and the prospect of having to leave this house makes her fearful. The threat becomes more and more precise. We are in the midst of wrangling between attorneys, and up till now we have not found a lodging in which to take refuge, but I have confidence in spite of all.

Dear Jacques, there is just enough space to tell you how much we love you, both Anne and I. Pray for us, for me who needs your prayers so much, "old dawdler" that I am.

I embrace you with all my heart.

JULIEN

⟨1. This article, originally published in the *Revue thomiste* (see 244.1), was reprinted as a chapter in Maritain's *Approches sans entraves* (Paris: Fayard, 1973).⟩

2. The ninth volume of Green's *Journal, Ce qui reste de jour,* was published by Plon (Pléiade V).

246

Kolbsheim
September 29, 1972

Dearest Julien,

May I have lunch with you on Tuesday, October 12th? (I will leave Kolbsheim on the 11th to return to Toulouse via Paris.)

Be good enough to answer quickly (a single line will suffice) so I may fix other appointments.

I embrace you and Anne with all my heart.

JACQUES

Pardon my writing so briefly; I am half dead with weariness.

247

October 6, 1972

Dearest Jacques,

I got Sister Pascale's letter on my return from Italy where I went for several days to rest up from a difficult summer.

It is very painful for me not to be able to tell you face to face how much I think of you, but if your stay in Alsace has done you some good, I am glad and I regret only that you cannot spend a few days in Paris. Above all, I don't want you to answer this letter, which has no other object than to tell you once again of the affection Anne and I have for you.

Anne is still very tired, but she rests as much as possible and is never alone. We speak of you so often, my dear Jacques, of you and all the light you have brought into our lives.

I am happy my books have pleased you. *Suite anglaise*[1] dates from my twenty-third year.

We still don't know where we are going to live, but I am still hunting. The owner has already demolished half of the building, not quite half really, for at the moment I judged best, I asked an expert to verify the solidity of the part we are still living in. We let the owner know that if he continued the demolition work, he would have to build a 120-foot retaining wall to keep us from falling into the void! And as if by a spell, the machines fell silent, but it is clear that one day or another we will be forced to leave. Anne suffers from this more than I do. Pray for us!

Dearest Jacques, I hope with all my heart that you are doing well and that you are not wearing yourself out. You know how much we love you—more and more.

I embrace you most affectionately.

JULIEN

I should be received into the Académie on November 16, and I dare not send you an invitation, but a word from you will suffice. . . . I know for sure you will be with me in your thoughts on that day.

1. The *Suite anglaise*, essays on Charles Lamb, William Blake, Samuel Johnson, and Charlotte Brontë—to which an essay on Nathaniel Hawthorne was added in the Pléiade (Volume I) edition—was published originally in 1927 (Paris: Cahiers Libres, 1927).

248

Toulouse
October 14, 1972

Beloved Julien,

Thank you for the news about you; I feel I have been waiting for
your acceptance speech, and this disturbed me a bit. I kept asking
myself how you were.

The doctor will not let me go to Paris, alas, on November 16th,
for, though some strength continues to come back little by little to
my poor body, my heart remains terribly weak. It is possible that in
two months it will make enough progress for me to dream of coming
to Paris and seeing you at the end of December. How can I tell you
with what tenderness I think of Anne and you!

I am afflicted by the savage demolition of your house which
causes you both so many cares. I thought that the only thing left
that the French respected was the Académie, and that from now on
the landlord would leave you in peace. It is horrible to find everywhere that money alone has importance for our contemporaries.

When certain ideas came into my head, I had the imprudence to
set myself to write a bit more, something that is not very convenient
at my age and with my fatigue, but I must try to hold on until the
end. After all, I am admirably assisted (a miracle of grace due to
Raïssa) by a Brother whom I love above all others, and to whom it
appears God has given extraordinary intellectual gifts (I consider
this son of poor German workers a true philosophic genius, and it
is on him that I count to do a really constructive work and to pass,
after my death, through the doors I have more or less clumsily tried
to open). I will tell you about all this. It is so astonishing. Heinz
will accompany me to Paris if I am permitted to make the trip at
the end of December; he has a deep admiration for you, and I wish
very much that you should meet him.

I am anxious to read your speech in *Le Monde*, the day after your
reception into the Académie.[1] In the meantime, I am sending you
an offprint of a talk which I gave to the Little Brothers last February and which might be of interest to you. (To my great surprise,

Revue thomiste asked to publish this text in its unusually familiar language.[2])

You know, Julien, that my friendship for Anne and for you is unique in this world. Pray for me. I embrace you and her with all my heart.

JACQUES

Heinz is preparing a book on Jakob Böhme[3] and German philosophy for which I have great hope. He has read all of Böhme, but translating quotations from this formidably delirious personage into French is such a difficulty that Koyré had to abandon doing so in his remarkable, but incomplete, work on him.[4] However, there exists a translation made in the eighteenth century by Louis-Claude Saint-Martin[5] (the "unknown philosopher"). Impossible to find it in Toulouse. May I ask you—if it doesn't bother you too much, if you could, either through some colleague at the Académie or through some book dealer of your acquaintance—to indicate to us how to get a hold of this translation in Paris? This would be a great service to Heinz. Forgive me for being so importunate like this!

⟨1. Green's acceptance speech was published by Plon in a volume entitled *Qui sommes nous? Discours de réception à l'Académie française et réponse de Pierre Gaxotte* (Paris, 1973).⟩

2. This talk was published as "En suivants de petits sentiers" in *Revue thomiste*, 72, No. 2 (April–June 1972), 233–52.

3. Jakob Böhme (1575–1642) was a German mystic and philosopher, ⟨nicknamed the *philosophus teutonicus.* Contrary to the Neoplatonists, who, beginning with the perfection and unity of the Supreme Being, described the successive degradations of being, Böhme tried to arrive at the Perfect One, taking imperfect beings as his point of departure.⟩ His words, like those of Martin Luther, influenced the German literary language, and his doctrine, influenced in part by Joachim of Fiore, made a deep impression on Novalis.

4. Alexander Koyré, *La Philosophie de Jacob Boehme,* was available in a reprint edition published in Paris by Vrin in 1929.

5. Louis-Claude de Saint-Martin (1743–1803) was a French philosopher and mystic who translated the works of Böhme. ⟨After studying law and serving in the army as a career officer, he became a Free Mason and helped to spread in France the mysticism and illuminism of Swedenborg.⟩ His writings influenced Balzac as much as those of Swedenborg had, and awakened echoes in many Christian romantics at the beginning of the nineteenth century.

249

October 24, 1972

My dearest Jacques,

I read with very great pleasure the pages you gave to the *Revue thomiste*. They are of great beauty, as is everything else that has come from your pen for many years now, but I don't want to begin singing the praises you deserve, otherwise I would never finish.

Certain things escape me, naturally, in this article. My ignorance is the culprit, but what I understood I found fascinating. The familiarity of tone reminded me sometimes of St. Vincent de Paul's talks to his religious and that adds a charm to your pages which in all other respects are so learned.

Concerning the glorified body, I was struck by what you said about the beauty that "God cherishes." This idea has been a part of my thinking for a long time now and has helped me resolve some very difficult problems. St. Gregory of Nyssa[1] has many things to say about the physical aspect before and after the Fall. At the end of His creation the Lord said that it was all very good. In the following chapter he says that it is not good for man to be alone, words which have led certain people to believe that between these two affirmations, something had happened—perhaps a first fall due to pride—but you know all this better than I. Without going into detail, there may have been a modification of the human body. It will be claimed no doubt that these are daydreams and the exegetes (who know everything . . .) will call them ridiculous. If I have the very great joy of seeing you in December,[2] which I hope I do with all my heart, we will be able to speak of these things.

What you say about space, of spaces and the nature of these spaces, seemed admirable to me. You make a bit clearer what is by its nature ineffable. I remember a conversation I had long ago with André George[3] about the notion of space. I asked him (a childish question, but children ask very curious questions) if there was a limit to the universe. Where does it end? (As if he knew!) If the universe has limits, what is there beyond it? A void? But the void can be conceived only in terms of space and as a sort of prolongation, which would still be space. Otherwise I don't see how one can form an idea of what the void is. With great finesse, and politely to put an end to these idiotic questions, he replied: "That's God's secret."

Whatever value this prattling may have, I insist on telling you once again that whatever you write has the effect of making God the object of love and *wonder*. You have never, very fortunately, undertaken to write in the edifying genre, for then you would not be Jacques Maritain, but you cannot help that what you write does edify and lead to God. This is your greatest gift, as I see it, and I am grateful to Him from Whom you got it. I embrace you as I love you, with all my heart.

JULIEN

"Another space that can in no way be represented . . ." This is the answer. It makes me dizzy.

Anne embraces you as I do. She is very tired but always brave. The prospect of being chased out of this house with me torments her. Where will we go? Pray for us, dearest Jacques.

How happy I would be to meet Brother Heinz! In December perhaps? Böhme translated by Saint-Martin is quite difficult to find, but I am looking.

1. Saint Gregory of Nyssa, one of the fourth-century Fathers of the Eastern Church, was an energetic opponent of the Arian heresies. He composed numerous homilies and explications of Biblical texts. It is most likely his *Dialogue on the Soul and on the Resurrection* to which Green refers.

2. Jacques Maritain came to see Julien Green in January, and this was his last visit to the rue de Varenne, for he died of a heart attack on April 28th in Toulouse.

3. André George (1890–1978) was a physicist and astrophysicist, a member of the Institut, a friend of Gabriel Marcel's, Max Planck's, and Louis de Broglie's, the author of works of science, a book on the *Oratoire* (Paris: Grasset, 1928), and articles on Einstein. He was a dear friend of Julien Green's and exchanged a long correspondence with him.

IN THE ETERNAL LIGHT

JULIEN GREEN

APRIL 28, 1973. 8:30 A.M. Éveline Garnier just telephoned me that our beloved Jacques Maritain died this morning of heart failure. He had said to his niece: "My heart is hanging on by no more than a thread." Yesterday evening, as I was turning the pages of my address book to pick out the names of those to whom I would send a card announcing my move to rue Vaneau, I fell upon the name of Jacques Maritain and a voice said to me very distinctly: "It's no use." We hear these messages without understanding them. Today the world is emptier than yesterday, and very much more so. The best are leaving. Jacques knew he was going to leave. He takes away with him a great measure of our hope. He no longer did any writing, but we knew he was there, that he was breathing. Now no more. I turn the dial of my radio to stop the noise of the world's news. Nothing makes sense for me any more. Maritain is dead. His hand will never again cover mine affectionately; he will never again throw kisses to Anne and me, when leaving us in the street. This wonderful tramp, the Prince of the Kingdom of God, with his angelic smile and his words, so tender and precise, and with all his soul in the depths of his pale blue eyes, he is now in the blessed regions with her whom he loved, in the Light of Jesus.

April 29, 1973. Thought a lot of Jacques. We do not understand right off the really bad news. The heart rejects it. But eventually it must come through to those who refuse it. This morning, in this house he loved so much and the sight of whose destruction and death he has been spared, I will never sit down next to him again. When I was disquieted, his clear eyes rested on me, dispelling every shadow. We believed the same things, and with that angelic simplicity of his, and that courtesy of a *grand seigneur*, he succeeded in making me understand difficult truths as if he had just discovered them himself on the instant. These poor sentences I write cannot really tell my sorrow.

April 30, 1973. Visit from Louis-Henri Parias who came to ask me several questions about Maritain. I remember that between Jacques and me there existed no familiarity whatsoever, only tenderness. We never felt the need to exchange useless banalities. He would ask me about my work, wanted to see everything I was writing. I sent him the texts. Three or four days later a wonderful letter would arrive, thought out and composed with care after a most attentive reading.

INDEX NOMINUM

The names of Anne Green, Raïssa Maritain, and Vera Oumansoff do not appear in this index, for one or another of them is mentioned in almost every letter. The references in **boldface** refer to the numbers of the Letters; those in lightface, to pages.